BLACK CAT

QUEEN IN BLACK

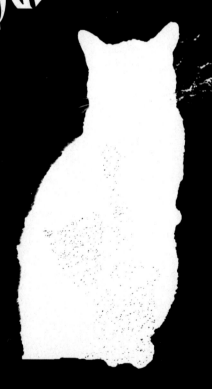

Knull, the primordial and malicious god of the symbiotes, has arrived on Earth with an army of symbiote dragons. Knull is the **King in Black**.

Fellcia Hardy and her crew of **Bruno** & **Doctor Korpse** have no idea what any of that means. Felicia's got a little experience with symbiotes from bad scrapes with **Eddie Brock** and **Lee Price** that she'd mostly like to forget. She's got plenty going on in her life as the greatest cat burglar in the world.

Felicia Hardy is...

collection editor **JENNIFER GRÜNWALD** ✦ assistant editor **DANIEL KIRCHHOFFER**

assistant managing editor **MAIA LOY** ✦ assistant managing editor **LISA MONTALBANO**

vp production & special projects **JEFF YOUNGQUIST** ✦ book designer **SARAH SPADACCINI** with **JAY BOWEN**

svp print, sales & marketing **DAVID GABRIEL** ✦ editor in chief **C.B. CEBULSKI**

BLACK CAT VOL. 4: QUEEN IN BLACK. Contains material originally published in magazine form as BLACK CAT (2020) #1-4 and X-MEN: TO SERVE AND PROTECT (2011) #4. First printing 2021. ISBN 978-1-302-92758-5. Published by MARVEL WORLDWIDE, INC., a subsidiary of MARVEL ENTERTAINMENT, LLC. OFFICE OF PUBLICATION: 1290 Avenue of the Americas, New York, NY 10104. © 2021 MARVEL No similarity between any of the names, characters, persons, and/or institutions in this magazine with those of any living or dead person or institution is intended, and any such similarity which may exist is purely coincidental. **Printed in Canada.** KEVIN FEIGE, Chief Creative Officer; DAN BUCKLEY, President, Marvel Entertainment; JOE QUESADA, EVP & Creative Director; DAVID BOGART, Associate Publisher & SVP of Talent Affairs; TOM BREVOORT, VP, Executive Editor; NICK LOWE, Executive Editor, VP of Content, Digital Publishing; DAVID GABRIEL, VP of Print & Digital Publishing; JEFF YOUNGQUIST, VP of Production & Special Projects; ALEX MORALES, Director of Publishing Operations; DAN EDINGTON, Managing Editor; RICKEY PURDIN, Director of Talent Relations; JENNIFER GRÜNWALD, Senior Editor, Special Projects; SUSAN CRESPI, Production Manager; STAN LEE, Chairman Emeritus. For information regarding advertising in Marvel Comics or on Marvel.com, please contact Vit DeBellis, Custom Solutions & Integrated Advertising Manager, at vdebellis@marvel.com. For Marvel subscription inquiries, please call 888-511-5480. **Manufactured between 4/9/2021 and 5/18/2021 by SOLISCO PRINTERS, SCOTT, QC, CANADA.**

10 9 8 7 6 5 4 3 2 1

BCAT

QUEEN IN BLACK

writer	**JED MacKAY**
artists	**C.F. VILLA** (#1-3), **NINA VAKUEVA** (#4) & **MICHAEL DOWLING** (#5)
color artist	**BRIAN REBER**
letterer	**FERRAN DELGADO**
cover art	**PEPE LARRAZ** & **MARTE GRACIA**
assistant editors	**LINDSEY COHICK**
editor	**NICK LOWE**

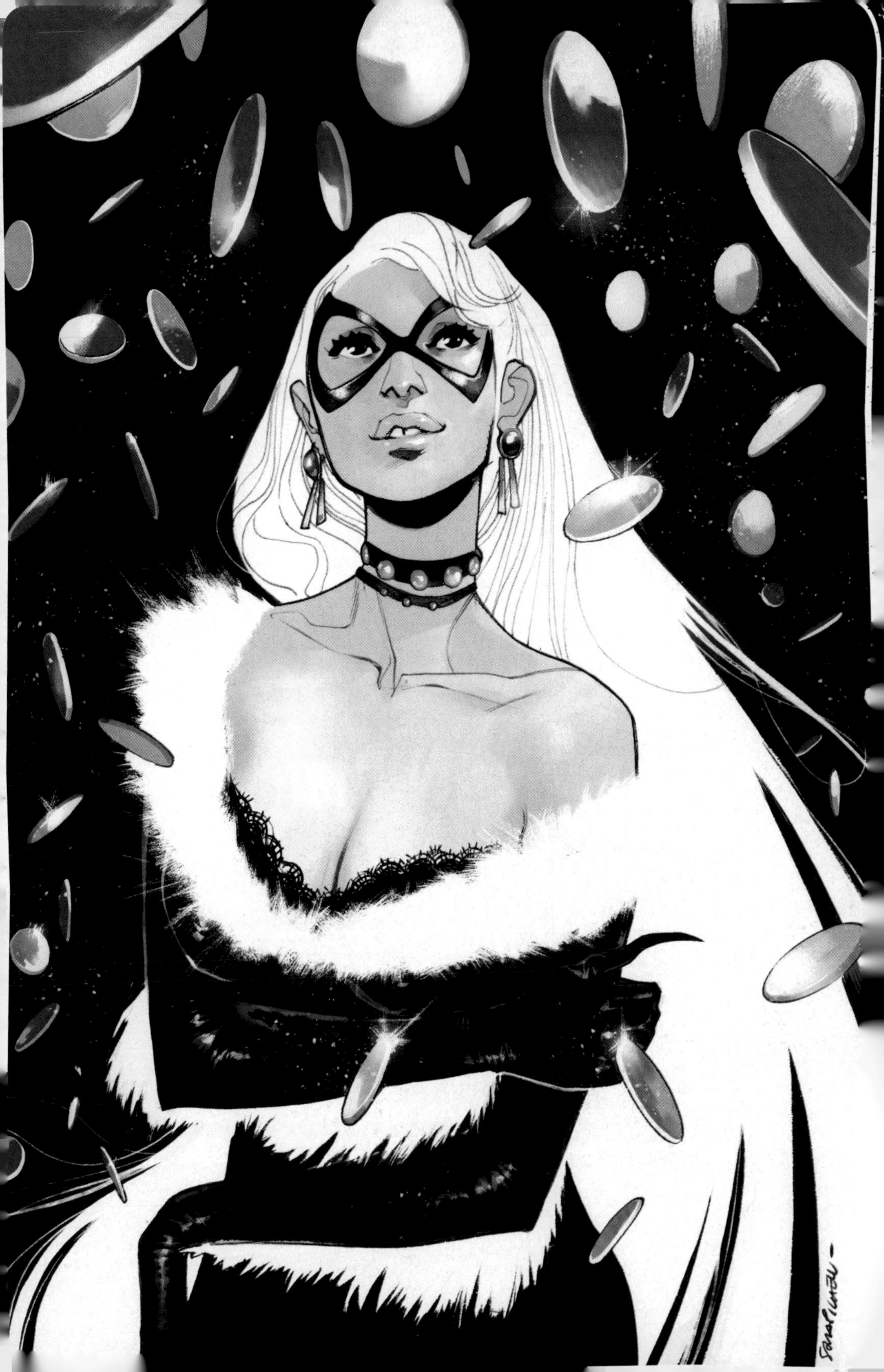

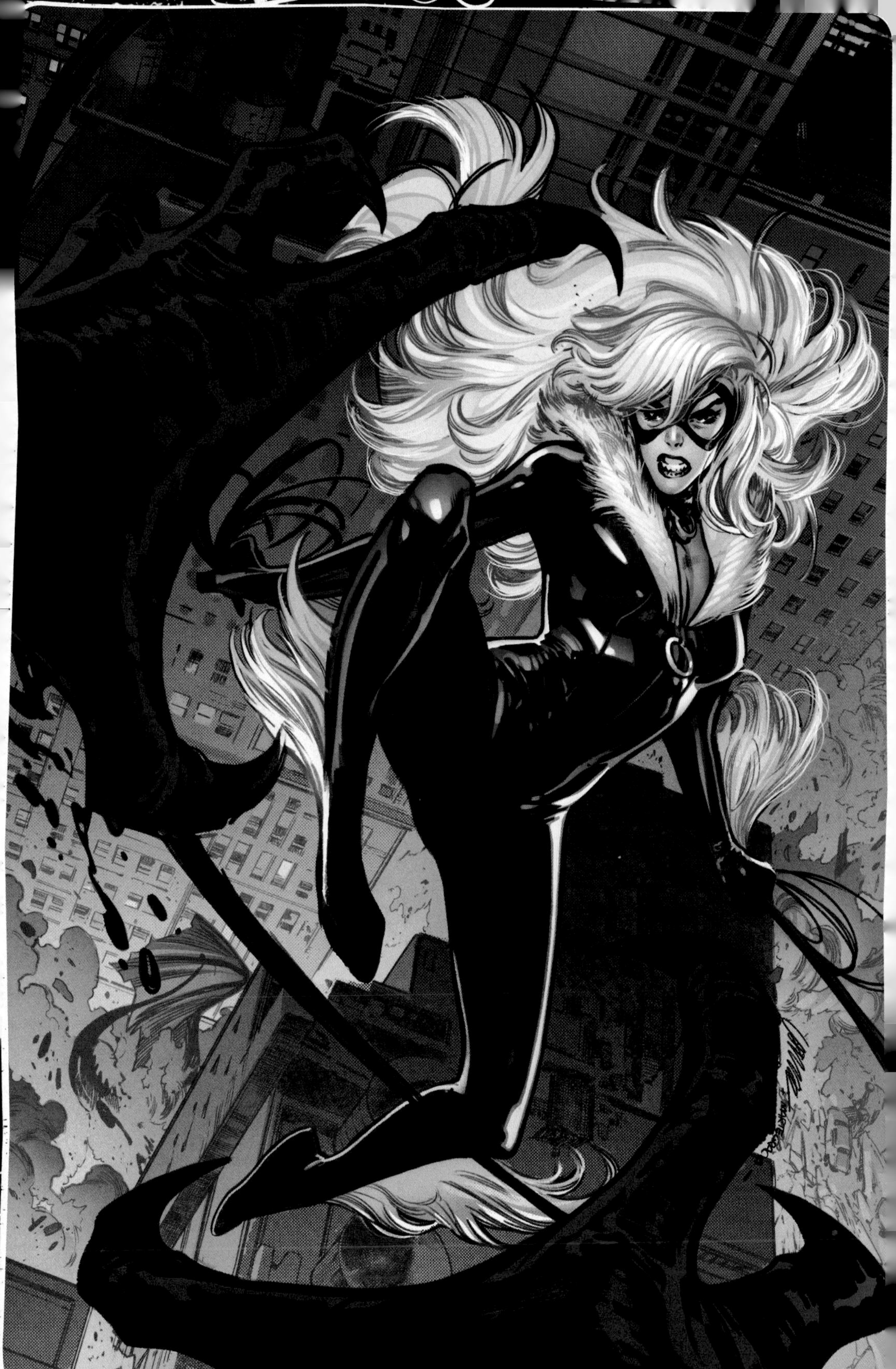

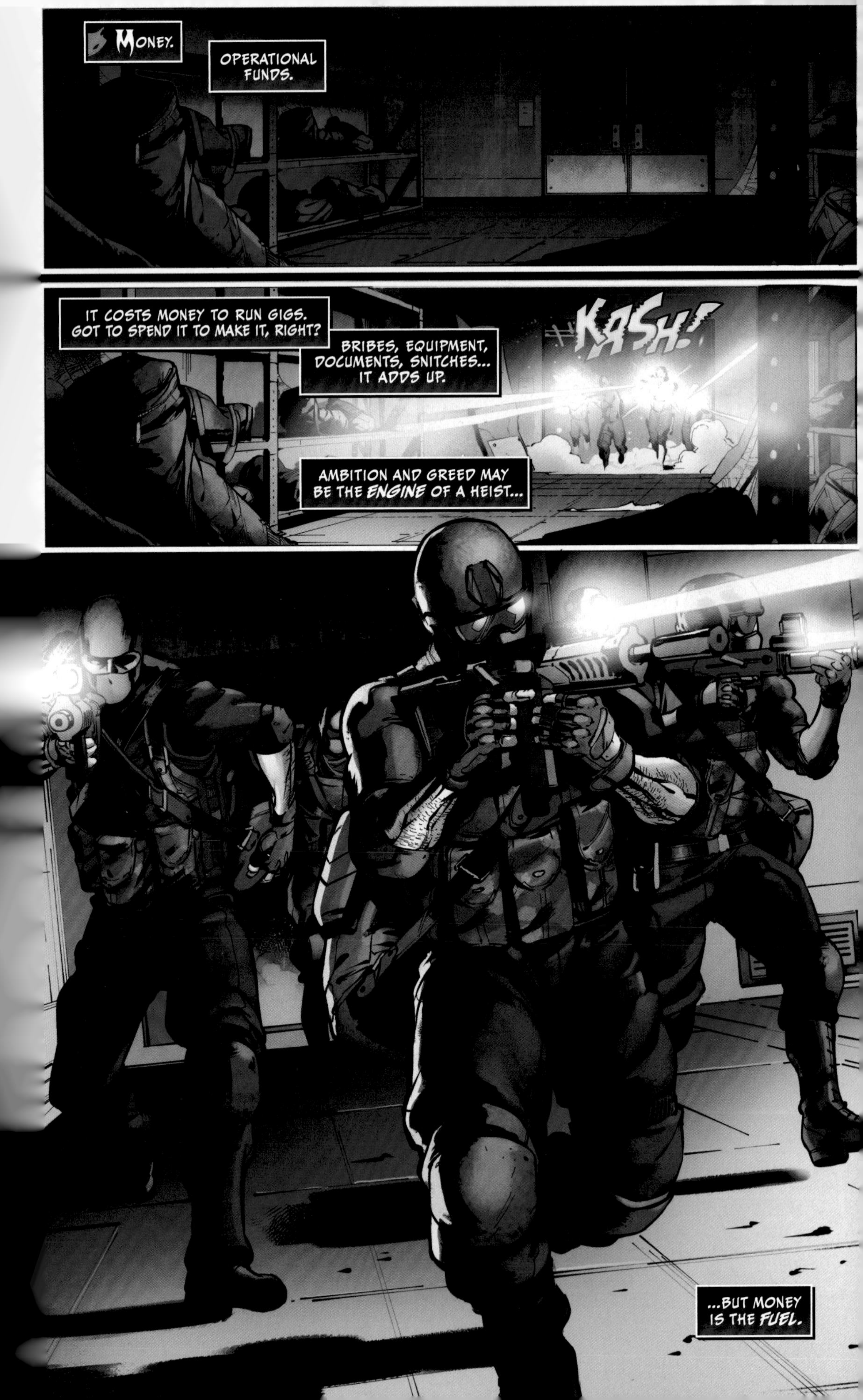
MONEY.
OPERATIONAL FUNDS.
IT COSTS MONEY TO RUN GIGS. GOT TO SPEND IT TO MAKE IT, RIGHT?
BRIBES, EQUIPMENT, DOCUMENTS, SNITCHES... IT ADDS UP.
KASH!
AMBITION AND GREED MAY BE THE ENGINE OF A HEIST...
...BUT MONEY IS THE FUEL.

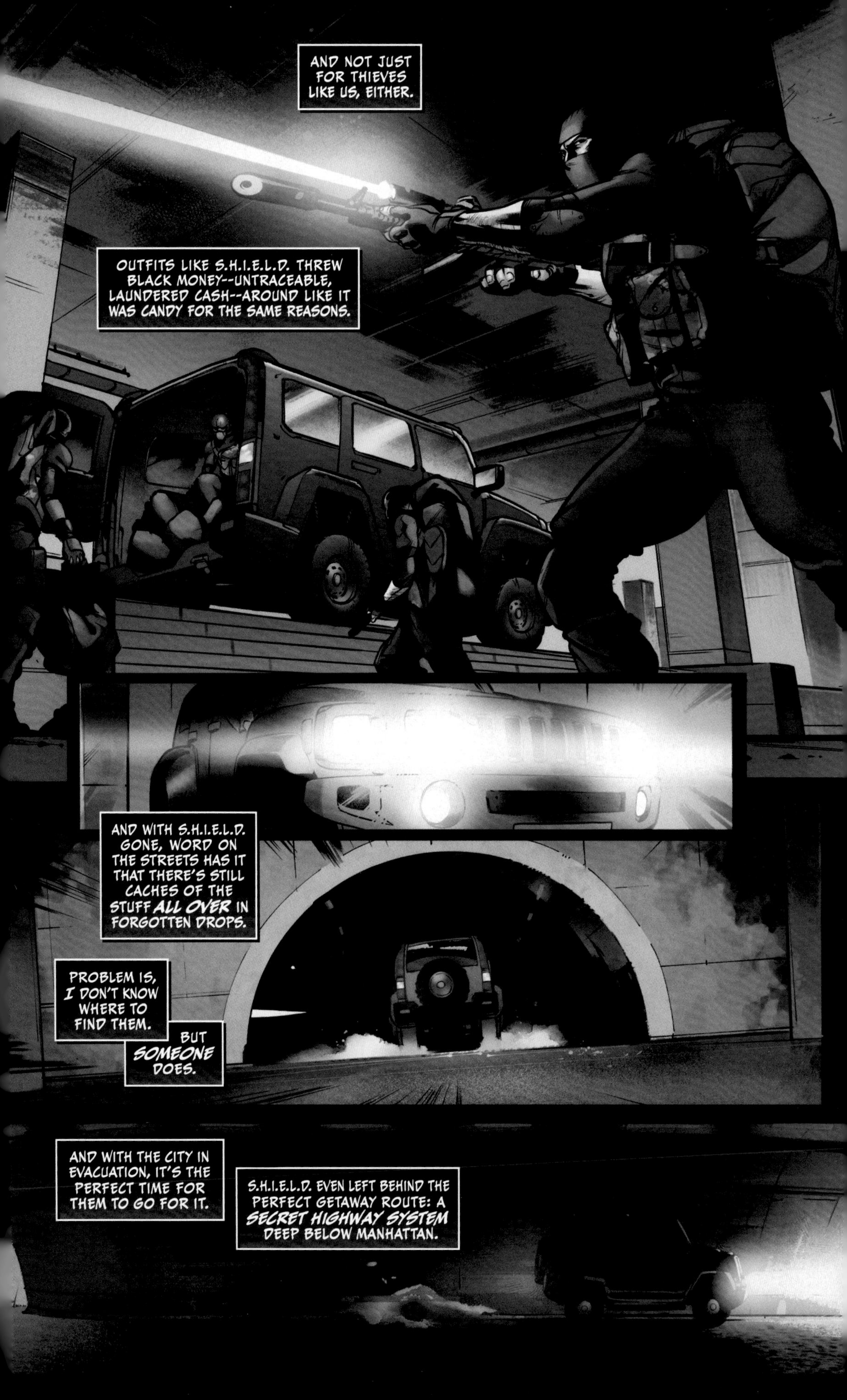

AND NOT JUST FOR THIEVES LIKE US, EITHER.
OUTFITS LIKE S.H.I.E.L.D. THREW BLACK MONEY--UNTRACEABLE, LAUNDERED CASH--AROUND LIKE IT WAS CANDY FOR THE SAME REASONS.
AND WITH S.H.I.E.L.D. GONE, WORD ON THE STREETS HAS IT THAT THERE'S STILL CACHES OF THE STUFF ALL OVER IN FORGOTTEN DROPS.
PROBLEM IS, I DON'T KNOW WHERE TO FIND THEM.
BUT SOMEONE DOES.
AND WITH THE CITY IN EVACUATION, IT'S THE PERFECT TIME FOR THEM TO GO FOR IT.
S.H.I.E.L.D. EVEN LEFT BEHIND THE PERFECT GETAWAY ROUTE: A SECRET HIGHWAY SYSTEM DEEP BELOW MANHATTAN.

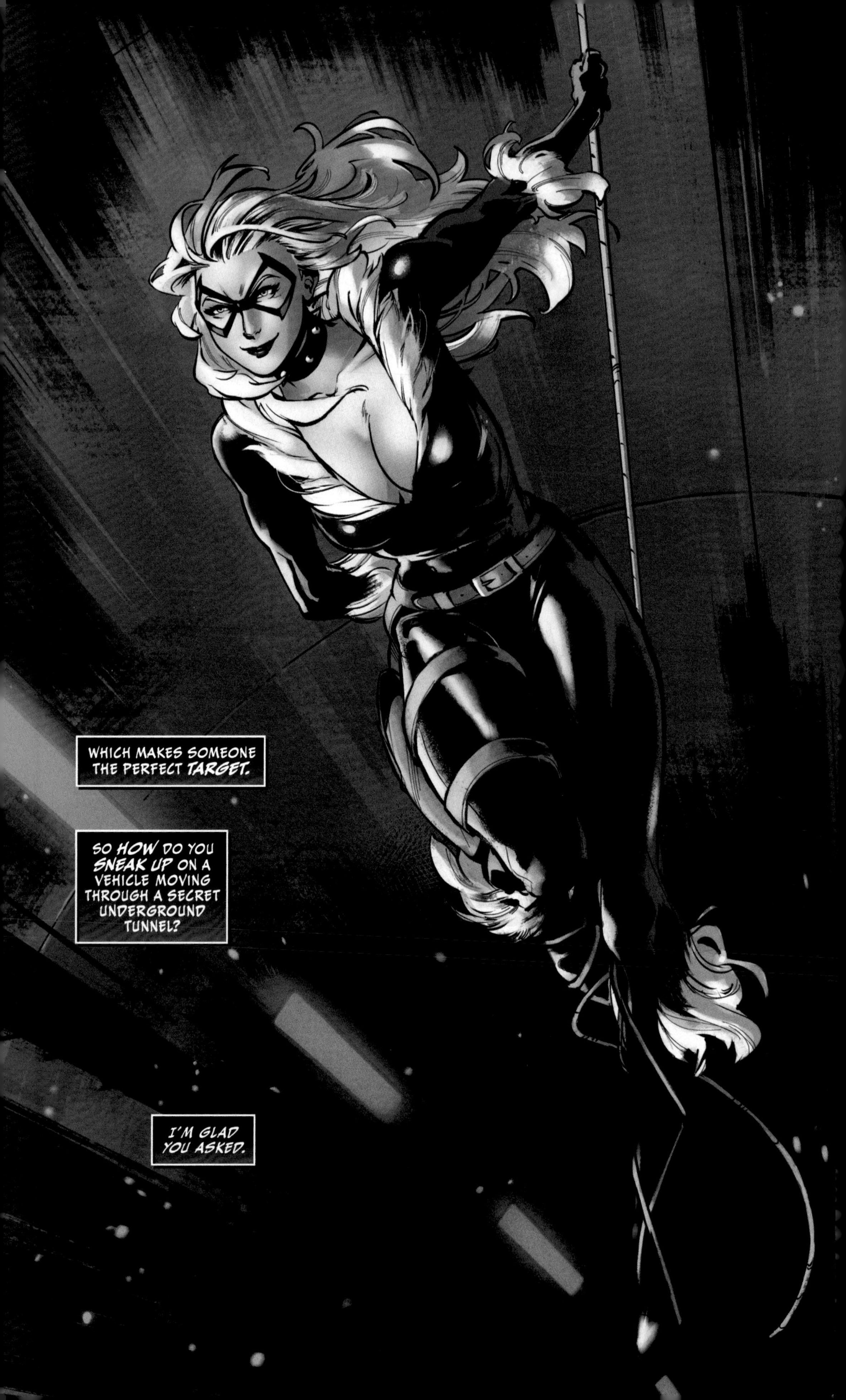
WHICH MAKES SOMEONE THE PERFECT TARGET.
SO HOW DO YOU SNEAK UP ON A VEHICLE MOVING THROUGH A SECRET UNDERGROUND TUNNEL?
I'M GLAD YOU ASKED.

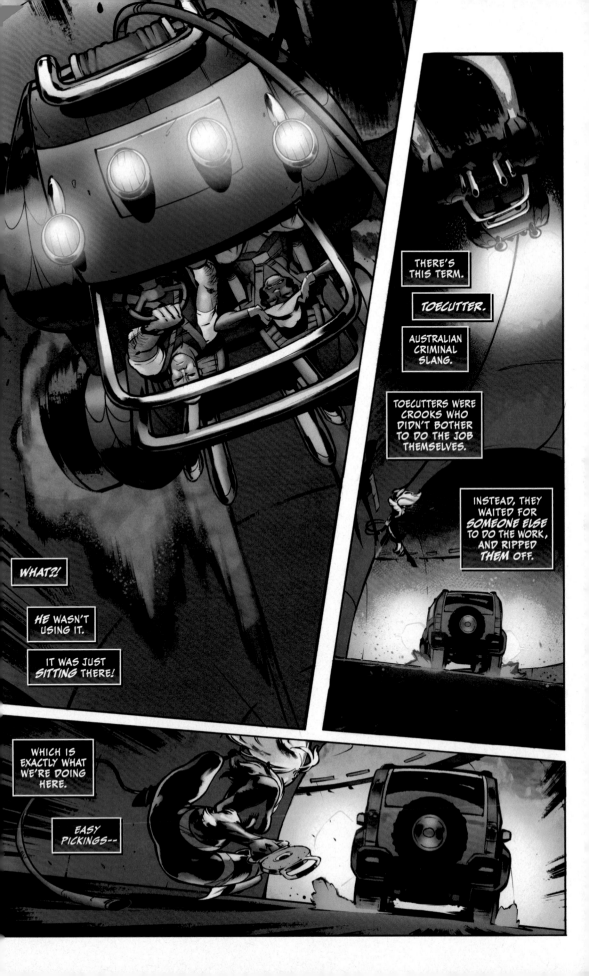

THERE'S THIS TERM.

TOECUTTER.

AUSTRALIAN CRIMINAL SLANG.

TOECUTTERS WERE CROOKS WHO DIDN'T BOTHER TO DO THE JOB THEMSELVES.

INSTEAD, THEY WAITED FOR *SOMEONE ELSE* TO DO THE WORK, AND RIPPED *THEM* OFF.

WHAT?!

HE WASN'T USING IT.

IT WAS JUST *SITTING* THERE!

WHICH IS EXACTLY WHAT WE'RE DOING HERE.

EASY PICKINGS--

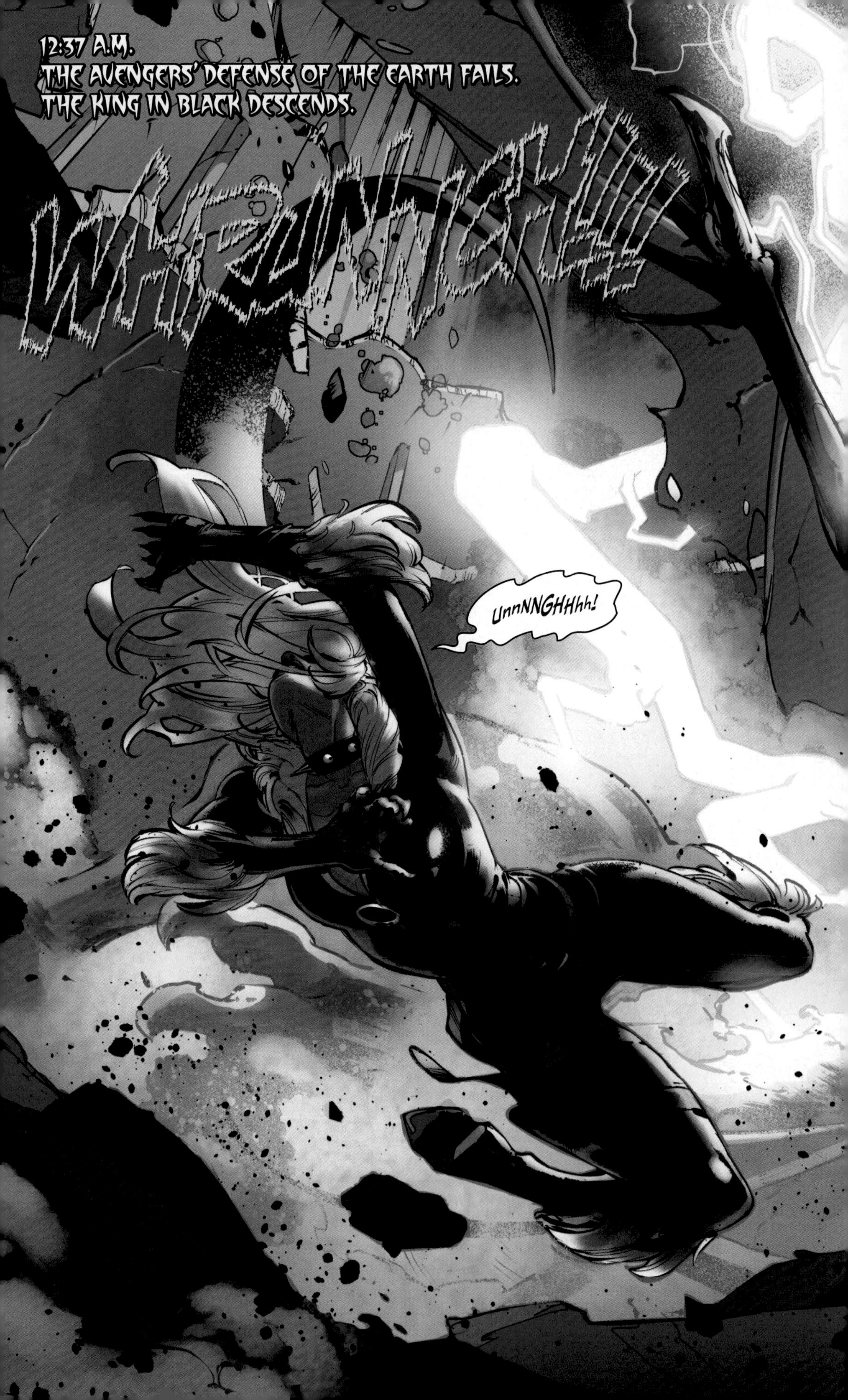
12:37 A.M.
THE AVENGERS' DEFENSE OF THE EARTH FAILS.
THE KING IN BLACK DESCENDS.
UnnNNGHHhh!

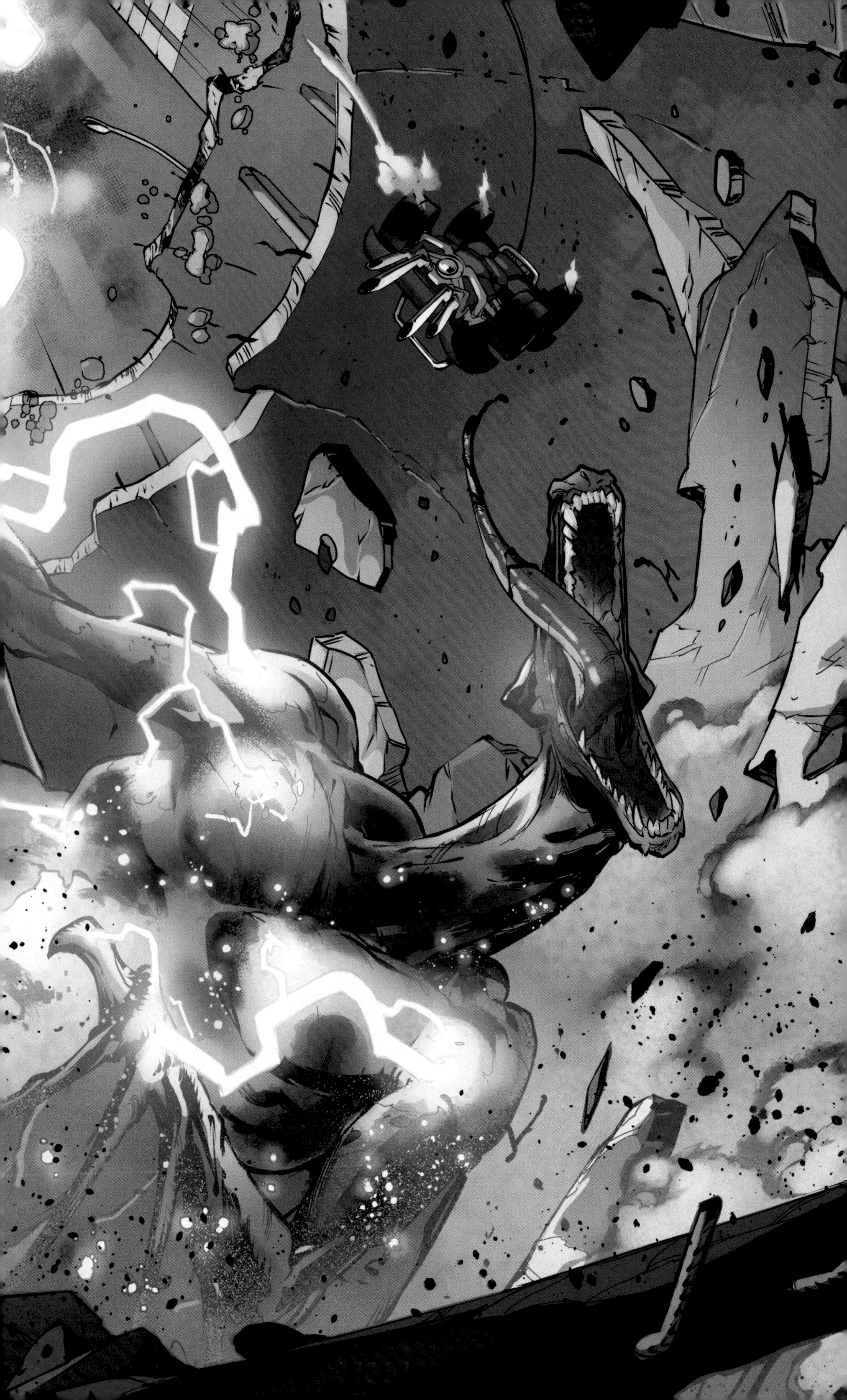

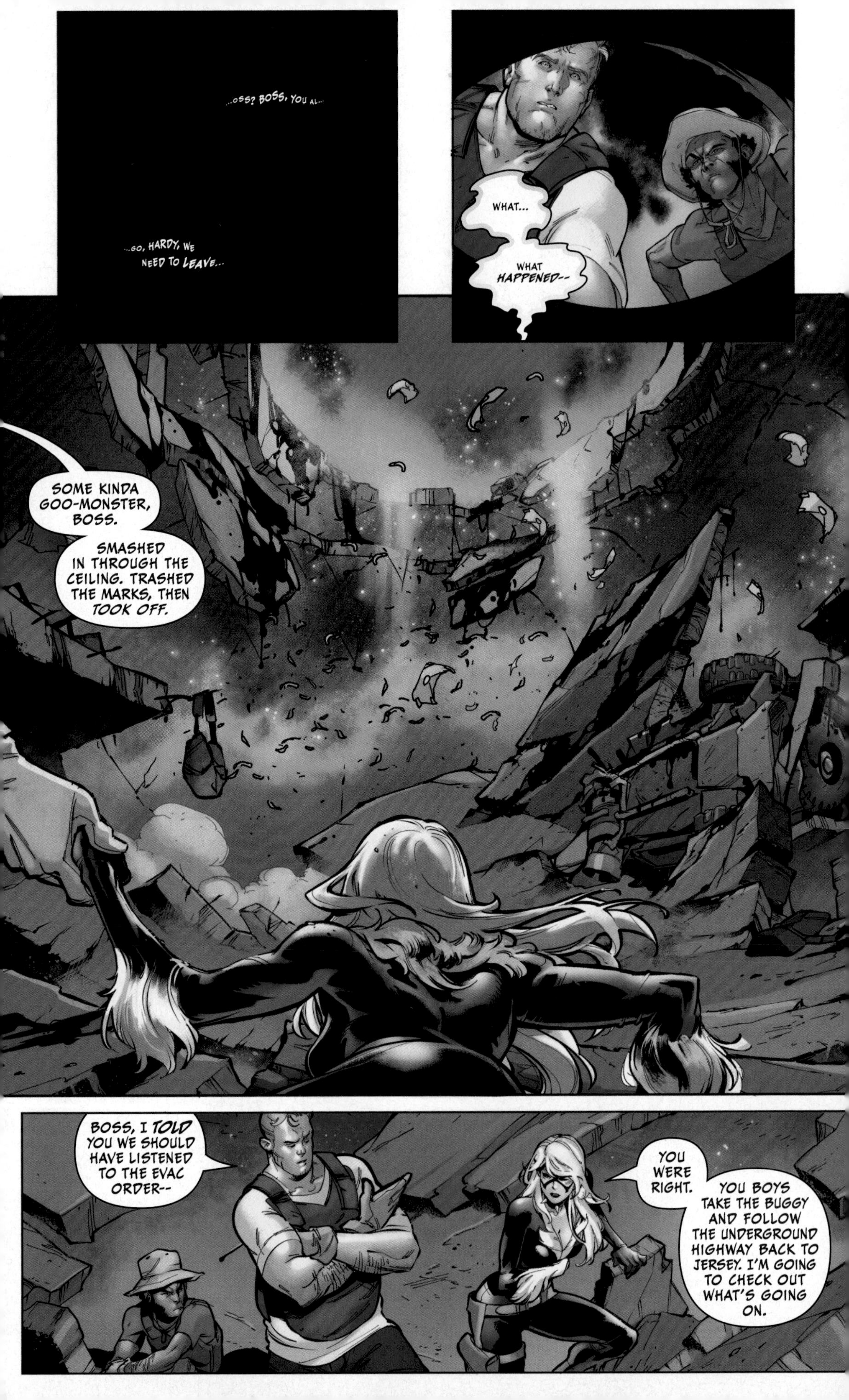
...OSS? BOSS, YOU AL...
...GO, HARDY, WE NEED TO LEAVE...
WHAT...
WHAT HAPPENED--
SOME KINDA GOO-MONSTER, BOSS.
SMASHED IN THROUGH THE CEILING. TRASHED THE MARKS, THEN TOOK OFF.
BOSS, I TOLD YOU WE SHOULD HAVE LISTENED TO THE EVAC ORDER--
YOU WERE RIGHT.
YOU BOYS TAKE THE BUGGY AND FOLLOW THE UNDERGROUND HIGHWAY BACK TO JERSEY. I'M GOING TO CHECK OUT WHAT'S GOING ON.

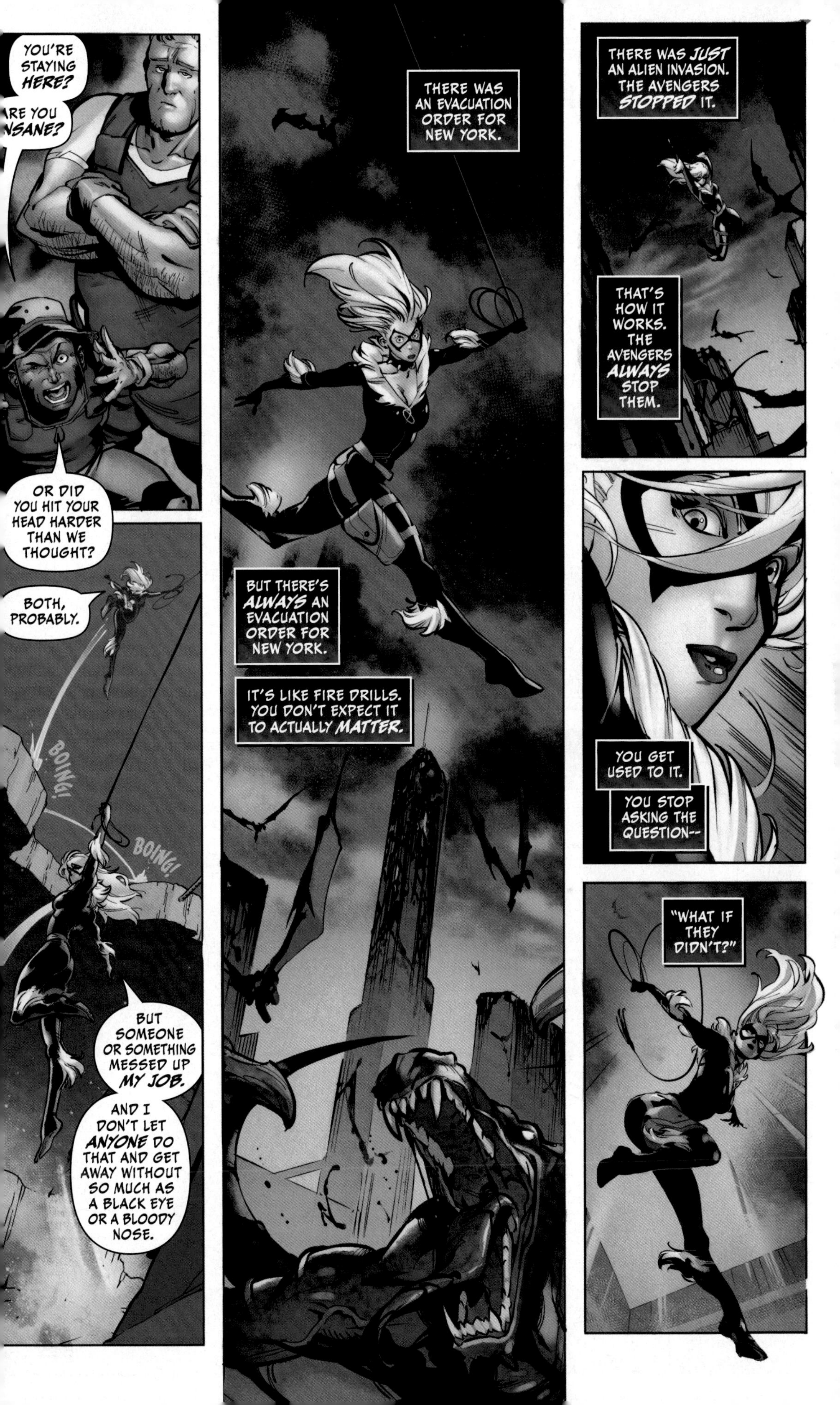

YOU'RE STAYING HERE?
ARE YOU INSANE?
OR DID YOU HIT YOUR HEAD HARDER THAN WE THOUGHT?
BOTH, PROBABLY.
BOING!
BOING!
BUT SOMEONE OR SOMETHING MESSED UP MY JOB.
AND I DON'T LET ANYONE DO THAT AND GET AWAY WITHOUT SO MUCH AS A BLACK EYE OR A BLOODY NOSE.
THERE WAS AN EVACUATION ORDER FOR NEW YORK.
BUT THERE'S ALWAYS AN EVACUATION ORDER FOR NEW YORK.
IT'S LIKE FIRE DRILLS. YOU DON'T EXPECT IT TO ACTUALLY MATTER.
THERE WAS JUST AN ALIEN INVASION. THE AVENGERS STOPPED IT.
THAT'S HOW IT WORKS. THE AVENGERS ALWAYS STOP THEM.
YOU GET USED TO IT.
YOU STOP ASKING THE QUESTION--
"WHAT IF THEY DIDN'T?"

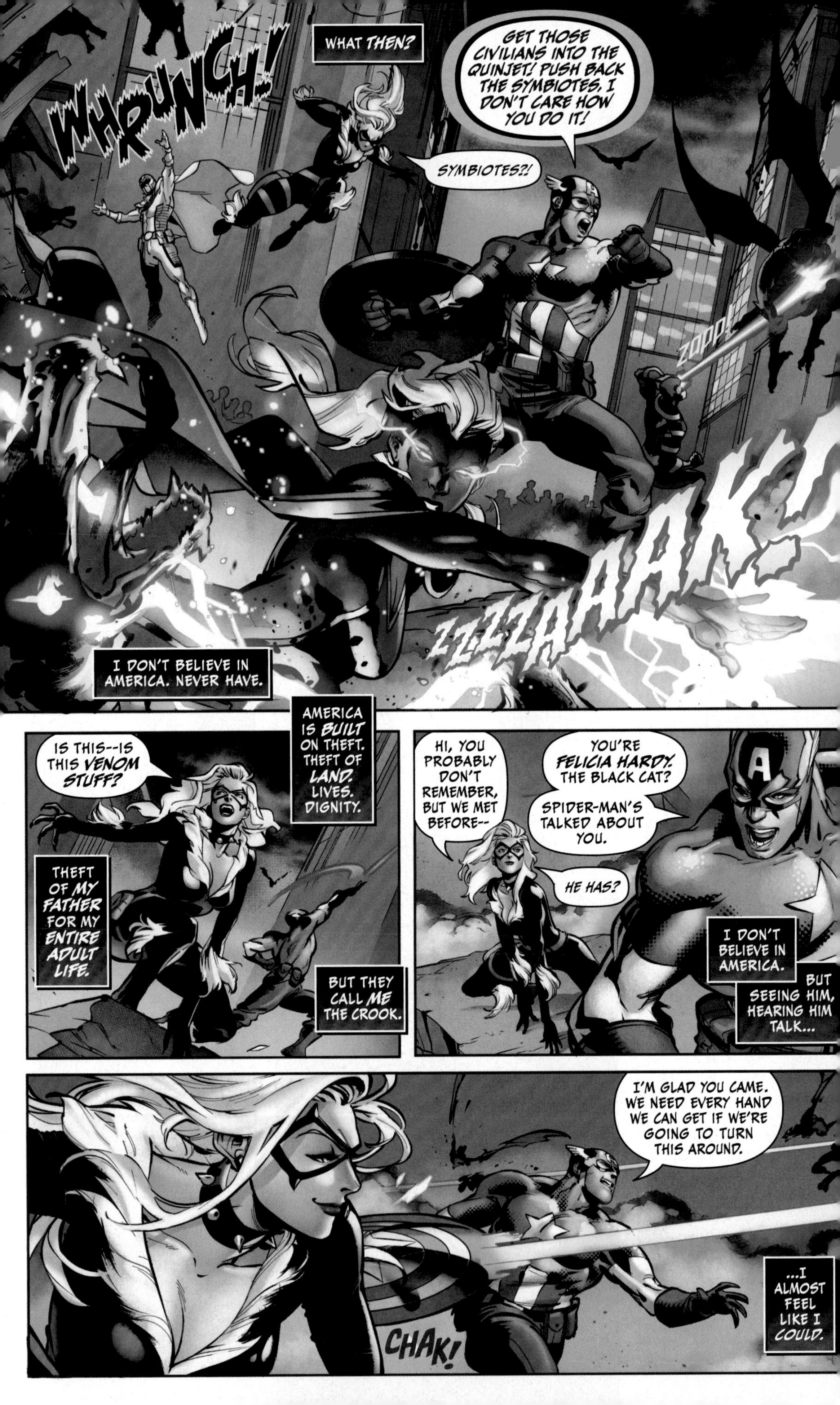
WHRUNCH!
WHAT THEN?
GET THOSE CIVILIANS INTO THE QUINJET! PUSH BACK THE SYMBIOTES. I DON'T CARE HOW YOU DO IT!
SYMBIOTES?!
ZOPP!
ZZZZAAAK!
I DON'T BELIEVE IN AMERICA. NEVER HAVE.
AMERICA IS BUILT ON THEFT. THEFT OF LAND. LIVES. DIGNITY.
IS THIS--IS THIS VENOM STUFF?
THEFT OF MY FATHER FOR MY ENTIRE ADULT LIFE.
BUT THEY CALL ME THE CROOK.
HI, YOU PROBABLY DON'T REMEMBER, BUT WE MET BEFORE--
YOU'RE FELICIA HARDY. THE BLACK CAT?
SPIDER-MAN'S TALKED ABOUT YOU.
HE HAS?
I DON'T BELIEVE IN AMERICA.
BUT SEEING HIM, HEARING HIM TALK...
I'M GLAD YOU CAME. WE NEED EVERY HAND WE CAN GET IF WE'RE GOING TO TURN THIS AROUND.
...I ALMOST FEEL LIKE I COULD.
CHAK!

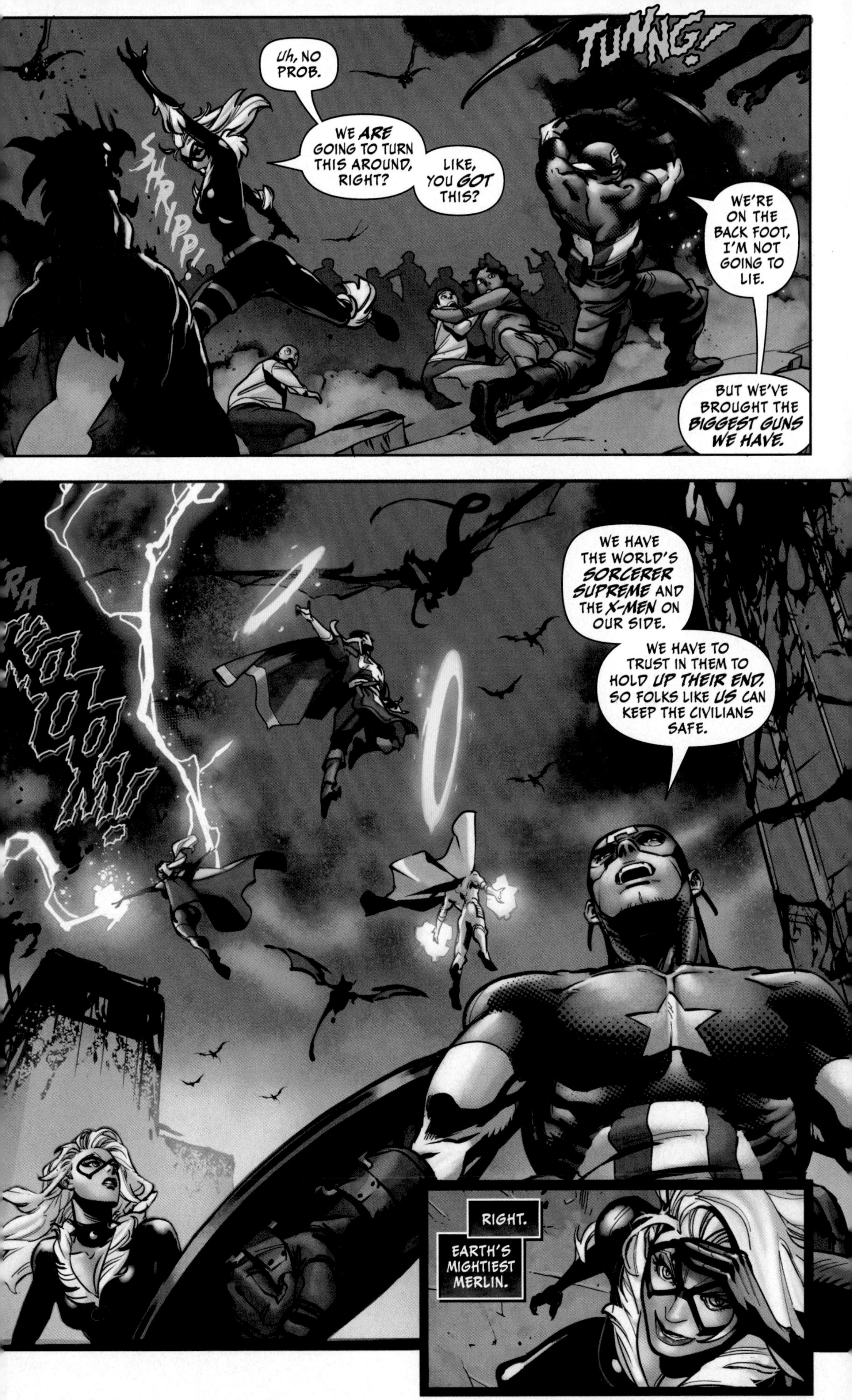
TUNNG!
SHRIPP!
Uh, NO PROB.
WE ARE GOING TO TURN THIS AROUND, RIGHT?
LIKE, YOU GOT THIS?
WE'RE ON THE BACK FOOT, I'M NOT GOING TO LIE.
BUT WE'VE BROUGHT THE BIGGEST GUNS WE HAVE.
RA
WE HAVE THE WORLD'S SORCERER SUPREME AND THE X-MEN ON OUR SIDE.
WE HAVE TO TRUST IN THEM TO HOLD UP THEIR END, SO FOLKS LIKE US CAN KEEP THE CIVILIANS SAFE.
RIGHT.
EARTH'S MIGHTIEST MERLIN.

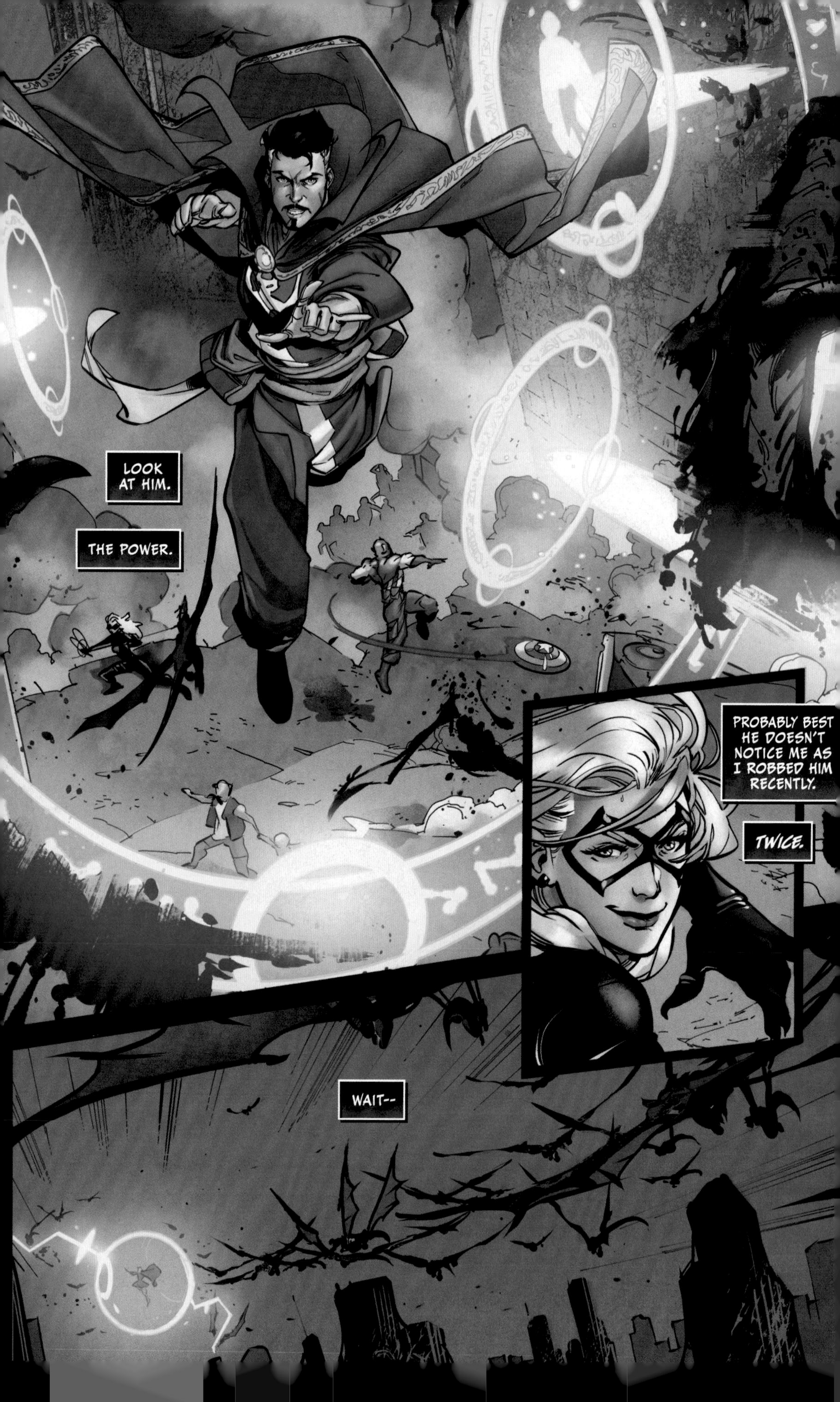
LOOK AT HIM.
THE POWER.
PROBABLY BEST HE DOESN'T NOTICE ME AS I ROBBED HIM RECENTLY.
TWICE.
WAIT--

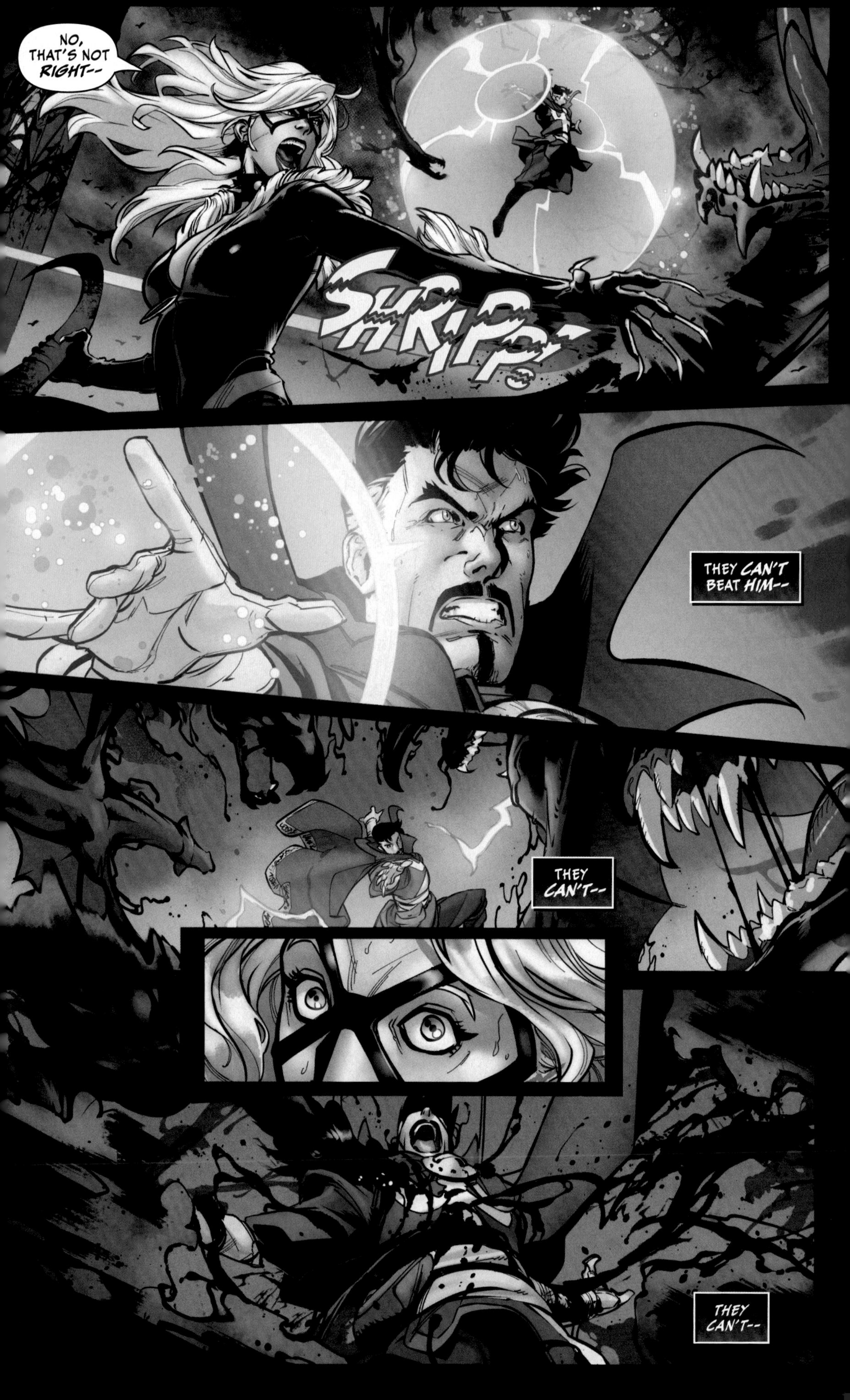
NO, THAT'S NOT RIGHT--
SHRIPP!
THEY CAN'T BEAT HIM--
THEY CAN'T--
THEY CAN'T--

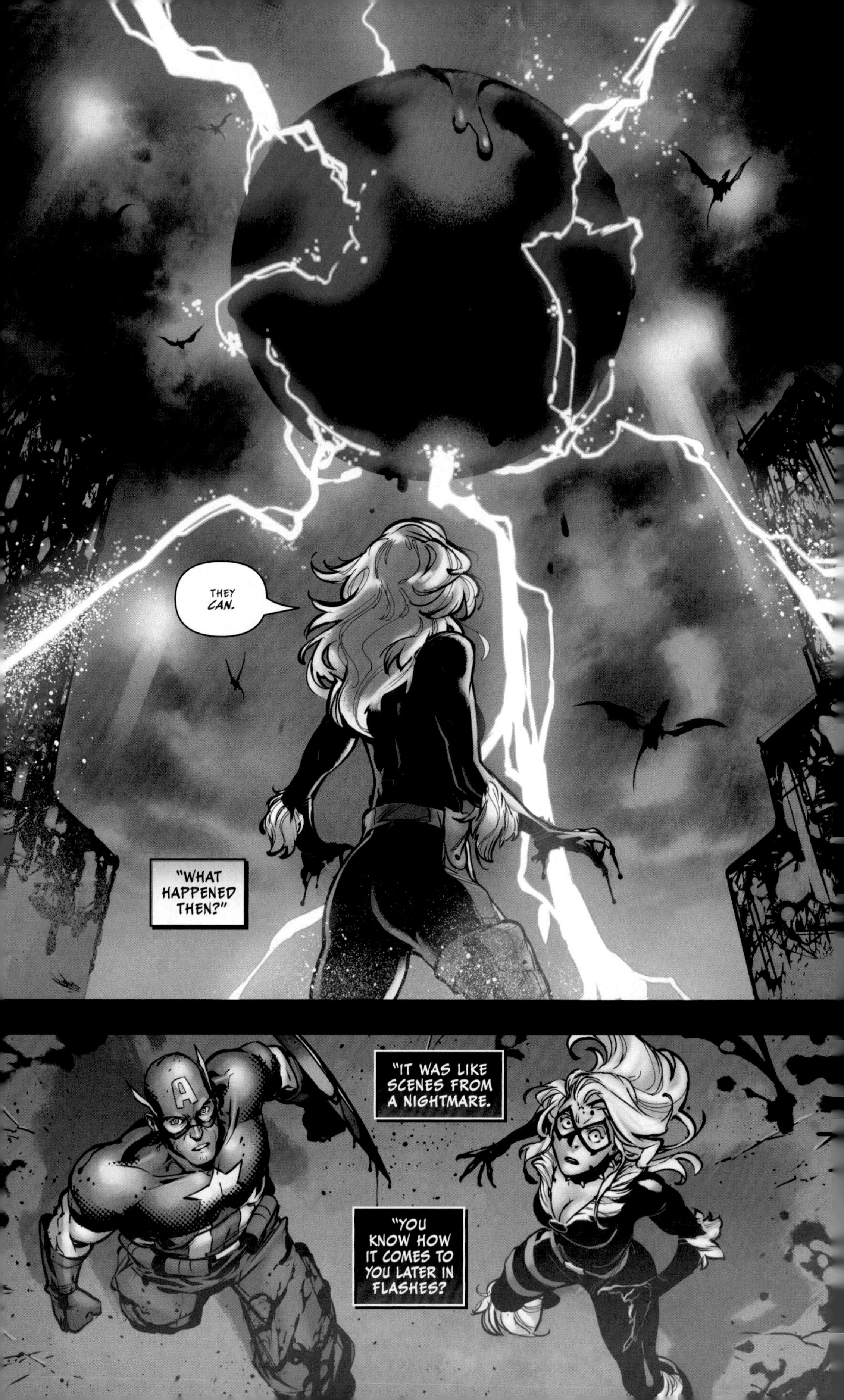
THEY CAN.
"WHAT HAPPENED THEN?"
"IT WAS LIKE SCENES FROM A NIGHTMARE.
"YOU KNOW HOW IT COMES TO YOU LATER IN FLASHES?

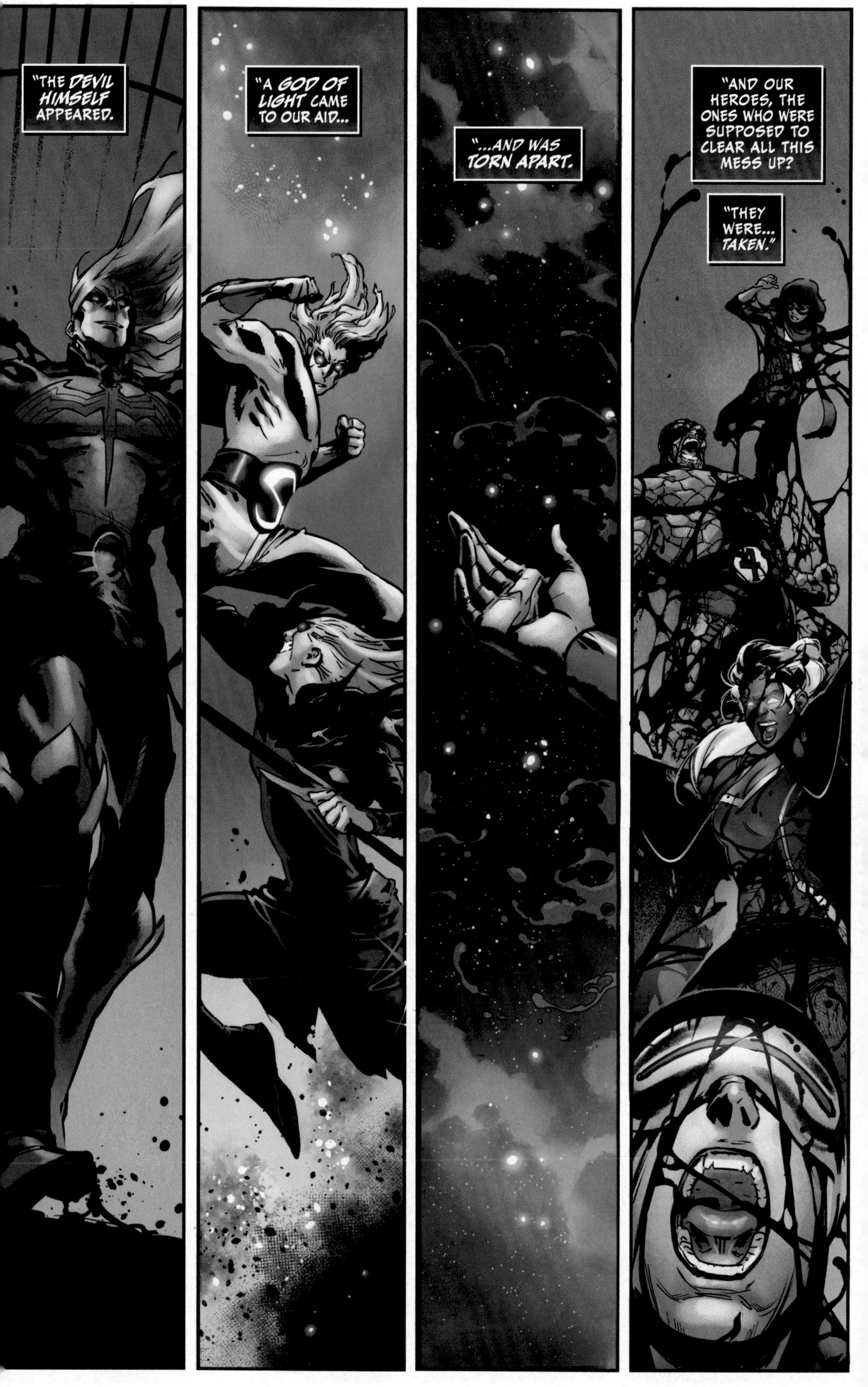
"THE DEVIL HIMSELF APPEARED.
"A GOD OF LIGHT CAME TO OUR AID...
"...AND WAS TORN APART.
"AND OUR HEROES, THE ONES WHO WERE SUPPOSED TO CLEAR ALL THIS MESS UP?
"THEY WERE... TAKEN."

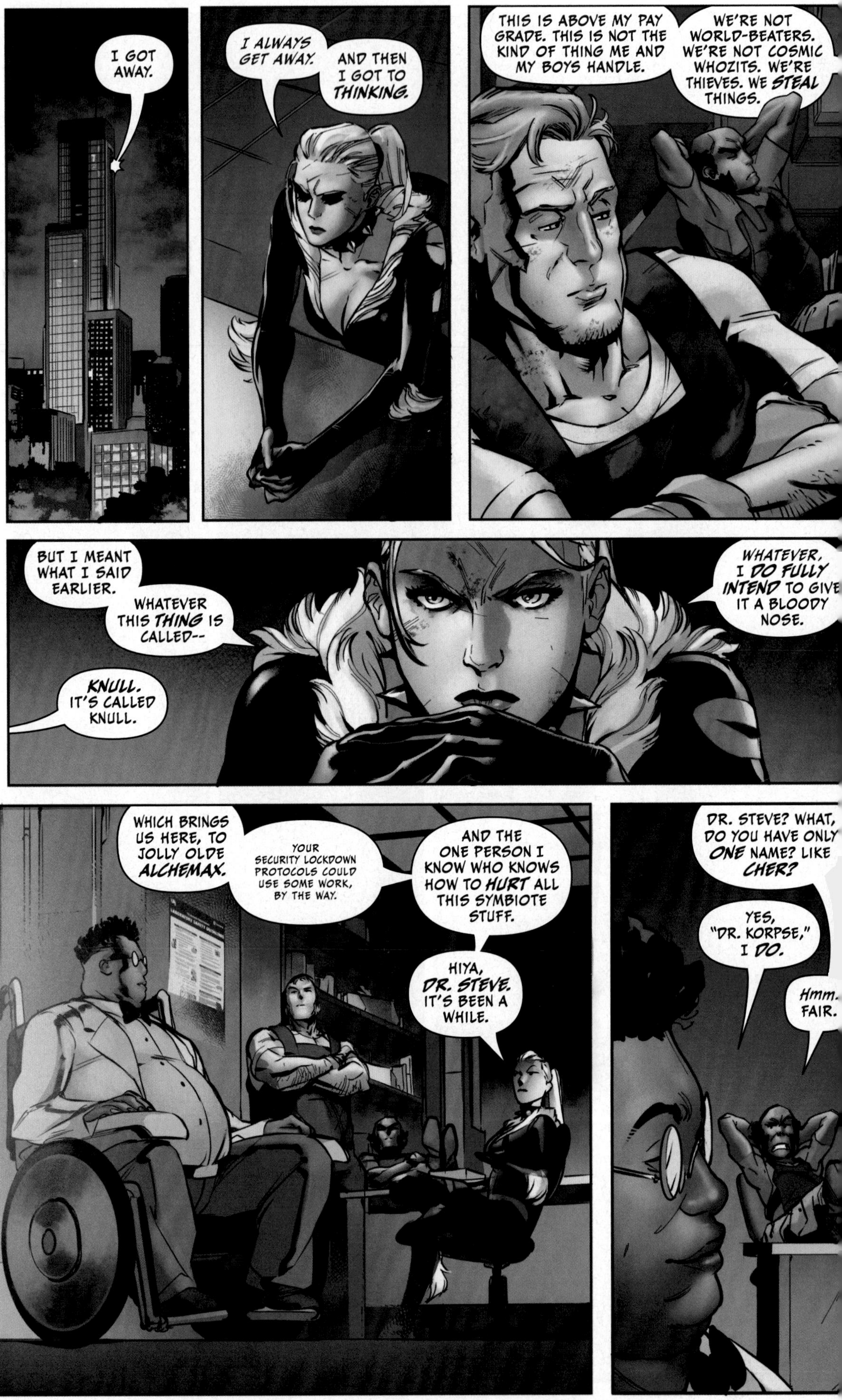

I GOT AWAY.
I ALWAYS GET AWAY.
AND THEN I GOT TO THINKING.
THIS IS ABOVE MY PAY GRADE. THIS IS NOT THE KIND OF THING ME AND MY BOYS HANDLE.
WE'RE NOT WORLD-BEATERS. WE'RE NOT COSMIC WHOZITS. WE'RE THIEVES. WE STEAL THINGS.
BUT I MEANT WHAT I SAID EARLIER.
WHATEVER THIS THING IS CALLED--
KNULL. IT'S CALLED KNULL.
WHATEVER. I DO FULLY INTEND TO GIVE IT A BLOODY NOSE.
WHICH BRINGS US HERE, TO JOLLY OLDE ALCHEMAX.
YOUR SECURITY LOCKDOWN PROTOCOLS COULD USE SOME WORK, BY THE WAY.
AND THE ONE PERSON I KNOW WHO KNOWS HOW TO HURT ALL THIS SYMBIOTE STUFF.
HIYA, DR. STEVE. IT'S BEEN A WHILE.
DR. STEVE? WHAT, DO YOU HAVE ONLY ONE NAME? LIKE CHER?
YES, "DR. KORPSE," I DO.
Hmm. FAIR.

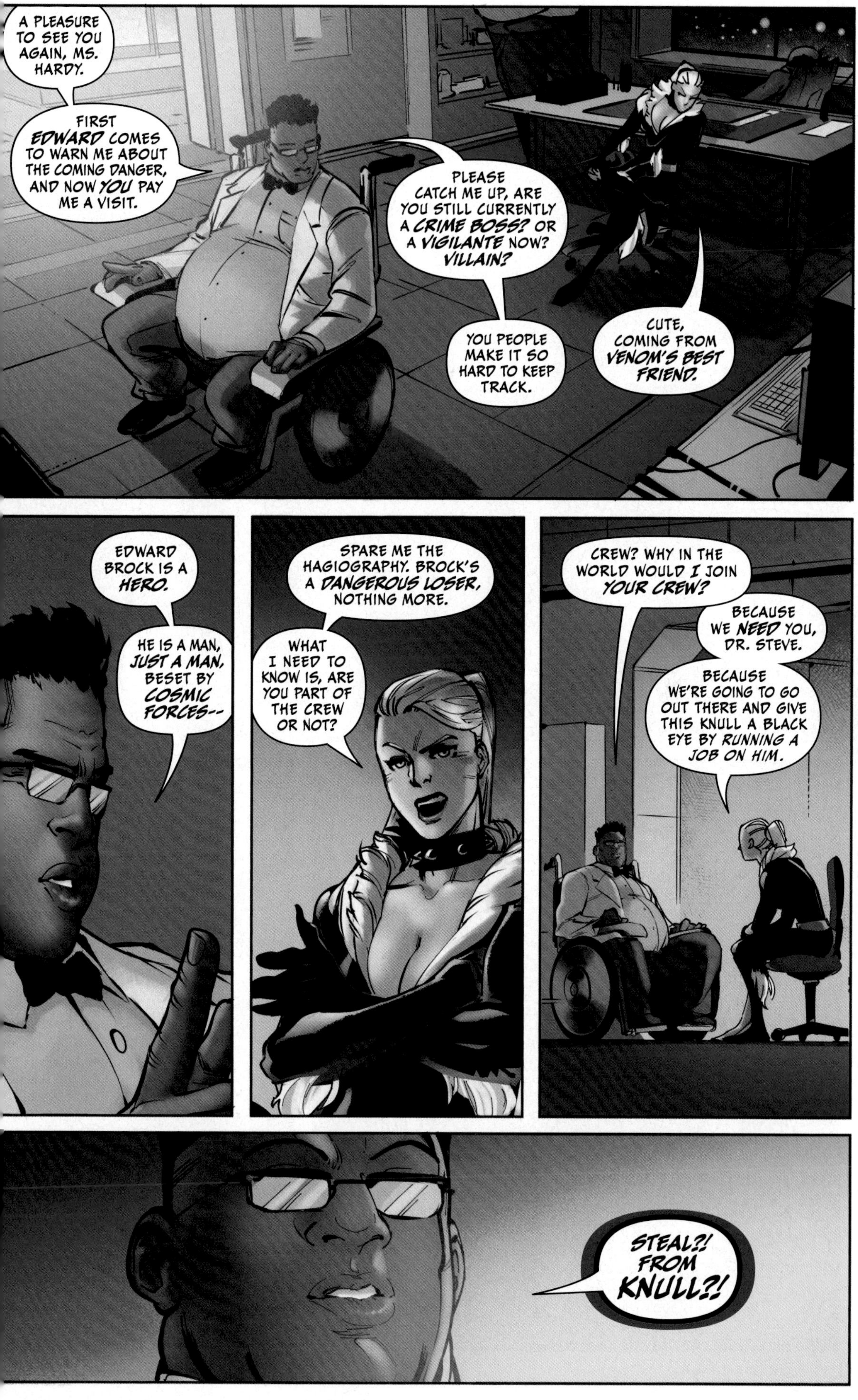

A PLEASURE TO SEE YOU AGAIN, MS. HARDY.
FIRST EDWARD COMES TO WARN ME ABOUT THE COMING DANGER, AND NOW YOU PAY ME A VISIT.
PLEASE CATCH ME UP, ARE YOU STILL CURRENTLY A CRIME BOSS? OR A VIGILANTE NOW? VILLAIN?
YOU PEOPLE MAKE IT SO HARD TO KEEP TRACK.
CUTE, COMING FROM VENOM'S BEST FRIEND.
EDWARD BROCK IS A HERO.
HE IS A MAN, JUST A MAN, BESET BY COSMIC FORCES--
SPARE ME THE HAGIOGRAPHY. BROCK'S A DANGEROUS LOSER, NOTHING MORE.
WHAT I NEED TO KNOW IS, ARE YOU PART OF THE CREW OR NOT?
CREW? WHY IN THE WORLD WOULD I JOIN YOUR CREW?
BECAUSE WE NEED YOU, DR. STEVE.
BECAUSE WE'RE GOING TO GO OUT THERE AND GIVE THIS KNULL A BLACK EYE BY RUNNING A JOB ON HIM.
STEAL?! FROM KNULL?!

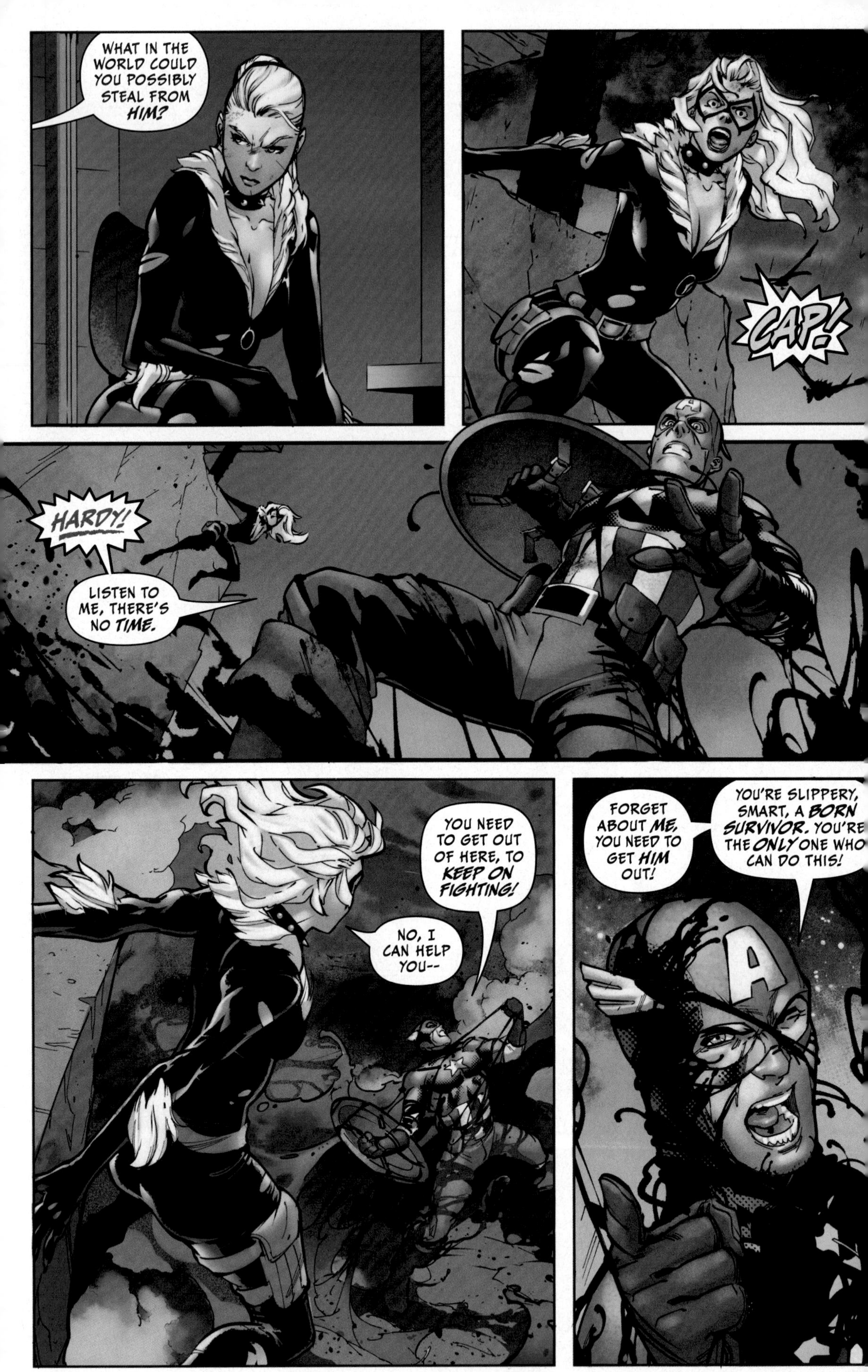
WHAT IN THE WORLD COULD YOU POSSIBLY STEAL FROM *HIM?*
CAP!
HARDY!
LISTEN TO ME, THERE'S NO *TIME.*
YOU NEED TO GET OUT OF HERE, TO *KEEP ON FIGHTING!*
NO, I CAN HELP YOU--
FORGET ABOUT *ME,* YOU NEED TO GET *HIM* OUT!
YOU'RE SLIPPERY, SMART, A *BORN SURVIVOR.* YOU'RE THE *ONLY* ONE WHO CAN DO THIS!

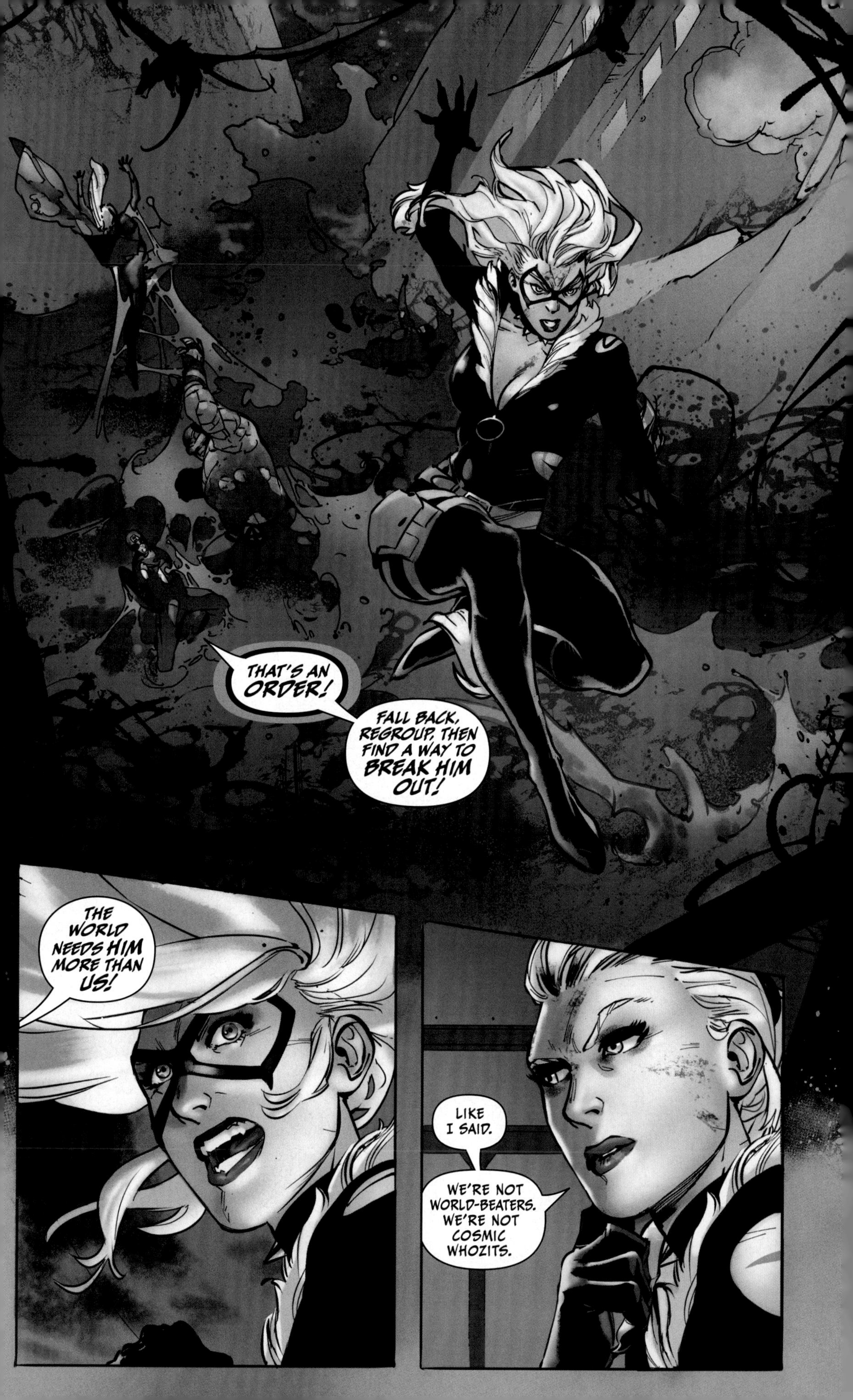
THAT'S AN ORDER!
FALL BACK, REGROUP, THEN FIND A WAY TO BREAK HIM OUT!
THE WORLD NEEDS HIM MORE THAN US!
LIKE I SAID.
WE'RE NOT WORLD-BEATERS. WE'RE NOT COSMIC WHOZITS.

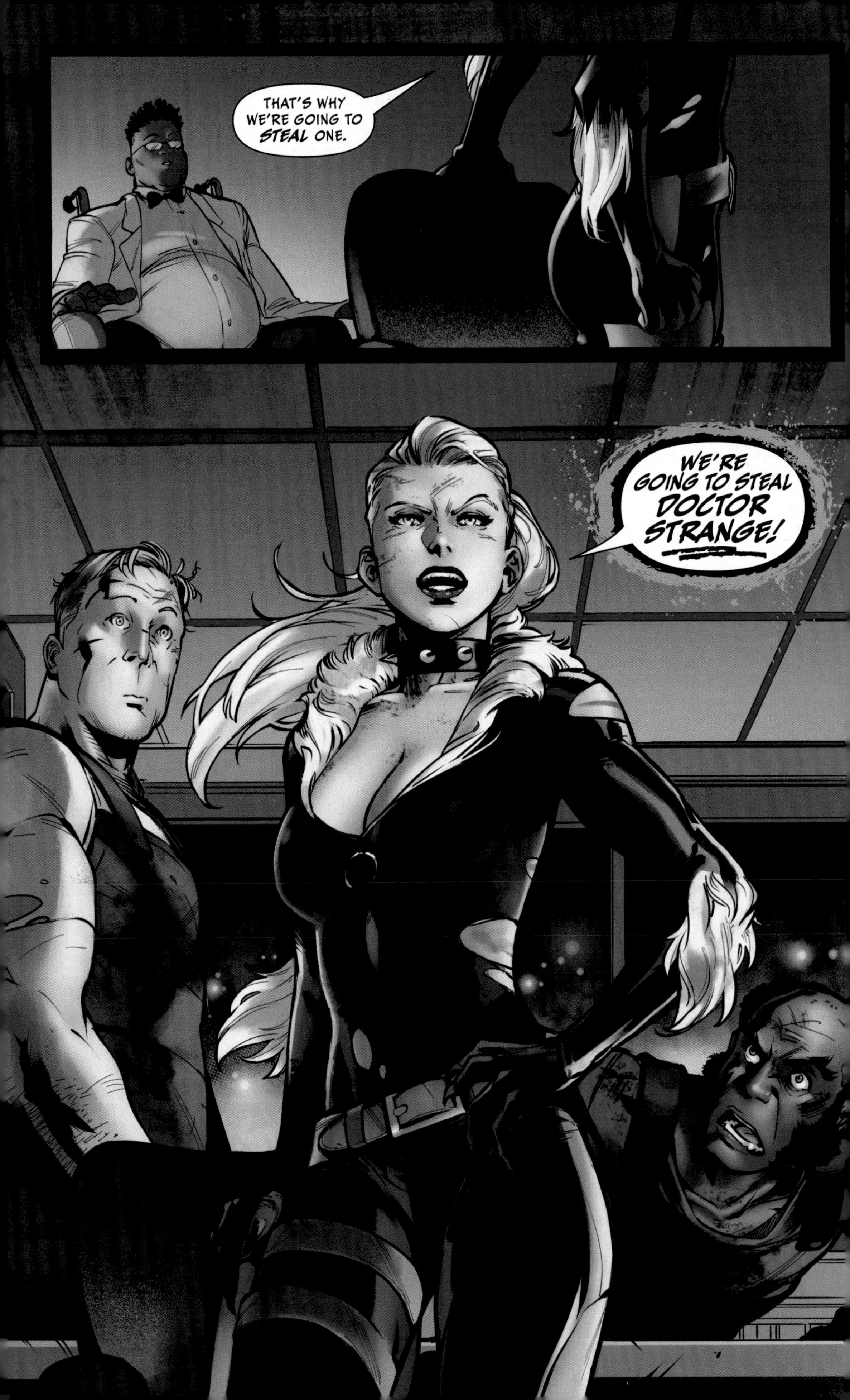
THAT'S WHY WE'RE GOING TO STEAL ONE.
WE'RE GOING TO STEAL DOCTOR STRANGE!

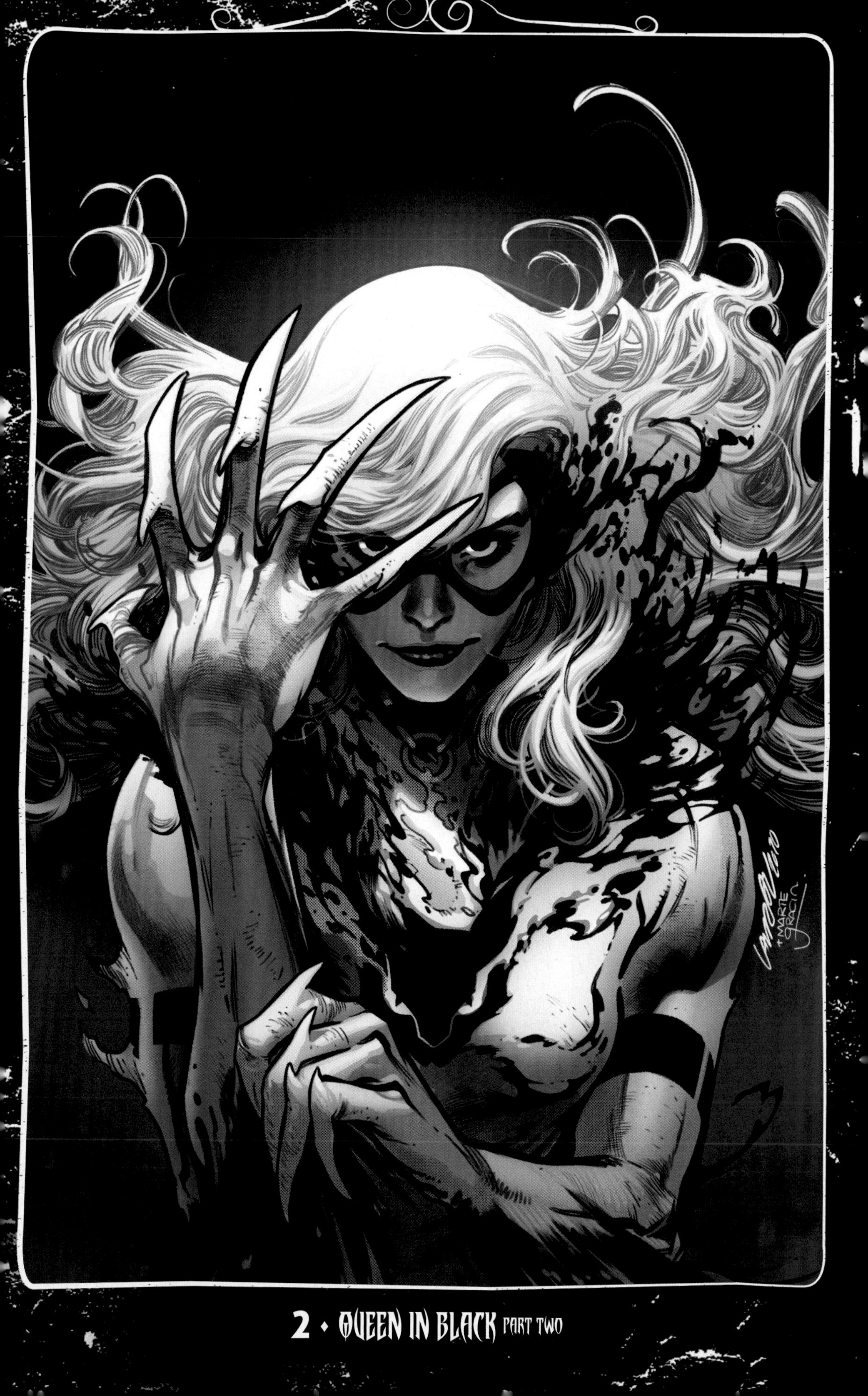

2 • QUEEN IN BLACK PART TWO

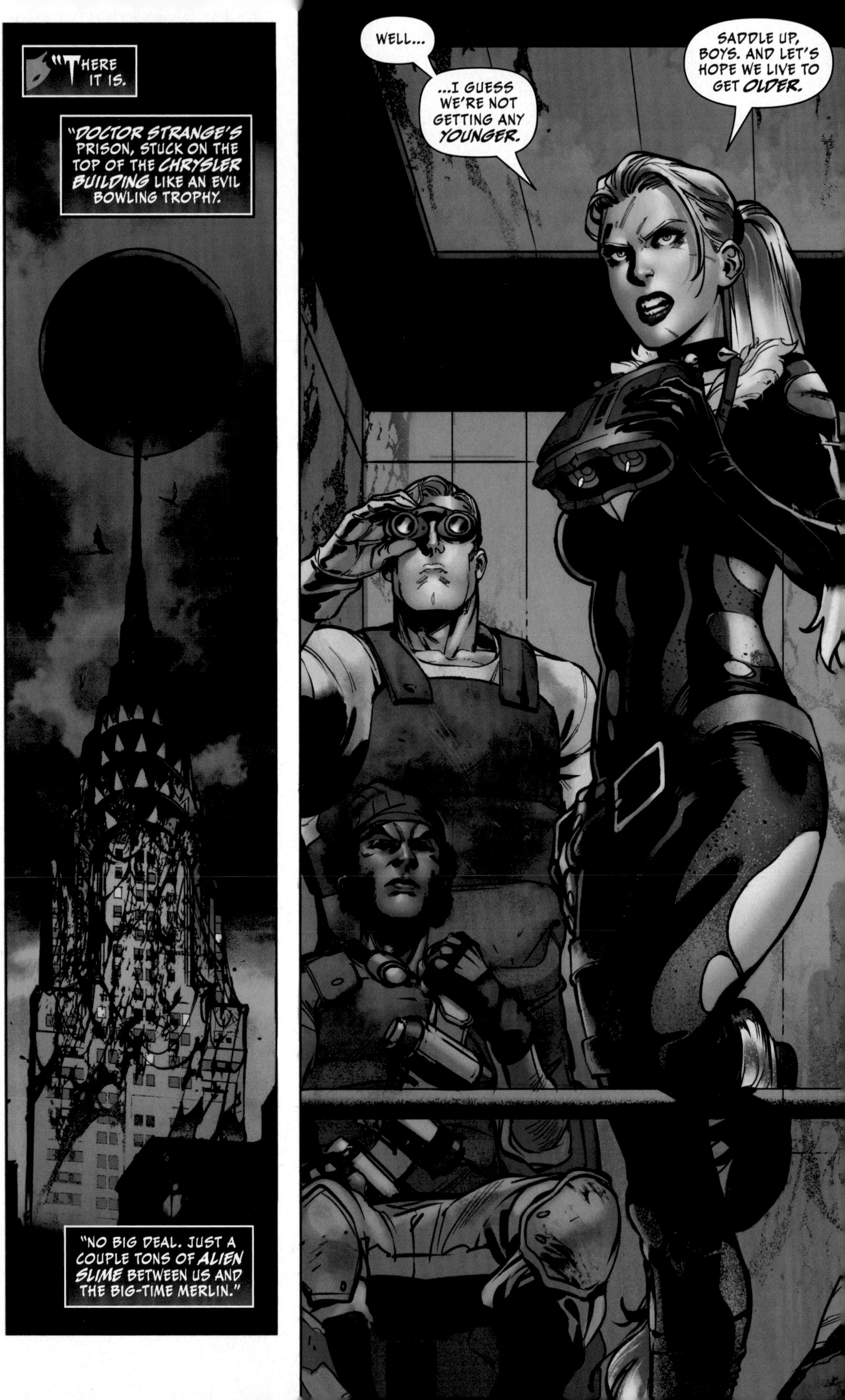
"THERE IT IS.
"DOCTOR STRANGE'S PRISON, STUCK ON THE TOP OF THE CHRYSLER BUILDING LIKE AN EVIL BOWLING TROPHY.
"NO BIG DEAL. JUST A COUPLE TONS OF ALIEN SLIME BETWEEN US AND THE BIG-TIME MERLIN."
WELL...
...I GUESS WE'RE NOT GETTING ANY YOUNGER.
SADDLE UP, BOYS. AND LET'S HOPE WE LIVE TO GET OLDER.

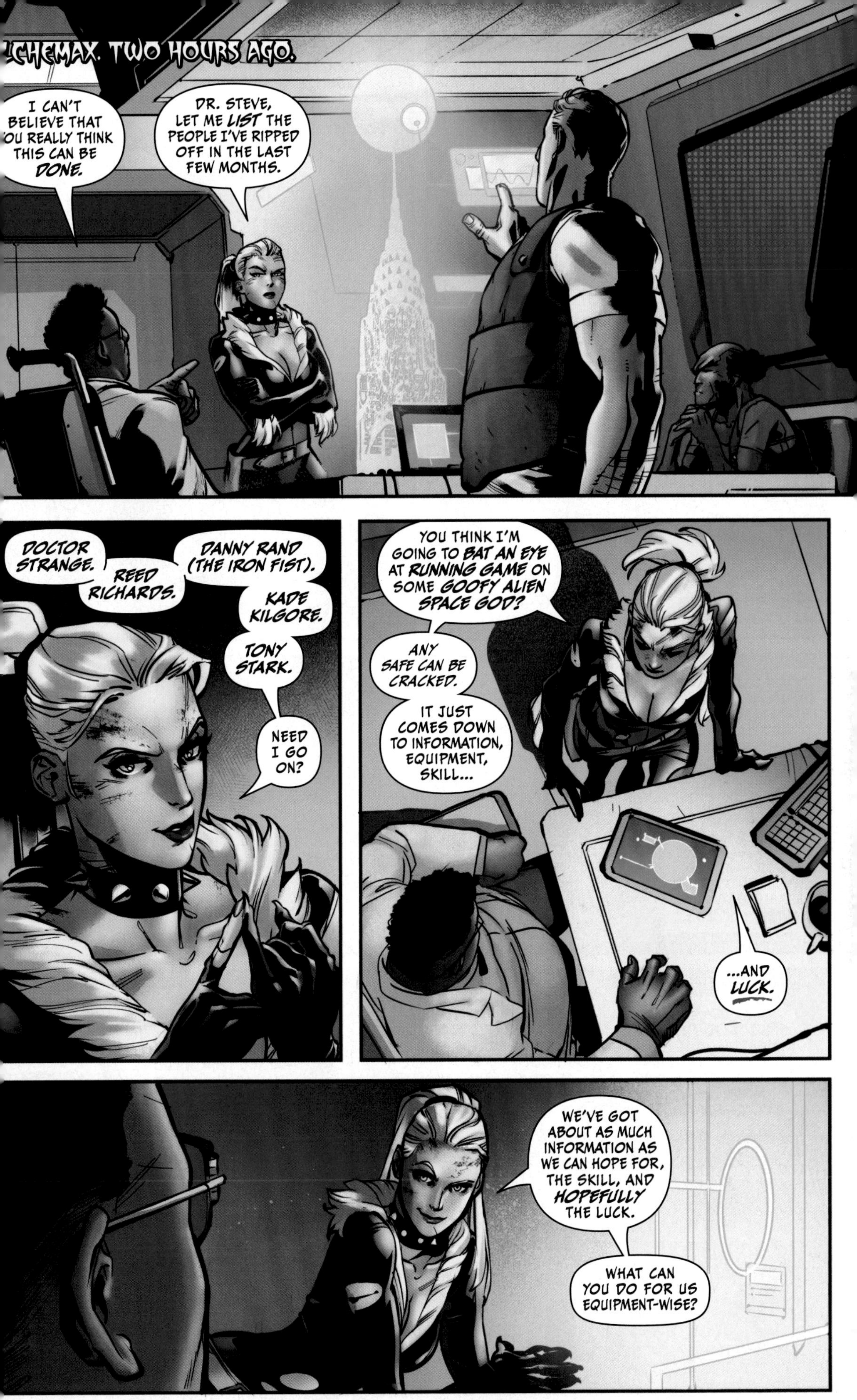

CHEMAX. TWO HOURS AGO.
I CAN'T BELIEVE THAT YOU REALLY THINK THIS CAN BE DONE.
DR. STEVE, LET ME LIST THE PEOPLE I'VE RIPPED OFF IN THE LAST FEW MONTHS.
DOCTOR STRANGE.
REED RICHARDS.
DANNY RAND (THE IRON FIST).
KADE KILGORE.
TONY STARK.
NEED I GO ON?
YOU THINK I'M GOING TO BAT AN EYE AT RUNNING GAME ON SOME GOOFY ALIEN SPACE GOD?
ANY SAFE CAN BE CRACKED.
IT JUST COMES DOWN TO INFORMATION, EQUIPMENT, SKILL...
...AND LUCK.
WE'VE GOT ABOUT AS MUCH INFORMATION AS WE CAN HOPE FOR, THE SKILL, AND HOPEFULLY THE LUCK.
WHAT CAN YOU DO FOR US EQUIPMENT-WISE?

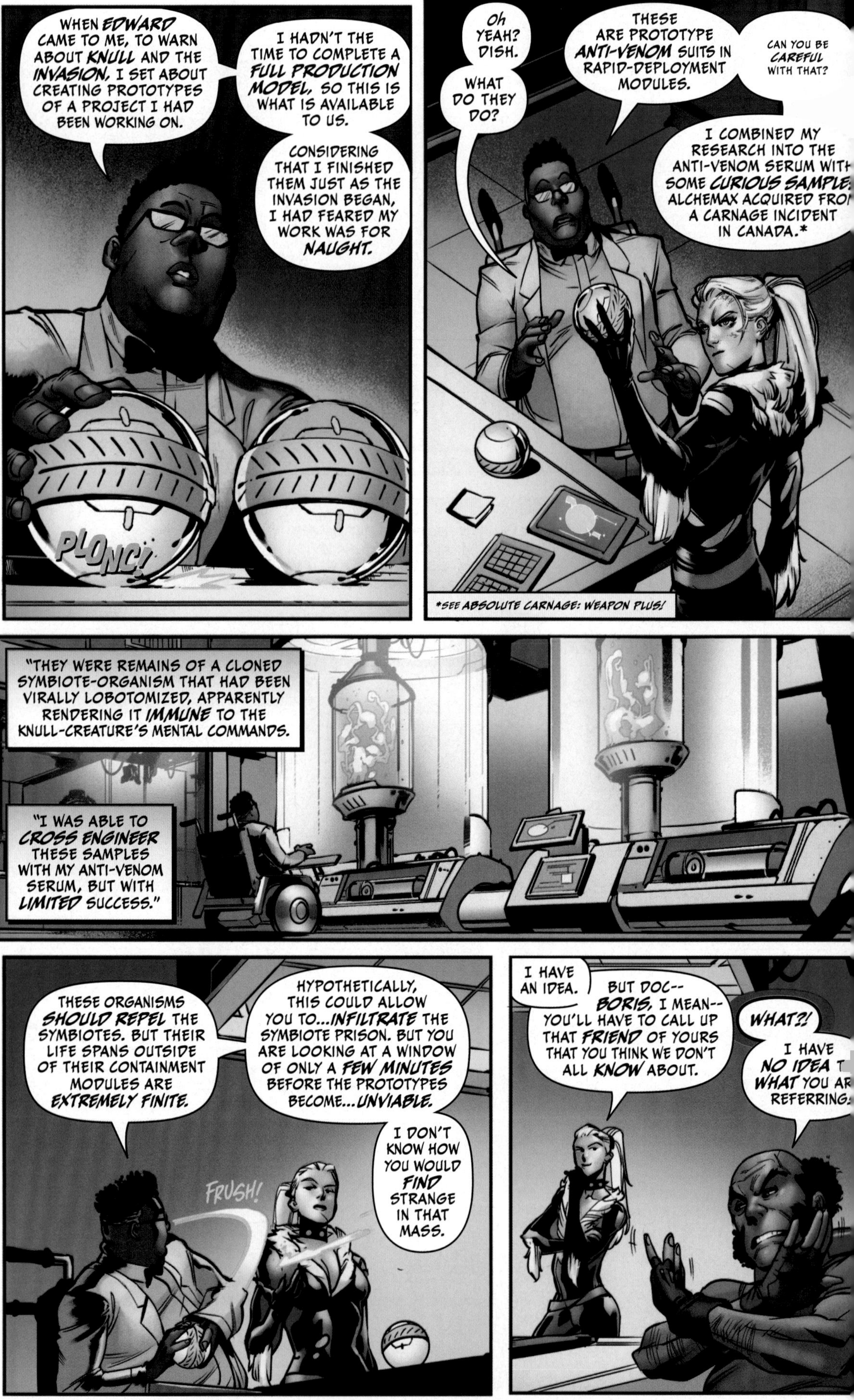
WHEN EDWARD CAME TO ME, TO WARN ABOUT KNULL AND THE INVASION, I SET ABOUT CREATING PROTOTYPES OF A PROJECT I HAD BEEN WORKING ON.
I HADN'T THE TIME TO COMPLETE A FULL PRODUCTION MODEL, SO THIS IS WHAT IS AVAILABLE TO US.
CONSIDERING THAT I FINISHED THEM JUST AS THE INVASION BEGAN, I HAD FEARED MY WORK WAS FOR NAUGHT.
PLONC!
Oh YEAH? DISH.
WHAT DO THEY DO?
THESE ARE PROTOTYPE ANTI-VENOM SUITS IN RAPID-DEPLOYMENT MODULES.
CAN YOU BE CAREFUL WITH THAT?
I COMBINED MY RESEARCH INTO THE ANTI-VENOM SERUM WITH SOME CURIOUS SAMPLES ALCHEMAX ACQUIRED FROM A CARNAGE INCIDENT IN CANADA.*
*SEE ABSOLUTE CARNAGE: WEAPON PLUS!
"THEY WERE REMAINS OF A CLONED SYMBIOTE-ORGANISM THAT HAD BEEN VIRALLY LOBOTOMIZED, APPARENTLY RENDERING IT IMMUNE TO THE KNULL-CREATURE'S MENTAL COMMANDS.
"I WAS ABLE TO CROSS ENGINEER THESE SAMPLES WITH MY ANTI-VENOM SERUM, BUT WITH LIMITED SUCCESS."
THESE ORGANISMS SHOULD REPEL THE SYMBIOTES. BUT THEIR LIFE SPANS OUTSIDE OF THEIR CONTAINMENT MODULES ARE EXTREMELY FINITE.
HYPOTHETICALLY, THIS COULD ALLOW YOU TO...INFILTRATE THE SYMBIOTE PRISON. BUT YOU ARE LOOKING AT A WINDOW OF ONLY A FEW MINUTES BEFORE THE PROTOTYPES BECOME...UNVIABLE.
I DON'T KNOW HOW YOU WOULD FIND STRANGE IN THAT MASS.
FRUSH!
I HAVE AN IDEA.
BUT DOC-- BORIS, I MEAN-- YOU'LL HAVE TO CALL UP THAT FRIEND OF YOURS THAT YOU THINK WE DON'T ALL KNOW ABOUT.
WHAT?!
I HAVE NO IDEA WHAT YOU ARE REFERRING

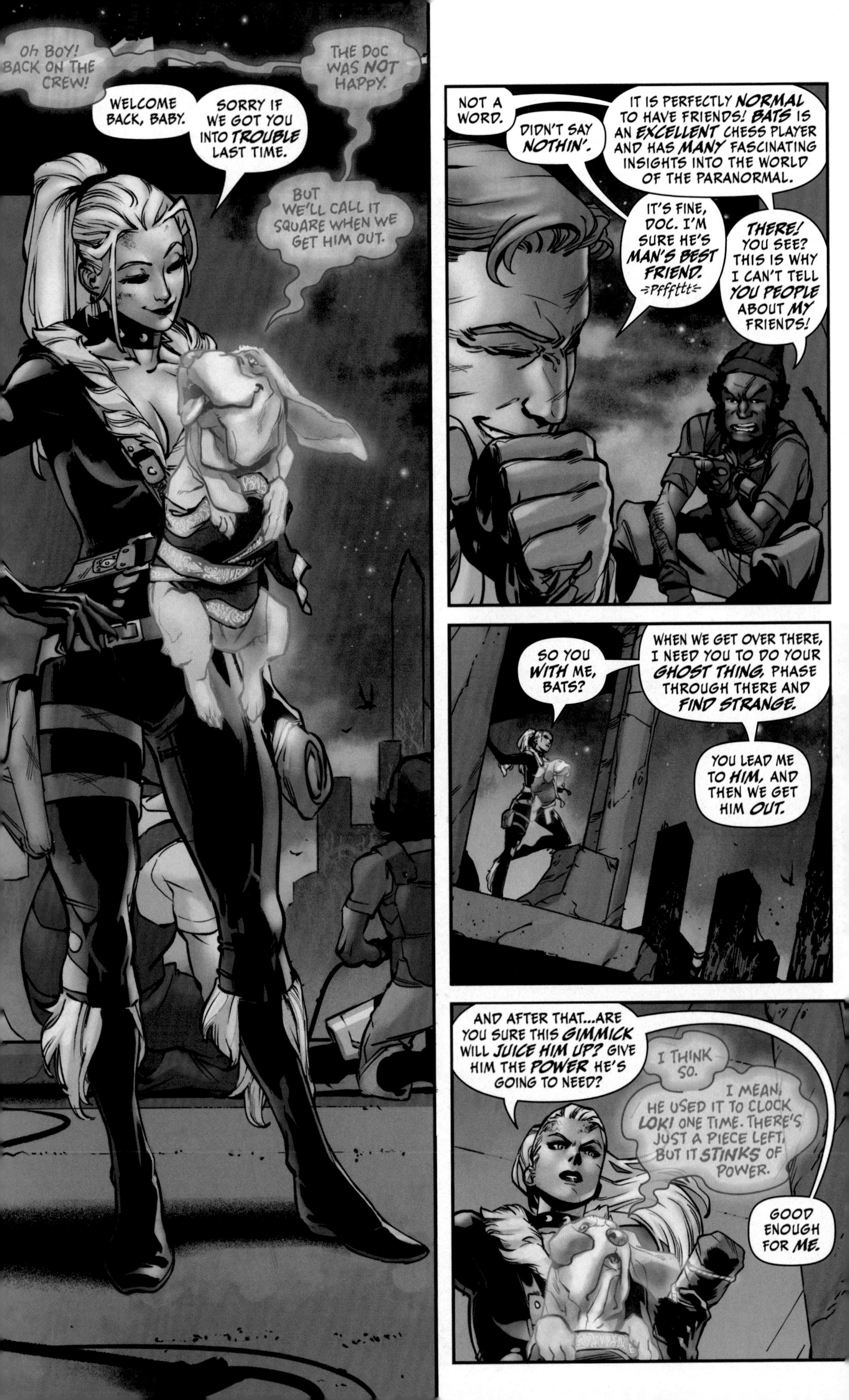
Oh BOY! BACK ON THE CREW!
THE DOC WAS NOT HAPPY.
WELCOME BACK, BABY.
SORRY IF WE GOT YOU INTO TROUBLE LAST TIME.
BUT WE'LL CALL IT SQUARE WHEN WE GET HIM OUT.
NOT A WORD.
DIDN'T SAY NOTHIN'.
IT IS PERFECTLY NORMAL TO HAVE FRIENDS! BATS IS AN EXCELLENT CHESS PLAYER AND HAS MANY FASCINATING INSIGHTS INTO THE WORLD OF THE PARANORMAL.
IT'S FINE, DOC. I'M SURE HE'S MAN'S BEST FRIEND.
=Pffftt=
THERE! YOU SEE? THIS IS WHY I CAN'T TELL YOU PEOPLE ABOUT MY FRIENDS!
SO YOU WITH ME, BATS?
WHEN WE GET OVER THERE, I NEED YOU TO DO YOUR GHOST THING. PHASE THROUGH THERE AND FIND STRANGE.
YOU LEAD ME TO HIM, AND THEN WE GET HIM OUT.
AND AFTER THAT...ARE YOU SURE THIS GIMMICK WILL JUICE HIM UP? GIVE HIM THE POWER HE'S GOING TO NEED?
I THINK SO.
I MEAN, HE USED IT TO CLOCK LOKI ONE TIME. THERE'S JUST A PIECE LEFT, BUT IT STINKS OF POWER.
GOOD ENOUGH FOR ME.

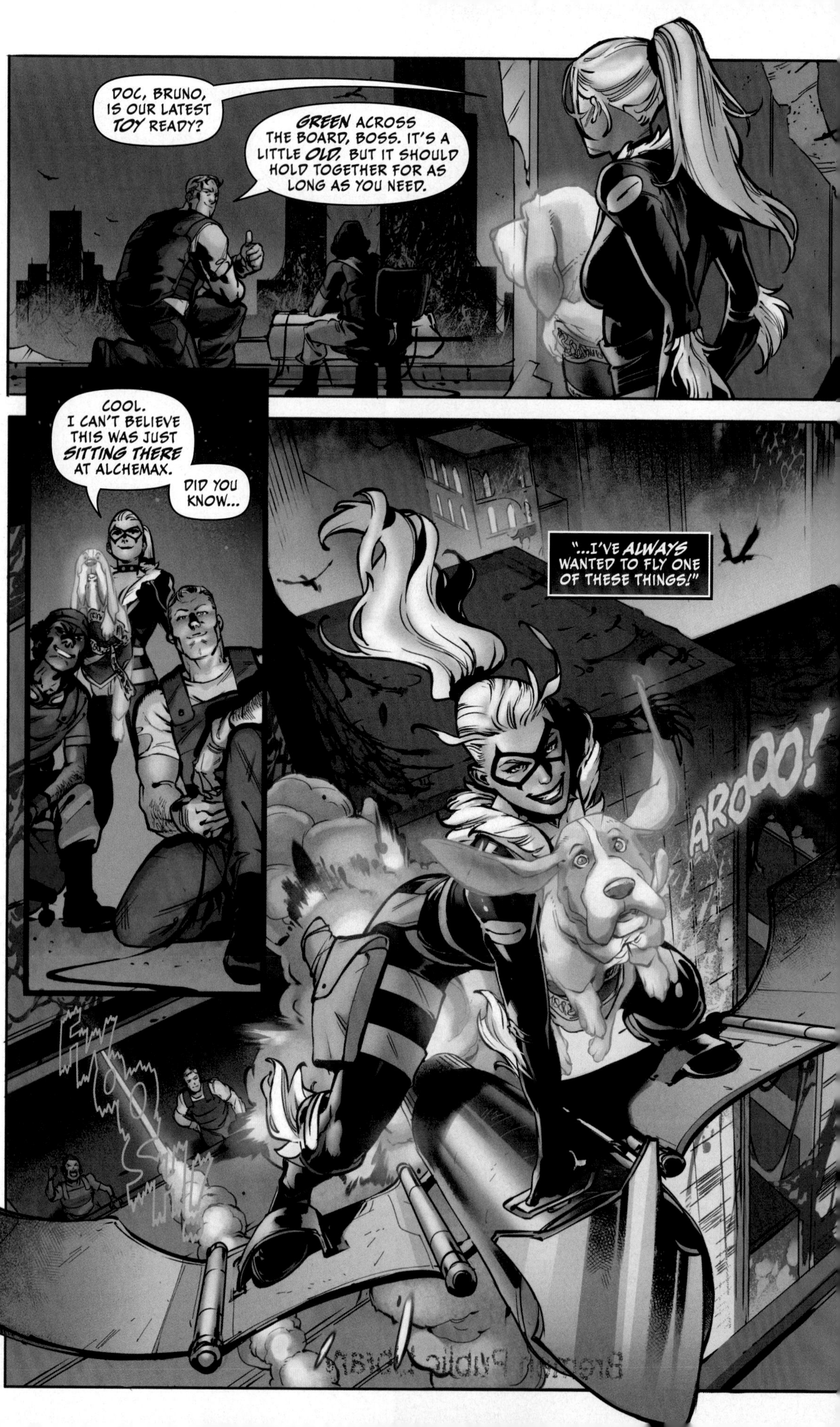
DOC, BRUNO, IS OUR LATEST TOY READY?
GREEN ACROSS THE BOARD, BOSS. IT'S A LITTLE OLD, BUT IT SHOULD HOLD TOGETHER FOR AS LONG AS YOU NEED.
COOL. I CAN'T BELIEVE THIS WAS JUST SITTING THERE AT ALCHEMAX.
DID YOU KNOW...
"...I'VE ALWAYS WANTED TO FLY ONE OF THESE THINGS!"
AROOO!

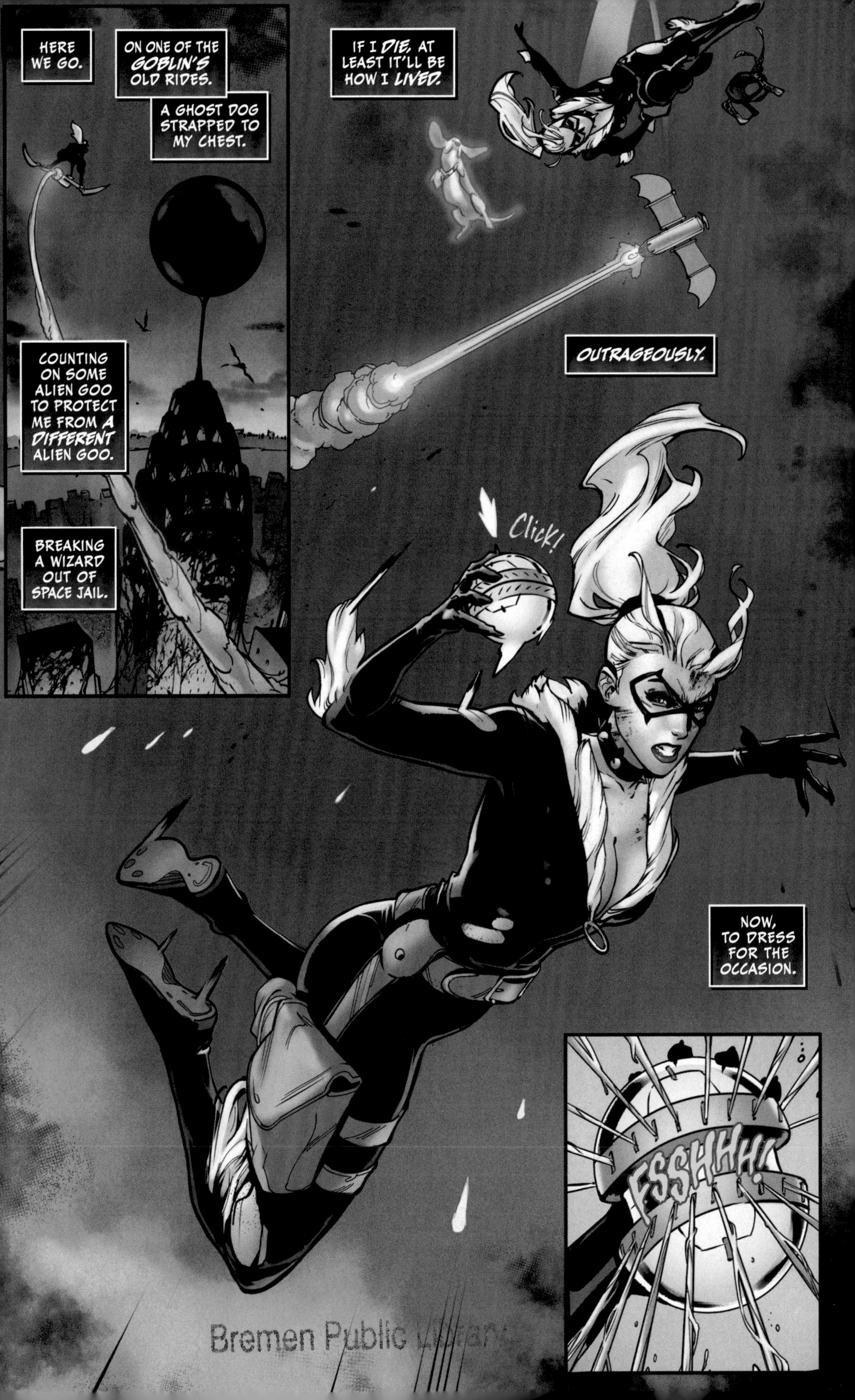
HERE WE GO.
ON ONE OF THE GOBLIN'S OLD RIDES.
A GHOST DOG STRAPPED TO MY CHEST.
COUNTING ON SOME ALIEN GOO TO PROTECT ME FROM A DIFFERENT ALIEN GOO.
BREAKING A WIZARD OUT OF SPACE JAIL.
IF I DIE, AT LEAST IT'LL BE HOW I LIVED.
OUTRAGEOUSLY.
Click!
NOW, TO DRESS FOR THE OCCASION.
FSSHHH!

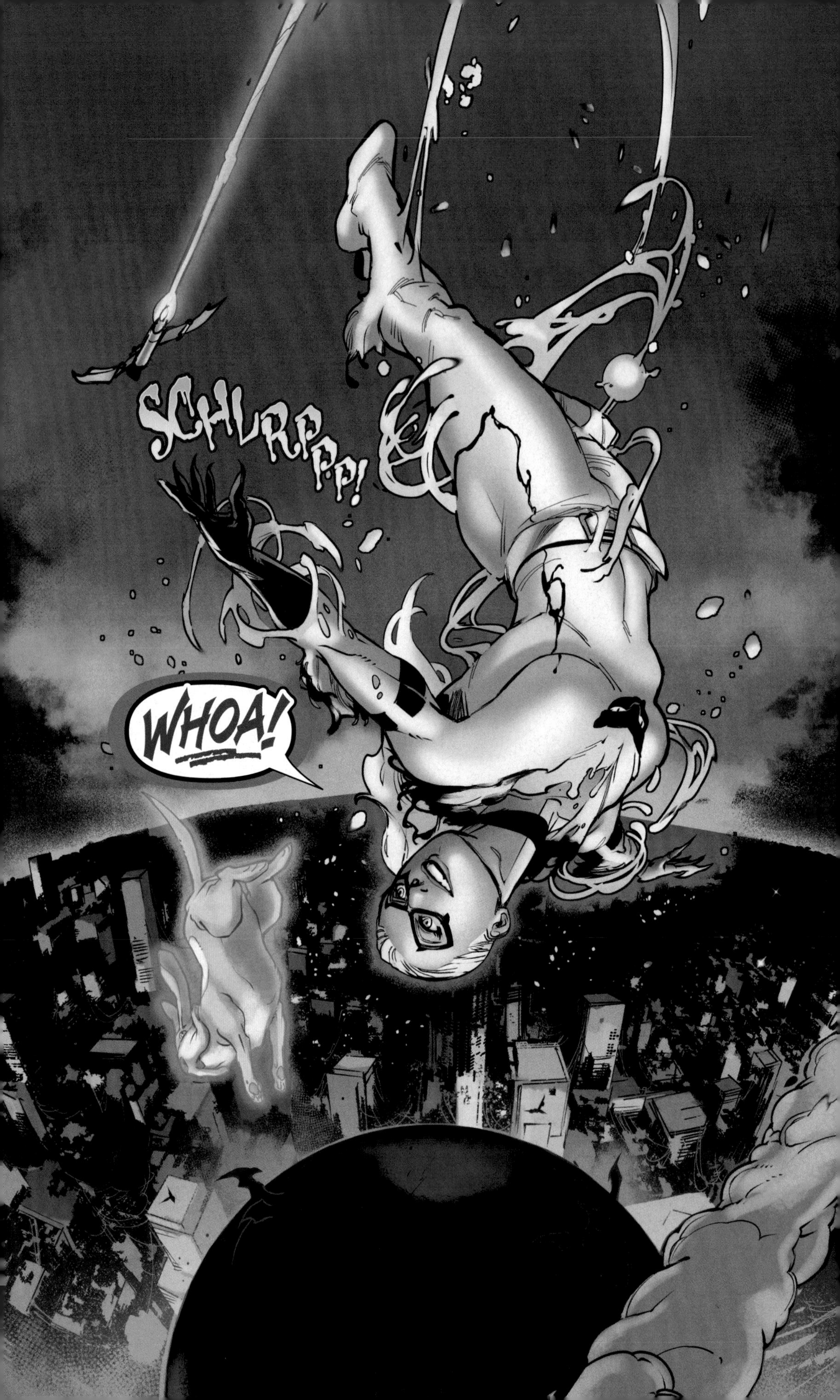
SCHLRPPP!
WHOA!

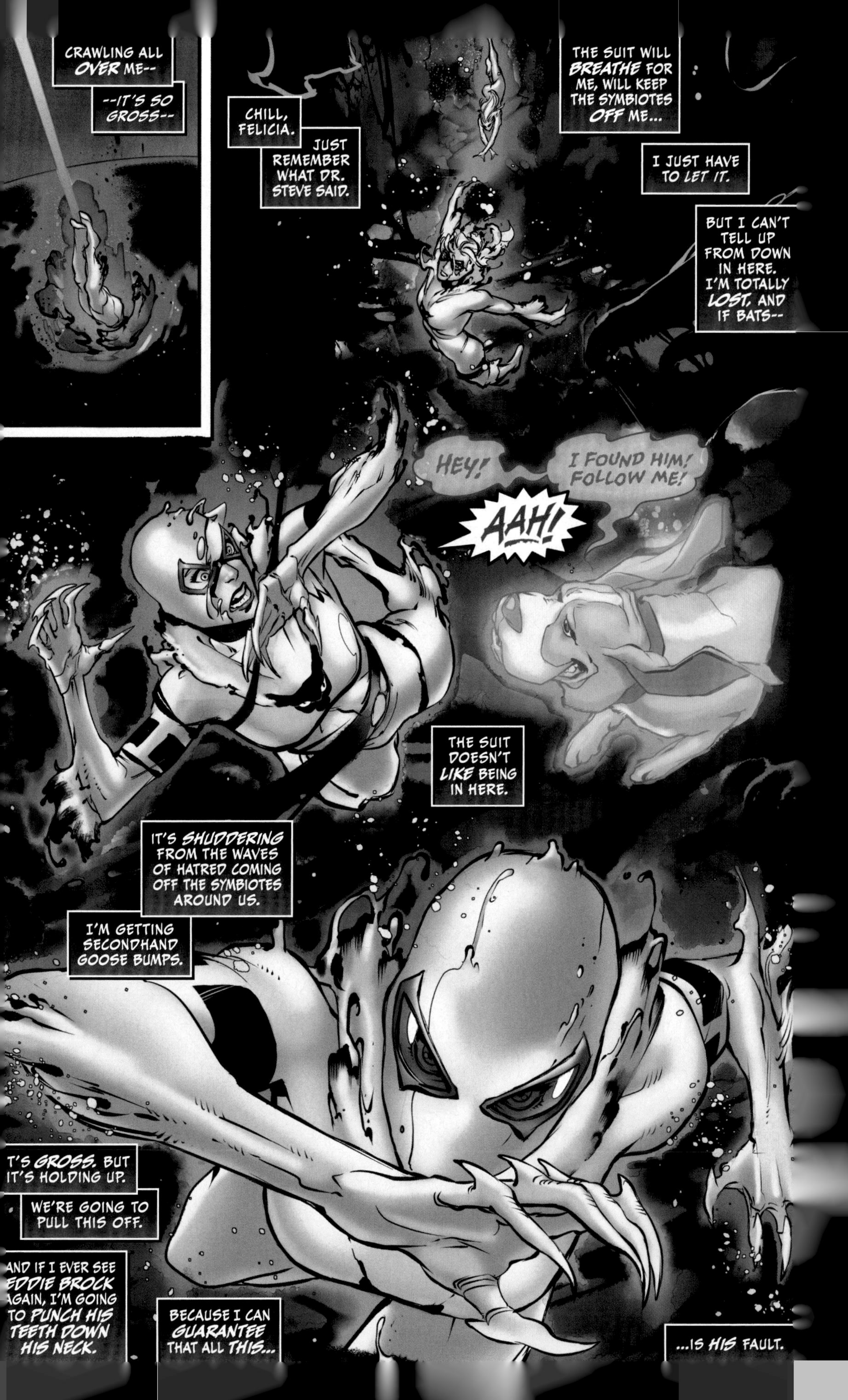
CRAWLING ALL OVER ME--
--IT'S SO GROSS--
CHILL, FELICIA.
JUST REMEMBER WHAT DR. STEVE SAID.
THE SUIT WILL BREATHE FOR ME, WILL KEEP THE SYMBIOTES OFF ME...
I JUST HAVE TO LET IT.
BUT I CAN'T TELL UP FROM DOWN IN HERE. I'M TOTALLY LOST, AND IF BATS--
HEY!
I FOUND HIM! FOLLOW ME!
AAH!
THE SUIT DOESN'T LIKE BEING IN HERE.
IT'S SHUDDERING FROM THE WAVES OF HATRED COMING OFF THE SYMBIOTES AROUND US.
I'M GETTING SECONDHAND GOOSE BUMPS.
T'S GROSS. BUT IT'S HOLDING UP.
WE'RE GOING TO PULL THIS OFF.
AND IF I EVER SEE EDDIE BROCK AGAIN, I'M GOING TO PUNCH HIS TEETH DOWN HIS NECK.
BECAUSE I CAN GUARANTEE THAT ALL THIS...
...IS HIS FAULT.

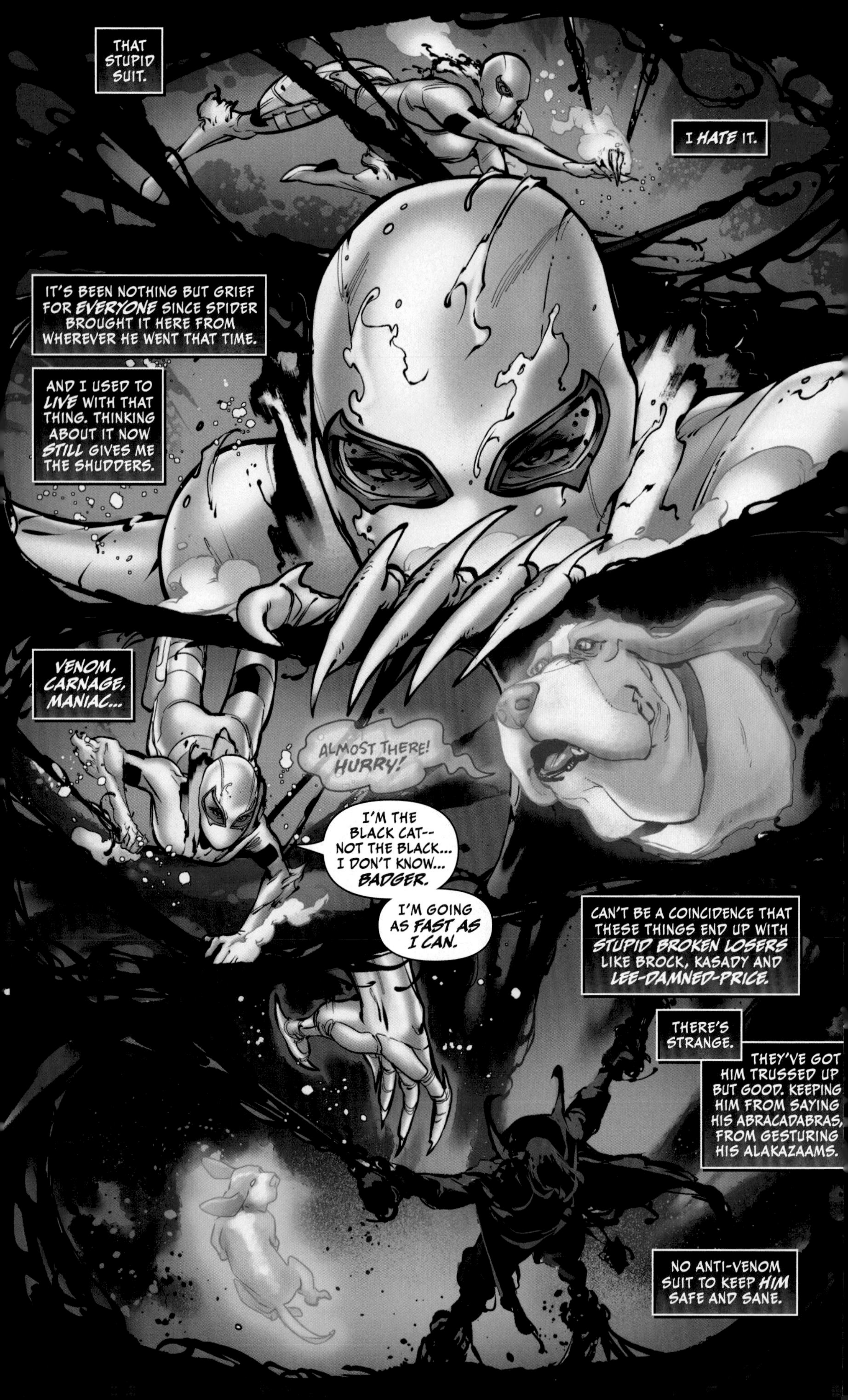
THAT STUPID SUIT.
I HATE IT.
IT'S BEEN NOTHING BUT GRIEF FOR EVERYONE SINCE SPIDER BROUGHT IT HERE FROM WHEREVER HE WENT THAT TIME.
AND I USED TO LIVE WITH THAT THING. THINKING ABOUT IT NOW STILL GIVES ME THE SHUDDERS.
VENOM, CARNAGE, MANIAC...
ALMOST THERE! HURRY!
I'M THE BLACK CAT-- NOT THE BLACK... I DON'T KNOW... BADGER.
I'M GOING AS FAST AS I CAN.
CAN'T BE A COINCIDENCE THAT THESE THINGS END UP WITH STUPID BROKEN LOSERS LIKE BROCK, KASADY AND LEE-DAMNED-PRICE.
THERE'S STRANGE.
THEY'VE GOT HIM TRUSSED UP BUT GOOD. KEEPING HIM FROM SAYING HIS ABRACADABRAS, FROM GESTURING HIS ALAKAZAAMS.
NO ANTI-VENOM SUIT TO KEEP HIM SAFE AND SANE.

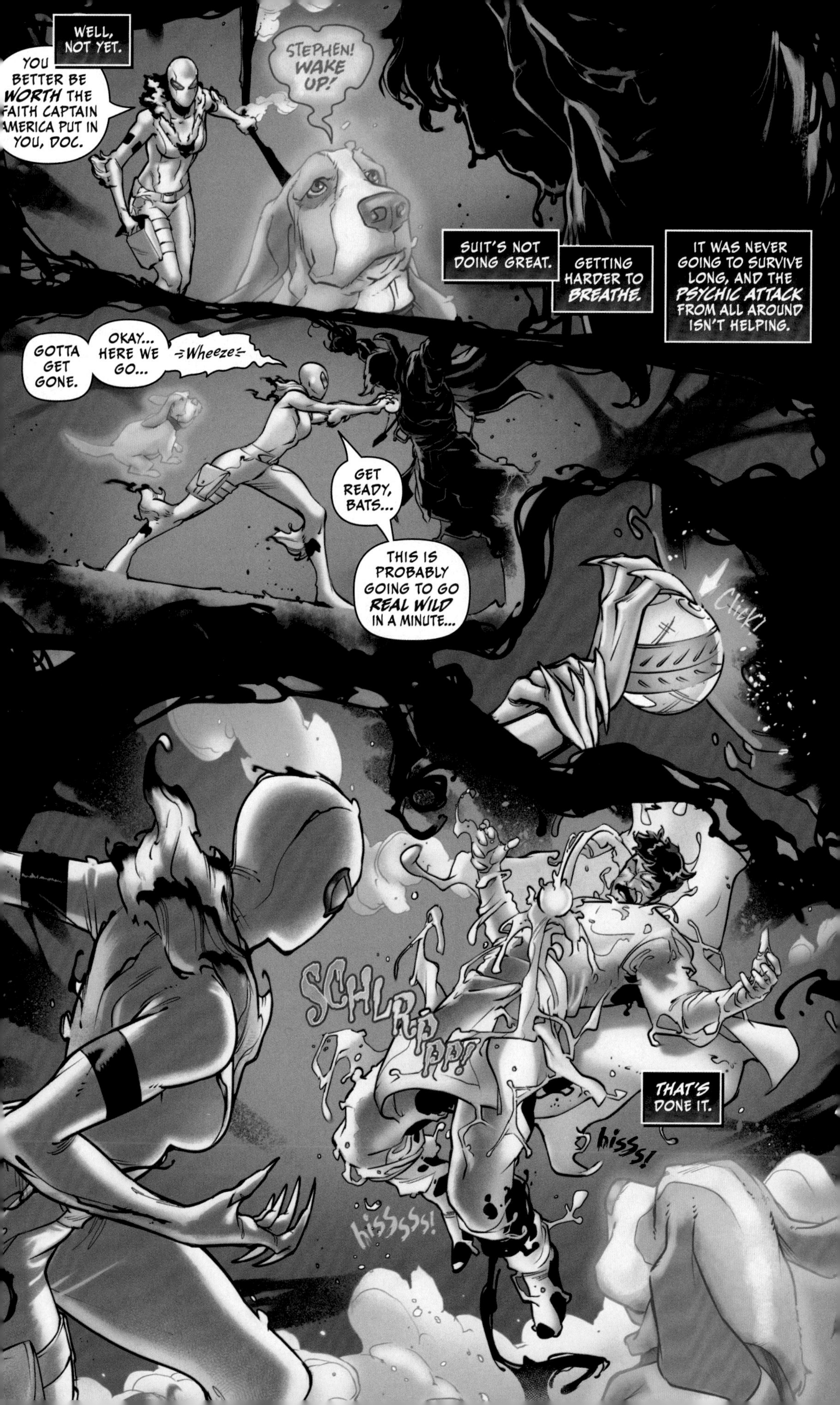
WELL, NOT YET.
YOU BETTER BE WORTH THE FAITH CAPTAIN AMERICA PUT IN YOU, DOC.
STEPHEN! WAKE UP!
SUIT'S NOT DOING GREAT.
GETTING HARDER TO BREATHE.
IT WAS NEVER GOING TO SURVIVE LONG, AND THE PSYCHIC ATTACK FROM ALL AROUND ISN'T HELPING.
GOTTA GET GONE.
OKAY... HERE WE GO...
Wheeze
GET READY, BATS...
THIS IS PROBABLY GOING TO GO REAL WILD IN A MINUTE...
Click!
SCHLRPPP!
THAT'S DONE IT.
hissss!
hissssss!

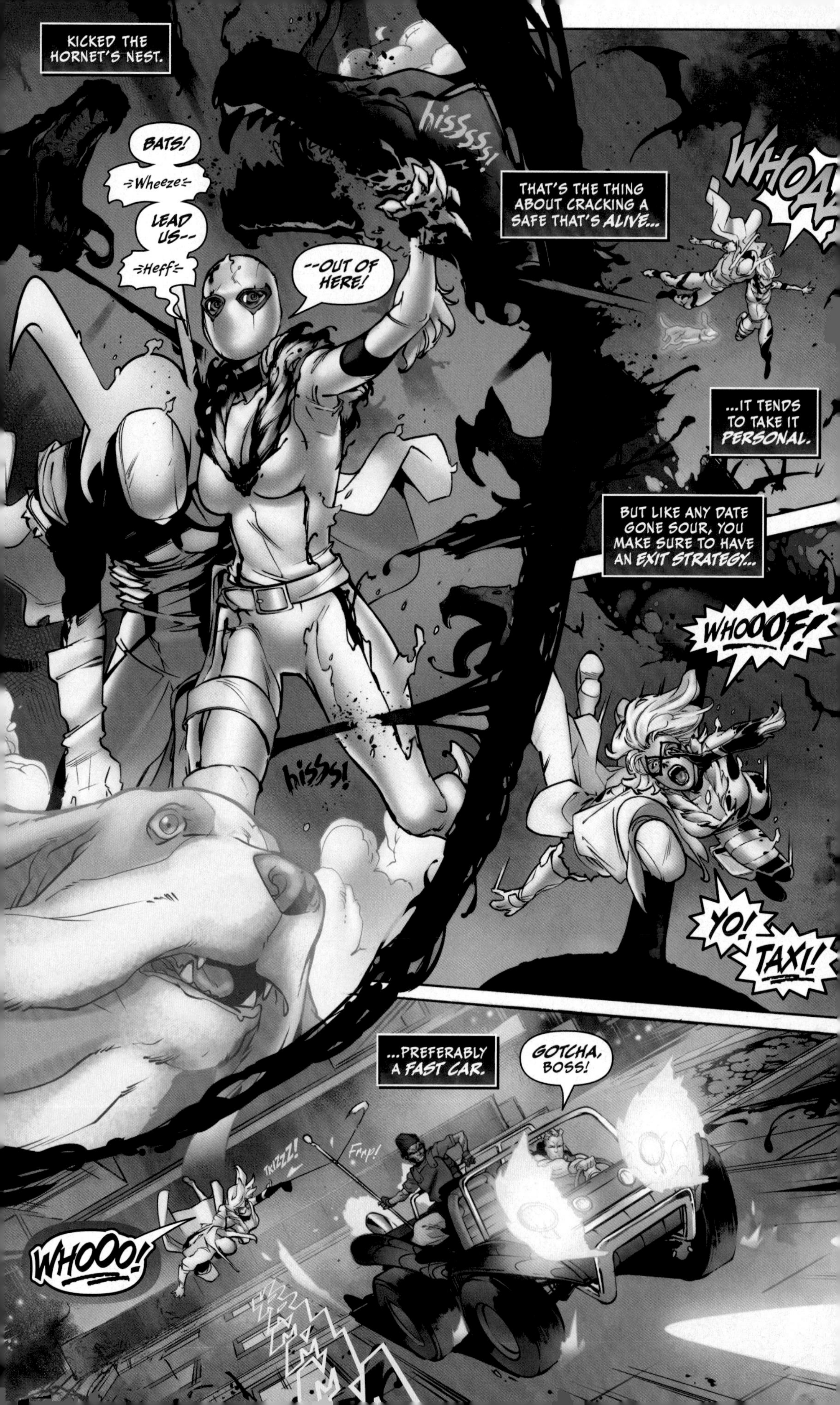
KICKED THE HORNET'S NEST.
hissssss!
BATS!
Wheeze
LEAD US--
Heff
--OUT OF HERE!
THAT'S THE THING ABOUT CRACKING A SAFE THAT'S ALIVE...
WHOA
...IT TENDS TO TAKE IT PERSONAL.
BUT LIKE ANY DATE GONE SOUR, YOU MAKE SURE TO HAVE AN EXIT STRATEGY...
WHOOOF!
hissss!
YO! TAXI!
...PREFERABLY A FAST CAR.
GOTCHA, BOSS!
TKIZZZ!
Frrp!
WHOOO!

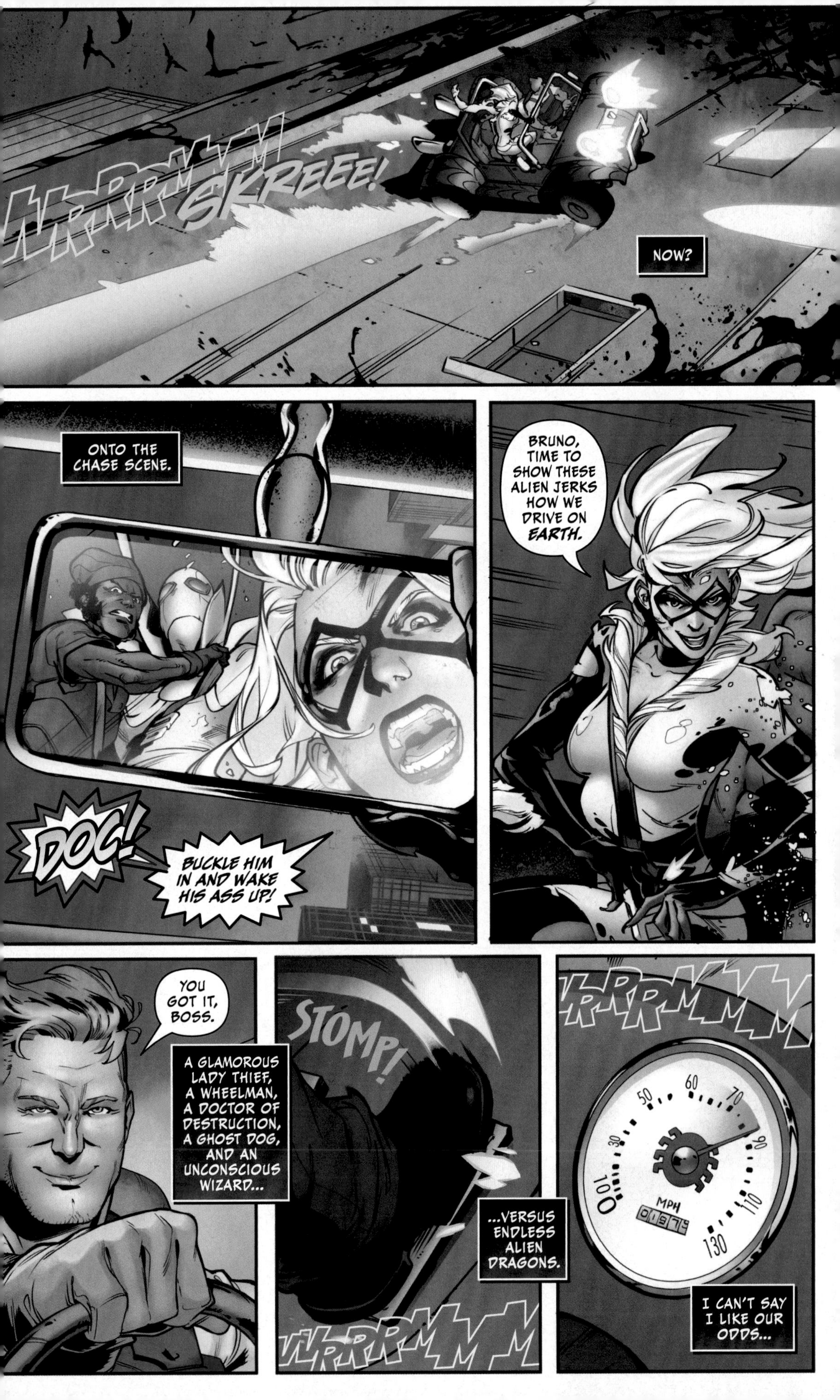

VRRRMMMM
SKREEE!
NOW?
ONTO THE CHASE SCENE.
BRUNO, TIME TO SHOW THESE ALIEN JERKS HOW WE DRIVE ON EARTH.
DOC!
BUCKLE HIM IN AND WAKE HIS ASS UP!
YOU GOT IT, BOSS.
A GLAMOROUS LADY THIEF, A WHEELMAN, A DOCTOR OF DESTRUCTION, A GHOST DOG, AND AN UNCONSCIOUS WIZARD...
STOMP!
...VERSUS ENDLESS ALIEN DRAGONS.
VRRRRMMMM
VRRRRMMMM
MPH
I CAN'T SAY I LIKE OUR ODDS...

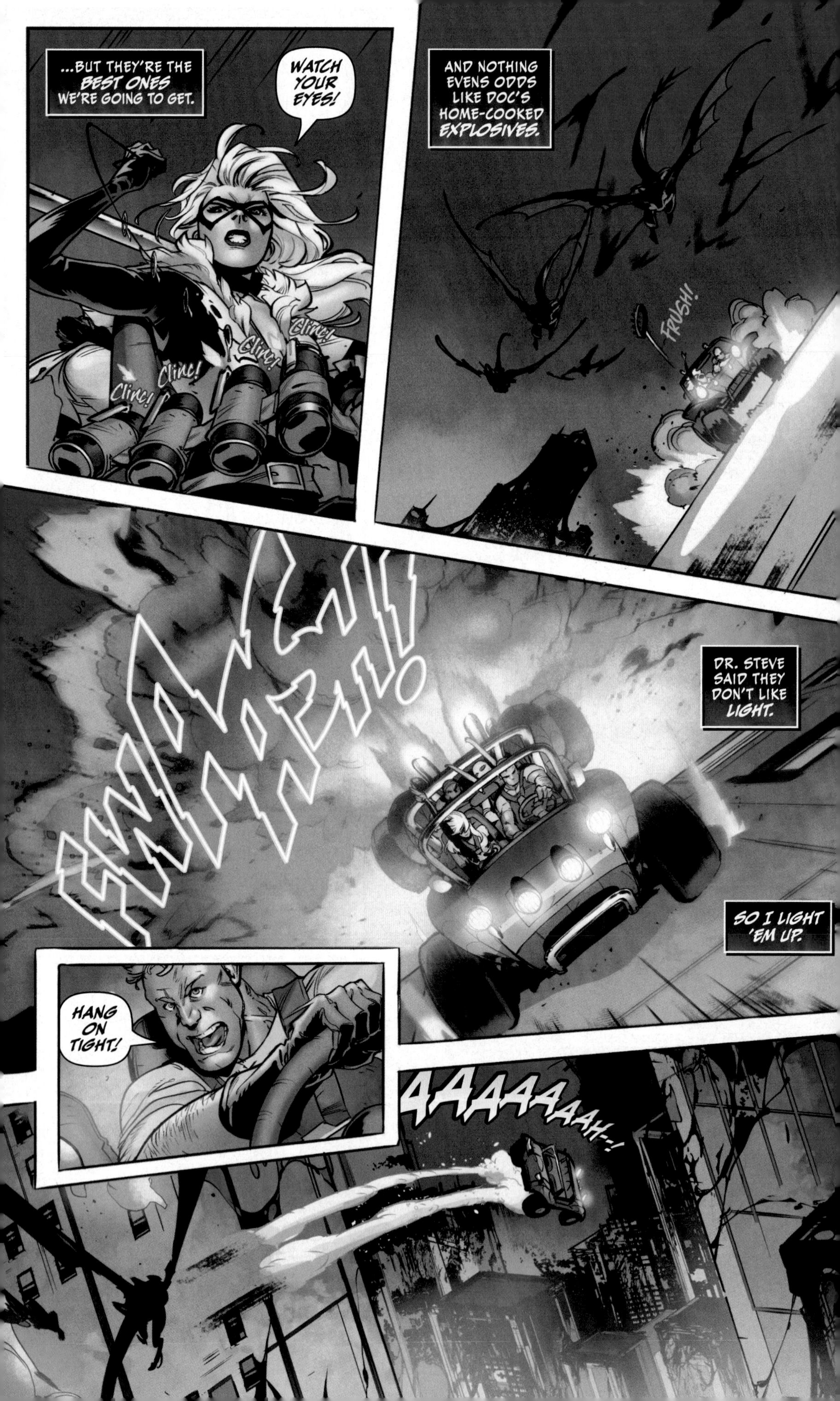
...BUT THEY'RE THE BEST ONES WE'RE GOING TO GET.
WATCH YOUR EYES!
Clinc!
Clinc!
Clinc!
Clinc!
AND NOTHING EVENS ODDS LIKE DOC'S HOME-COOKED EXPLOSIVES.
FRUSH!
DR. STEVE SAID THEY DON'T LIKE LIGHT.
SO I LIGHT 'EM UP.
HANG ON TIGHT!
AAAAAAAAH--!

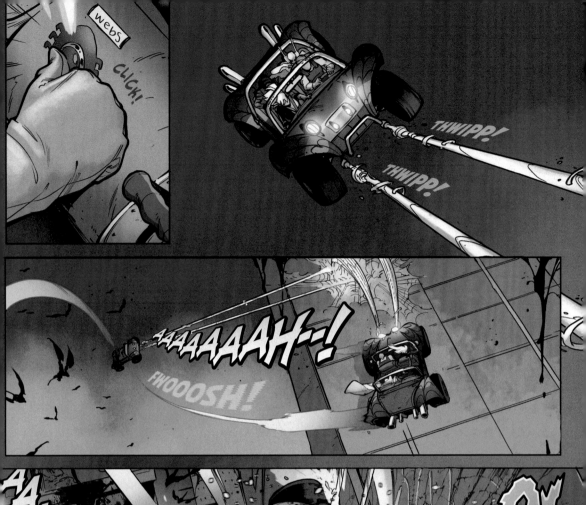

webs

CLICK!

THWIPP!

THWIPP!

AAAAAAAH--!

FWOOOSH!

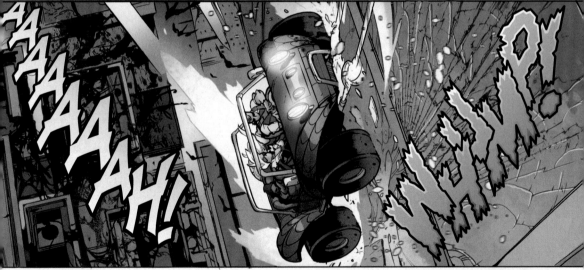

AAAAAAAH!

NNNNP?!

DOC! I TOLD YOU TO WAKE HIM UP!

I AM NOT A MEDICAL DOCTOR!

I AM A BLOWING-THINGS-UP DOCTOR!

INCOMING!

BTOOM! BTOOM! BTOOM! BTOOM!

DAMN IT--

IF HE'S NOT *AWAKE,* HE CAN'T USE THE *THING* AND SAVE OUR *BUTTS*--

WWRRRM!

--SO THAT MEANS WE'RE GOING TO HAVE TO IMPROVISE.

KRREESH!

WHICH, GRANTED, IS NORMALLY MY STRONG SUIT.

WHUMP!

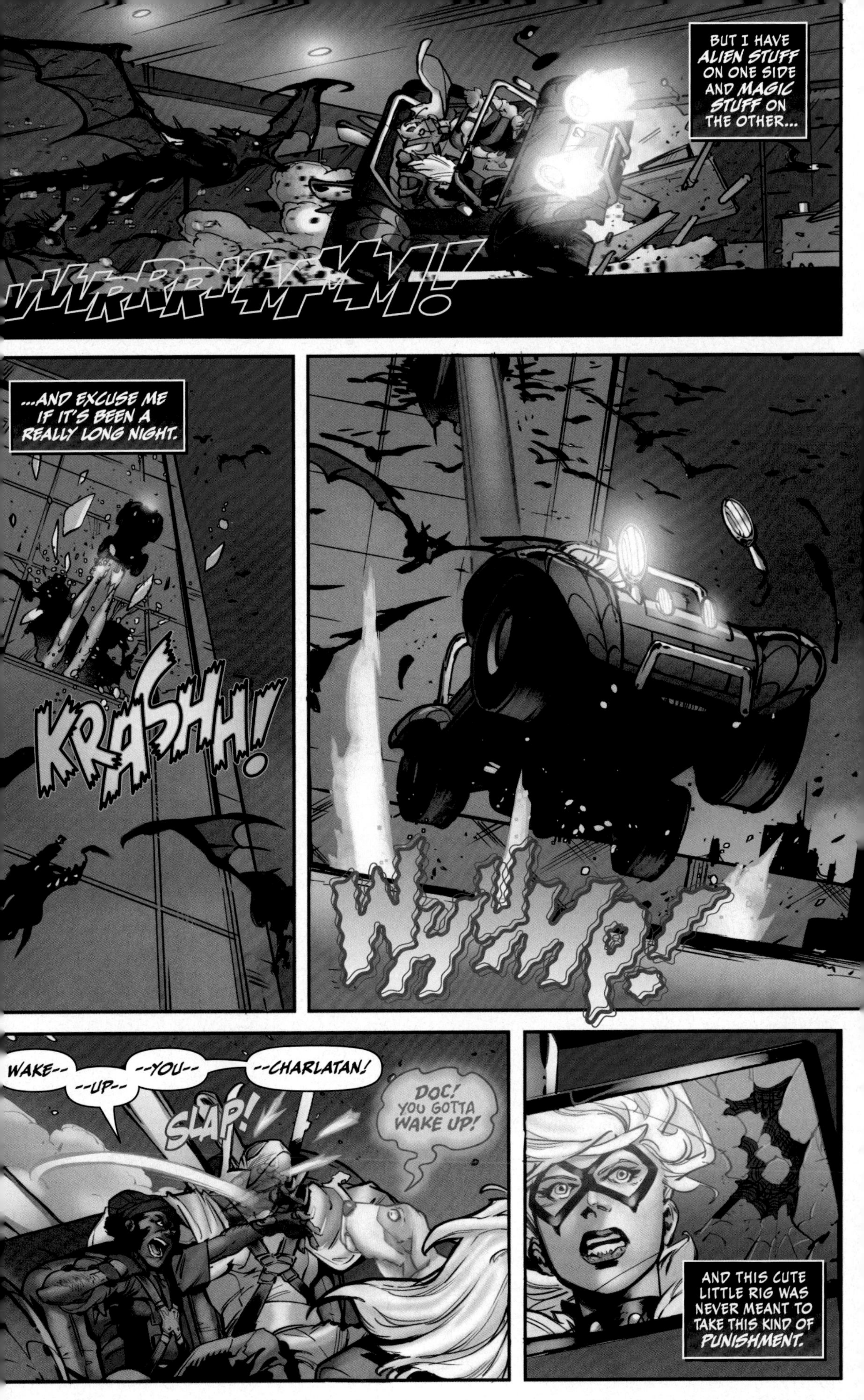
BUT I HAVE ALIEN STUFF ON ONE SIDE AND MAGIC STUFF ON THE OTHER...
VVVRRRRMMMMM!
...AND EXCUSE ME IF IT'S BEEN A REALLY LONG NIGHT.
KRASHH!
WHUMP!
WAKE--
--UP--
--YOU--
--CHARLATAN!
SLAP!
DOC! YOU GOTTA WAKE UP!
AND THIS CUTE LITTLE RIG WAS NEVER MEANT TO TAKE THIS KIND OF PUNISHMENT.

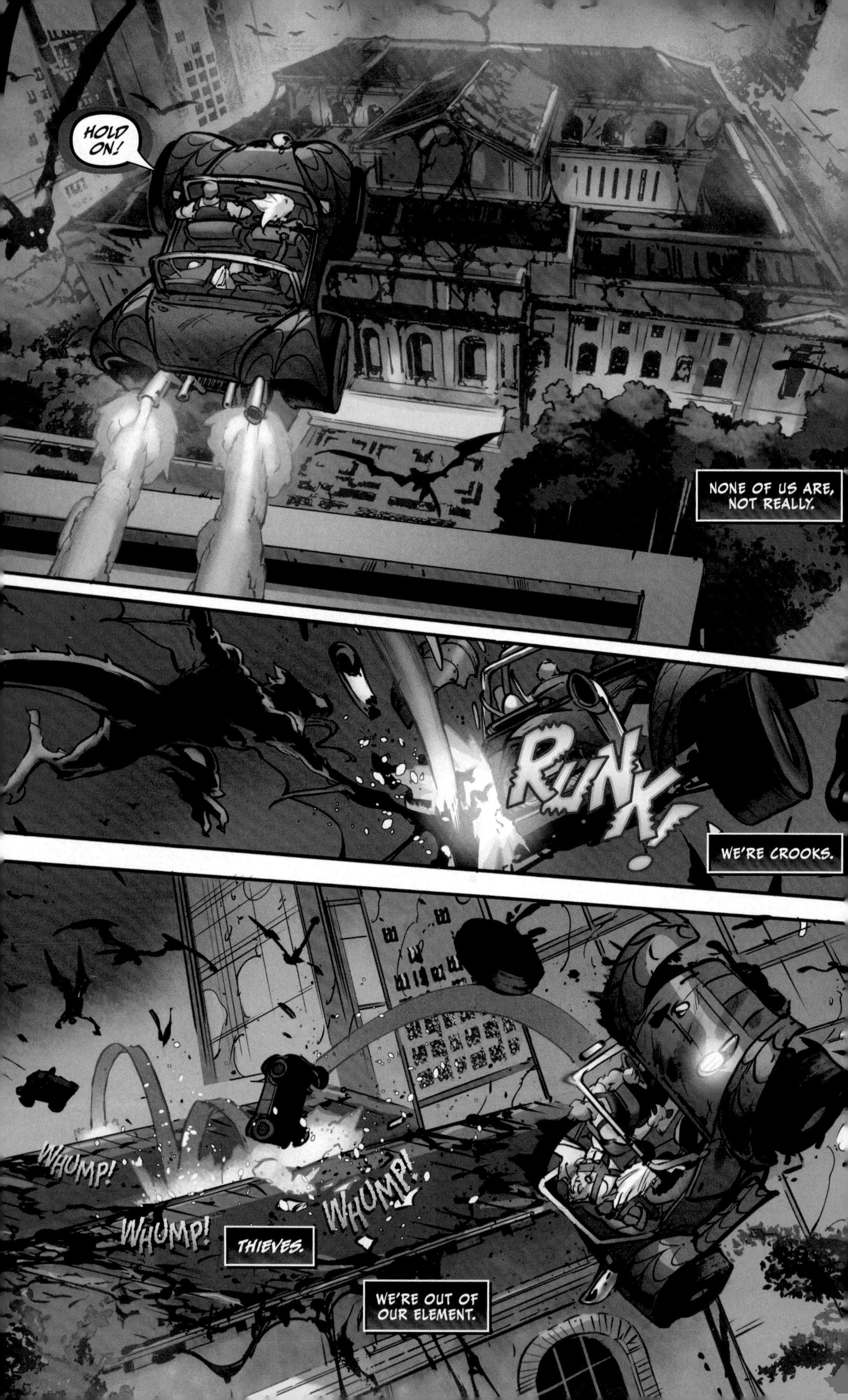
HOLD ON!
NONE OF US ARE, NOT REALLY.
RUNK!
WE'RE CROOKS.
WHUMP!
WHUMP!
WHUMP!
THIEVES.
WE'RE OUT OF OUR ELEMENT.

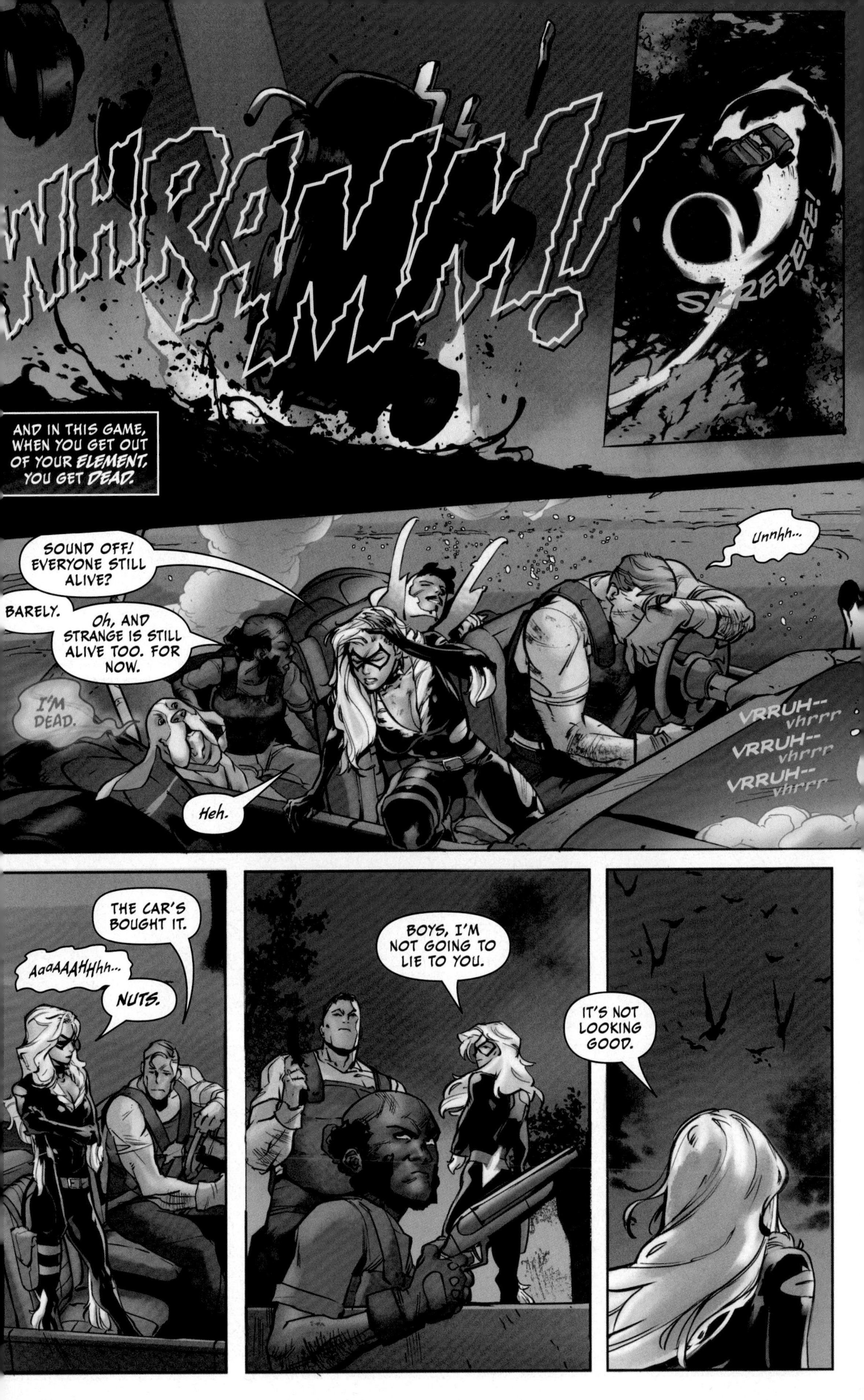
WHRAMM!!
SKREEEEEE!
AND IN THIS GAME, WHEN YOU GET OUT OF YOUR ELEMENT, YOU GET DEAD.
SOUND OFF! EVERYONE STILL ALIVE?
Unnhh...
BARELY.
Oh, AND STRANGE IS STILL ALIVE TOO. FOR NOW.
I'M DEAD.
Heh.
VRRUH-- vhrrr
VRRUH-- vhrrr
VRRUH-- vhrrr
THE CAR'S BOUGHT IT.
AaaAAAHHhh...
NUTS.
BOYS, I'M NOT GOING TO LIE TO YOU.
IT'S NOT LOOKING GOOD.

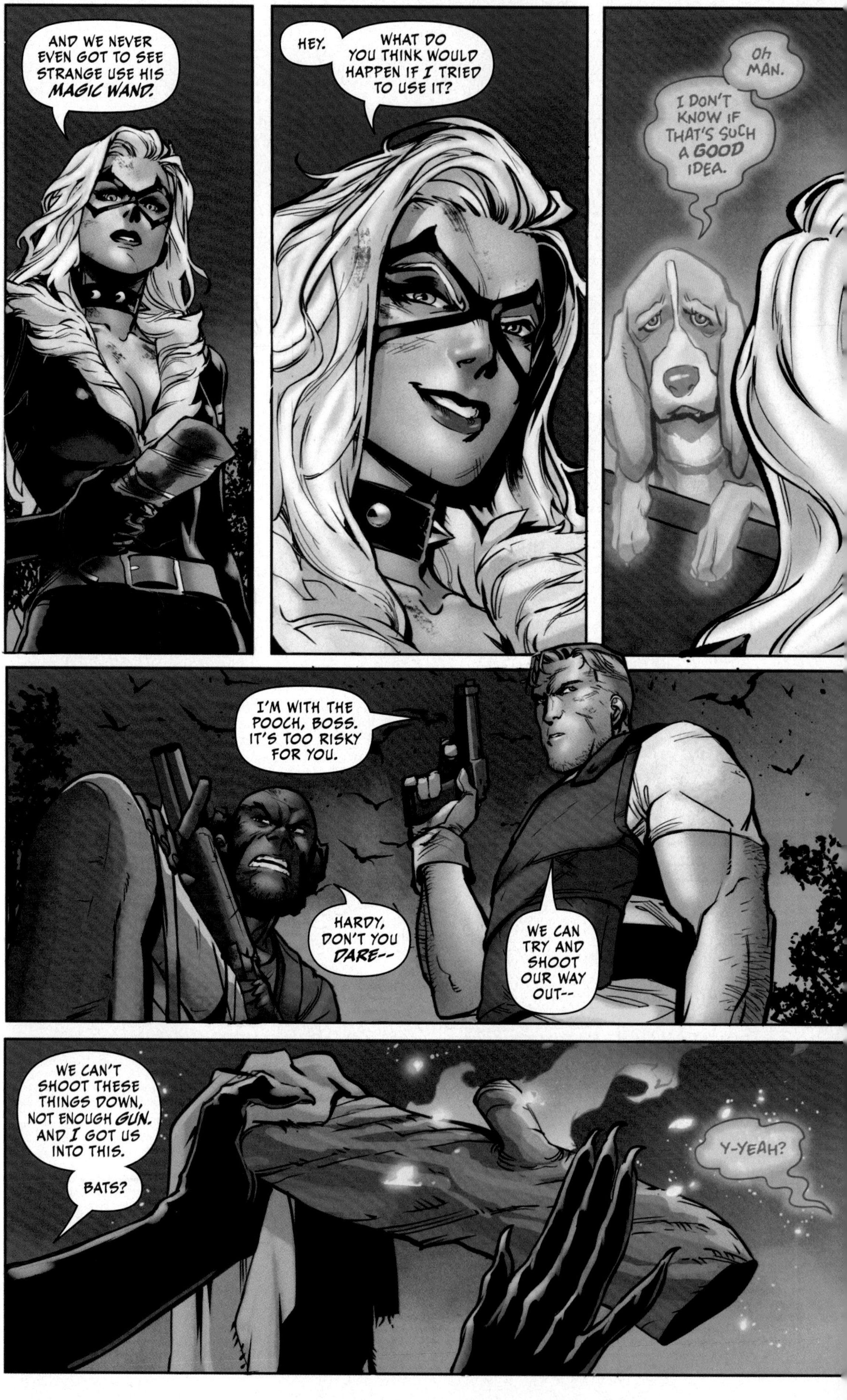
AND WE NEVER EVEN GOT TO SEE STRANGE USE HIS MAGIC WAND.
HEY.
WHAT DO YOU THINK WOULD HAPPEN IF I TRIED TO USE IT?
Oh MAN.
I DON'T KNOW IF THAT'S SUCH A GOOD IDEA.
I'M WITH THE POOCH, BOSS. IT'S TOO RISKY FOR YOU.
HARDY, DON'T YOU DARE--
WE CAN TRY AND SHOOT OUR WAY OUT--
WE CAN'T SHOOT THESE THINGS DOWN, NOT ENOUGH GUN. AND I GOT US INTO THIS.
BATS?
Y-YEAH?

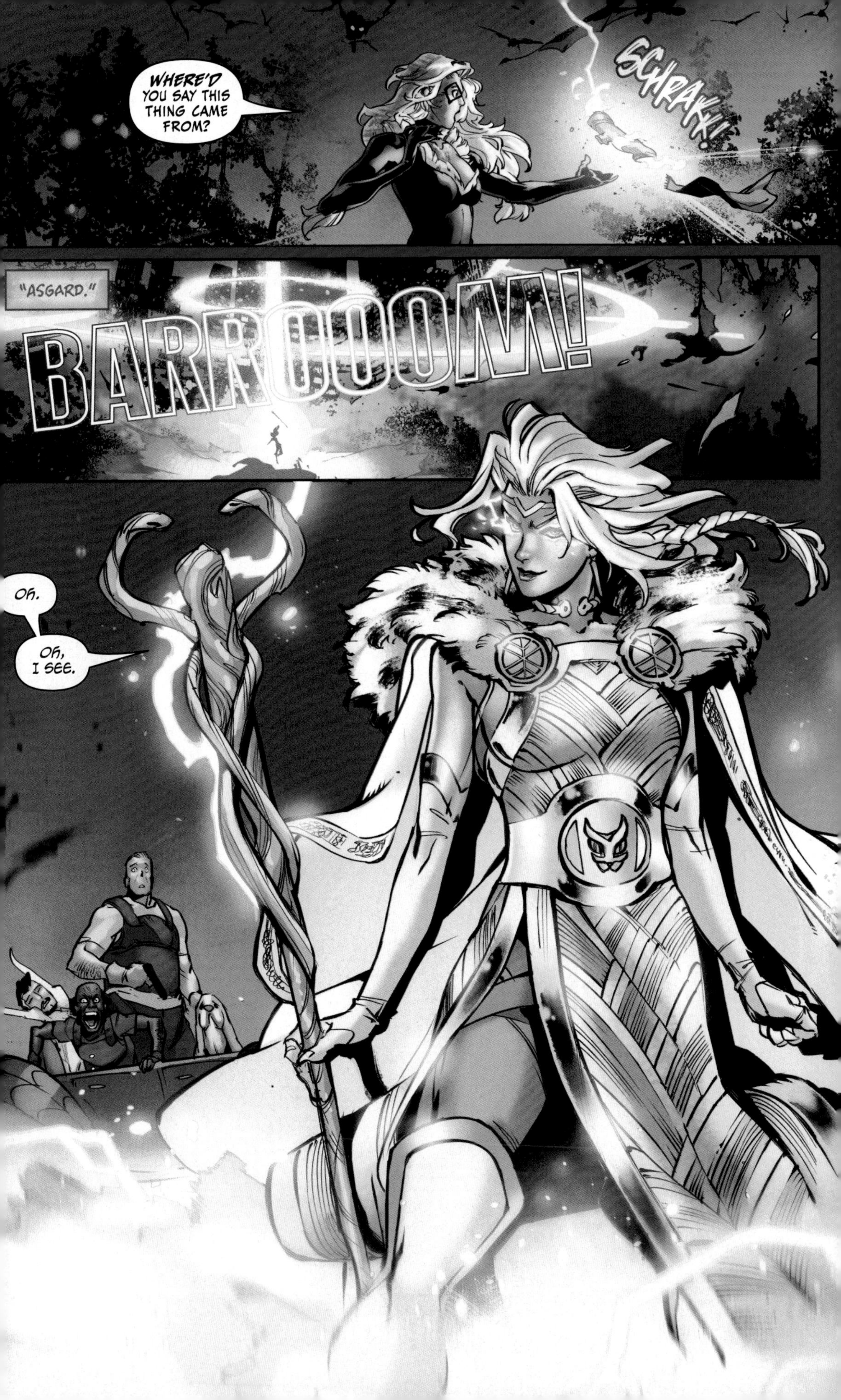
WHERE'D YOU SAY THIS THING CAME FROM?
SCHRAKK!
"ASGARD."
BARROOOM!
OH.
OH, I SEE.

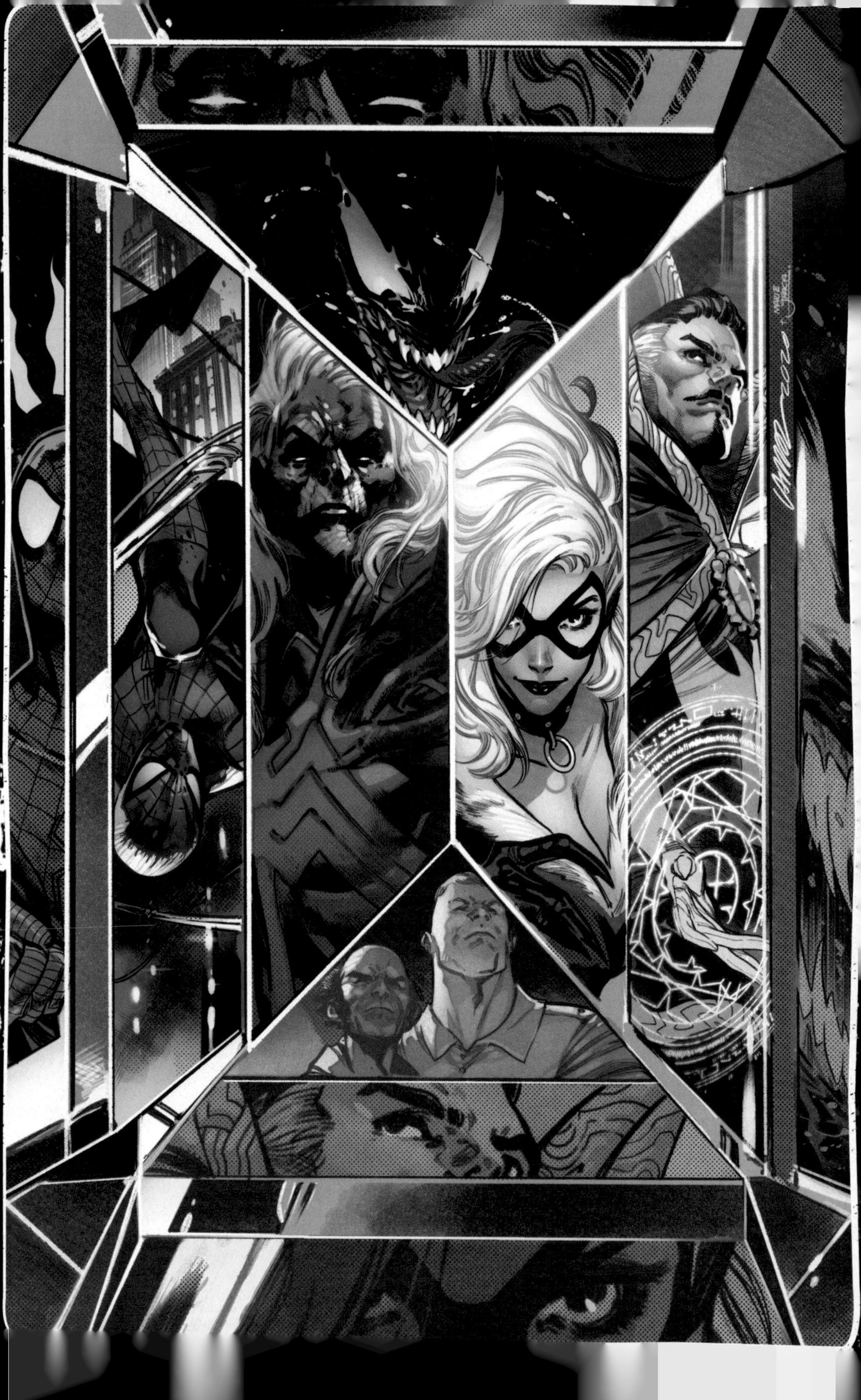

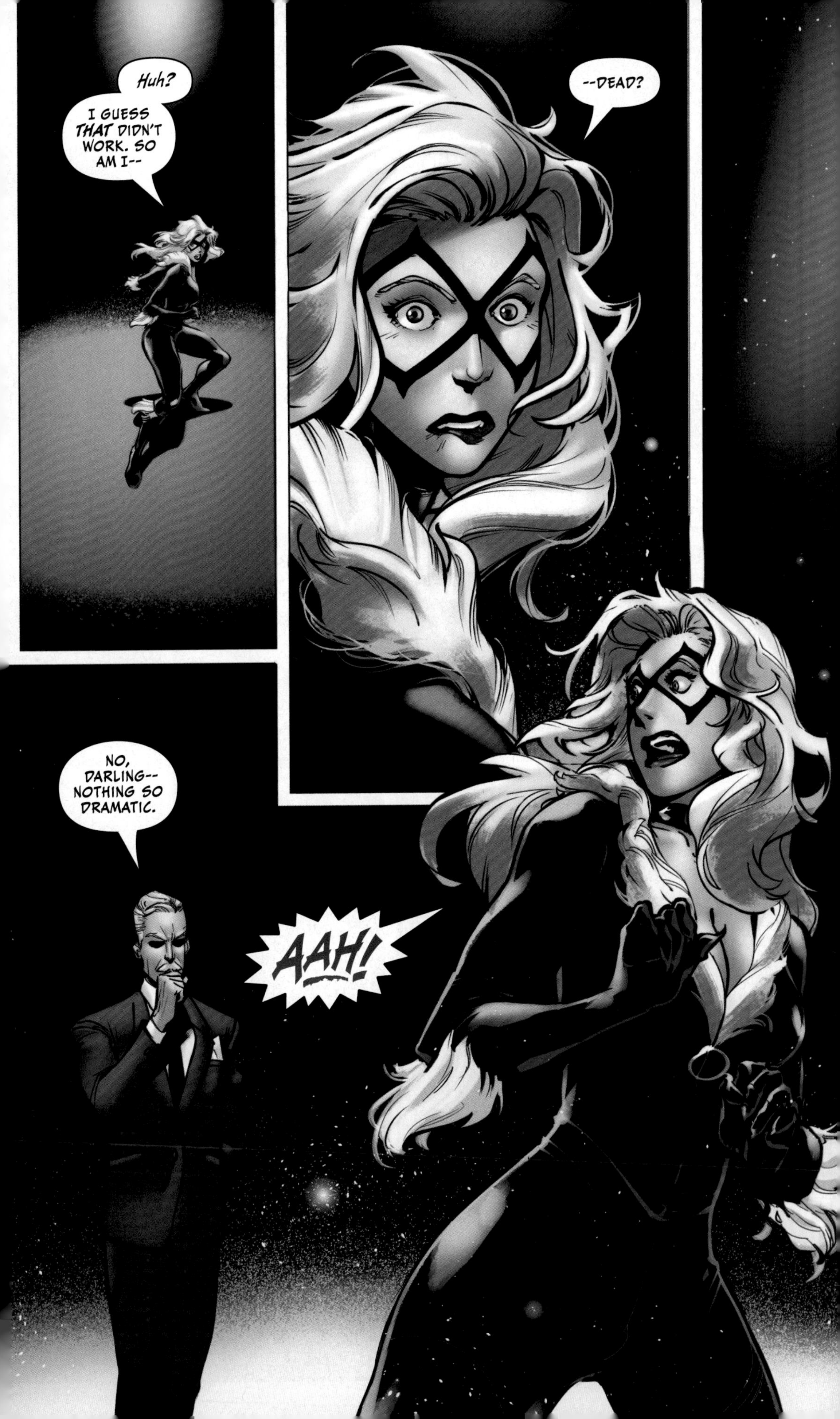
Huh?
I GUESS THAT DIDN'T WORK. SO AM I--
--DEAD?
NO, DARLING-- NOTHING SO DRAMATIC.
AAH!

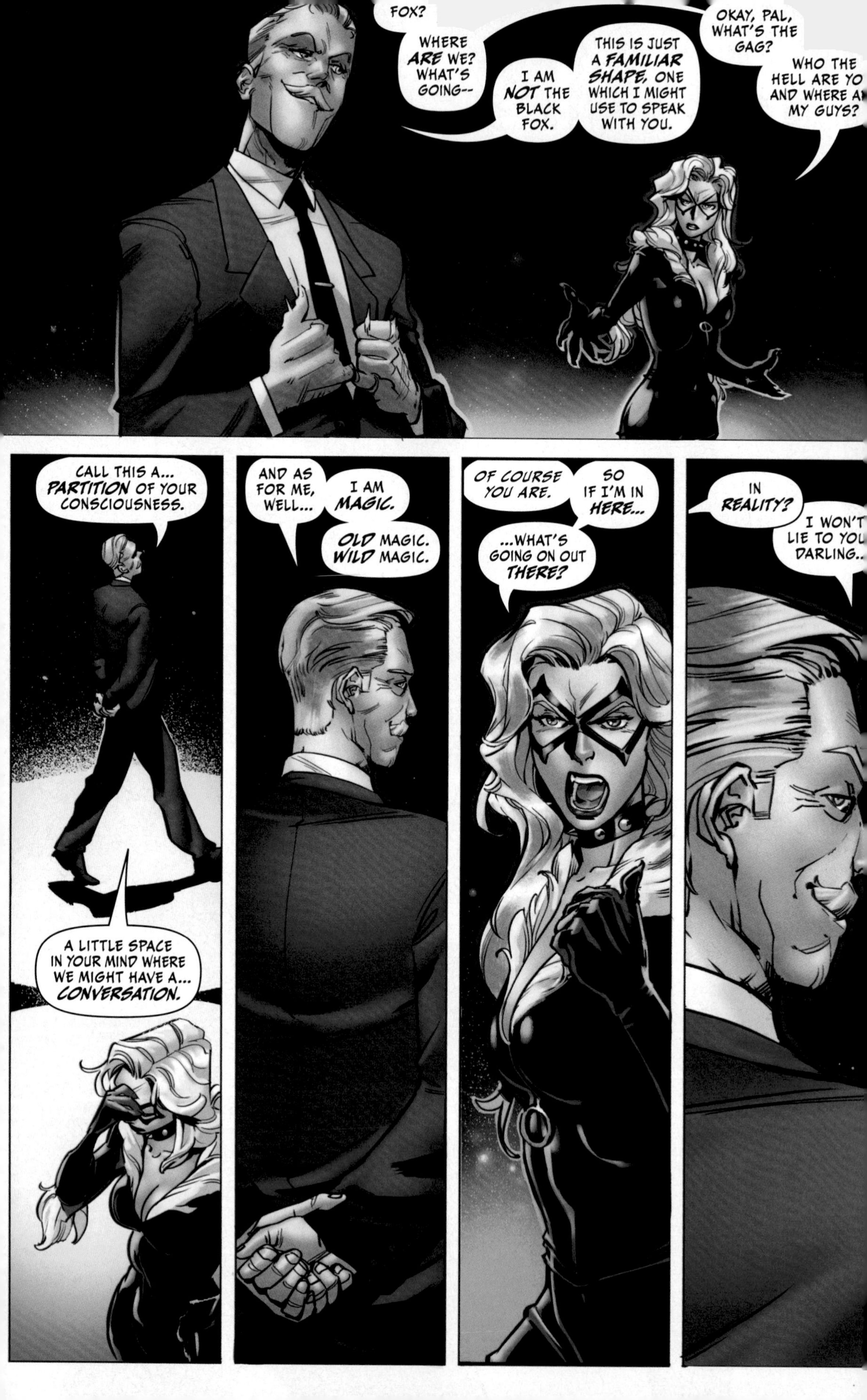
FOX?
WHERE *ARE* WE? WHAT'S GOING--
I AM *NOT* THE BLACK FOX.
THIS IS JUST A *FAMILIAR SHAPE,* ONE WHICH I MIGHT USE TO SPEAK WITH YOU.
OKAY, PAL, WHAT'S THE GAG?
WHO THE HELL ARE YO AND WHERE A MY GUYS?
CALL THIS A... *PARTITION* OF YOUR CONSCIOUSNESS.
A LITTLE SPACE IN YOUR MIND WHERE WE MIGHT HAVE A... *CONVERSATION.*
AND AS FOR ME, WELL...
I AM *MAGIC.*
OLD MAGIC. *WILD* MAGIC.
OF COURSE YOU ARE.
SO IF I'M IN *HERE...*
...WHAT'S GOING ON OUT *THERE?*
IN *REALITY?*
I WON'T LIE TO YOU DARLING...

"...IT'S LOOKING BAD."

HARDYYY!

WHAT THE *HELL* DO YOU THINK YOU'RE PLAYING AT UP THERE?!

FZZZIGGGSSSKKKKK!

"QUITE BAD."

OH NO.

"OH NO" INDEED.

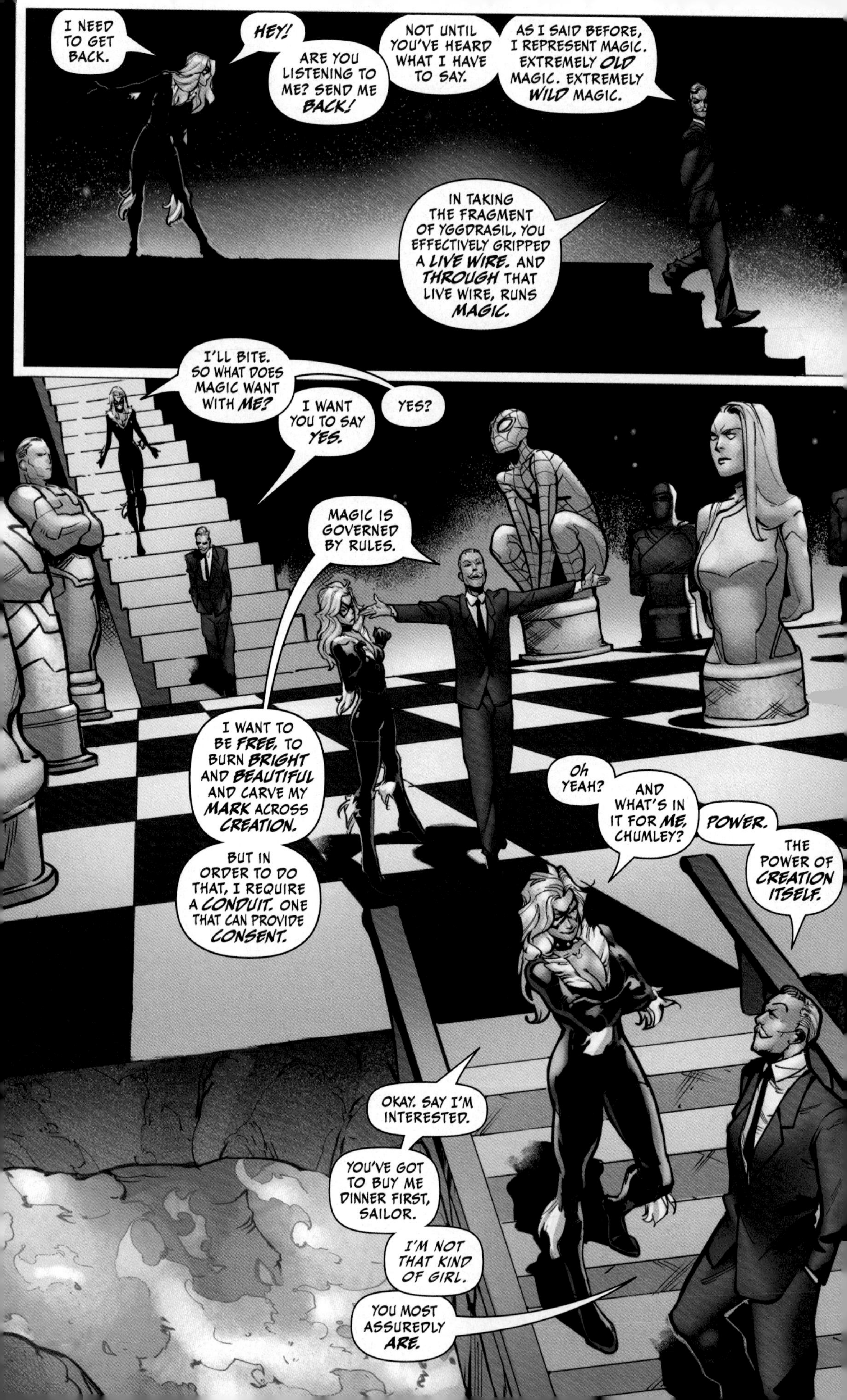
I NEED TO GET BACK.
HEY!
ARE YOU LISTENING TO ME? SEND ME BACK!
NOT UNTIL YOU'VE HEARD WHAT I HAVE TO SAY.
AS I SAID BEFORE, I REPRESENT MAGIC. EXTREMELY OLD MAGIC. EXTREMELY WILD MAGIC.
IN TAKING THE FRAGMENT OF YGGDRASIL, YOU EFFECTIVELY GRIPPED A LIVE WIRE. AND THROUGH THAT LIVE WIRE, RUNS MAGIC.
I'LL BITE. SO WHAT DOES MAGIC WANT WITH ME?
I WANT YOU TO SAY YES.
YES?
MAGIC IS GOVERNED BY RULES.
I WANT TO BE FREE, TO BURN BRIGHT AND BEAUTIFUL AND CARVE MY MARK ACROSS CREATION.
BUT IN ORDER TO DO THAT, I REQUIRE A CONDUIT. ONE THAT CAN PROVIDE CONSENT.
Oh YEAH?
AND WHAT'S IN IT FOR ME, CHUMLEY?
POWER.
THE POWER OF CREATION ITSELF.
OKAY. SAY I'M INTERESTED.
YOU'VE GOT TO BUY ME DINNER FIRST, SAILOR.
I'M NOT THAT KIND OF GIRL.
YOU MOST ASSUREDLY ARE.

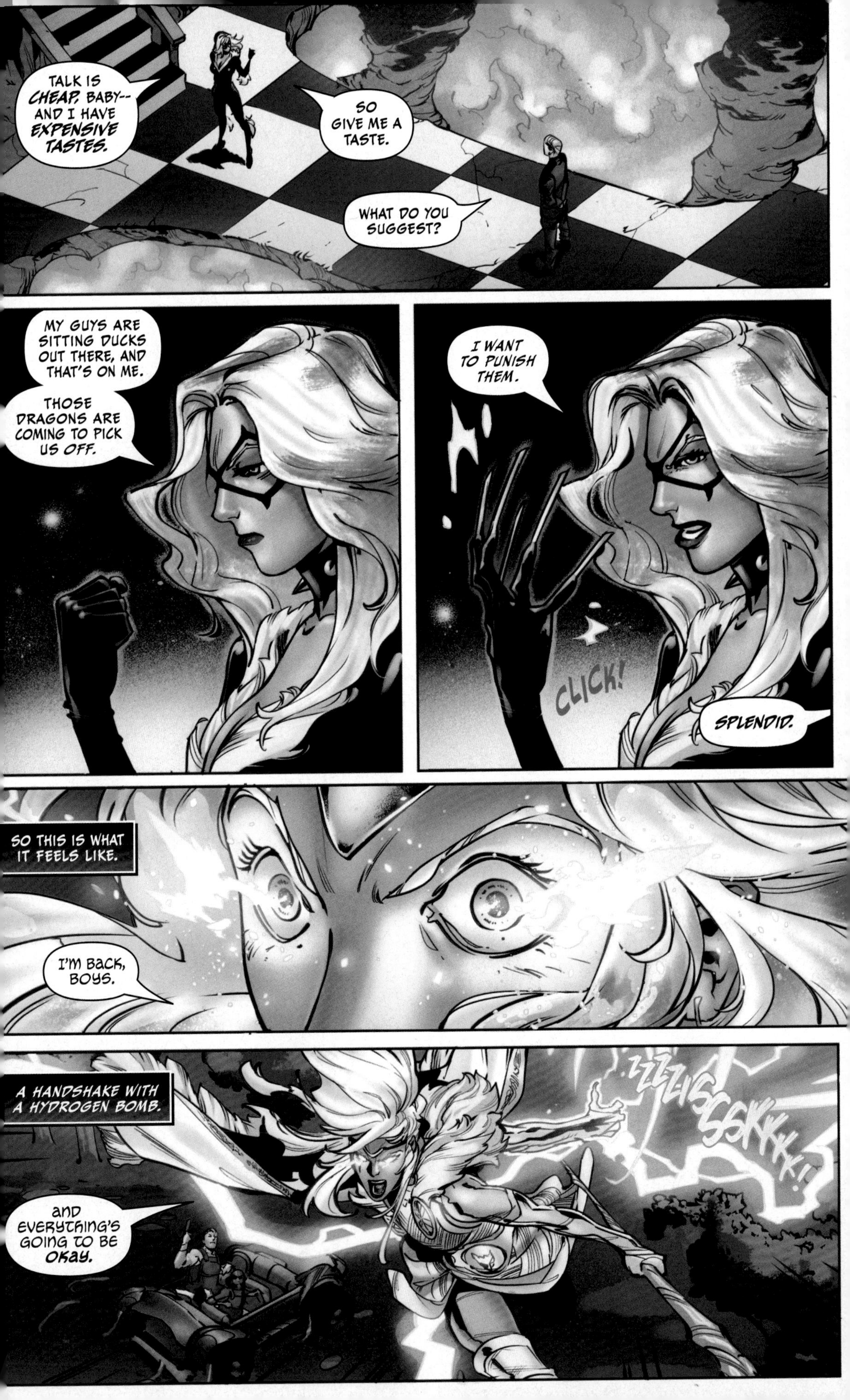

TALK IS CHEAP, BABY-- AND I HAVE EXPENSIVE TASTES.
SO GIVE ME A TASTE.
WHAT DO YOU SUGGEST?
MY GUYS ARE SITTING DUCKS OUT THERE, AND THAT'S ON ME.
THOSE DRAGONS ARE COMING TO PICK US OFF.
I WANT TO PUNISH THEM.
CLICK!
SPLENDID.
SO THIS IS WHAT IT FEELS LIKE.
I'M BACK, BOYS.
A HANDSHAKE WITH A HYDROGEN BOMB.
ZZZZSSSKKKK!
AND EVERYTHING'S GOING TO BE OKAY.

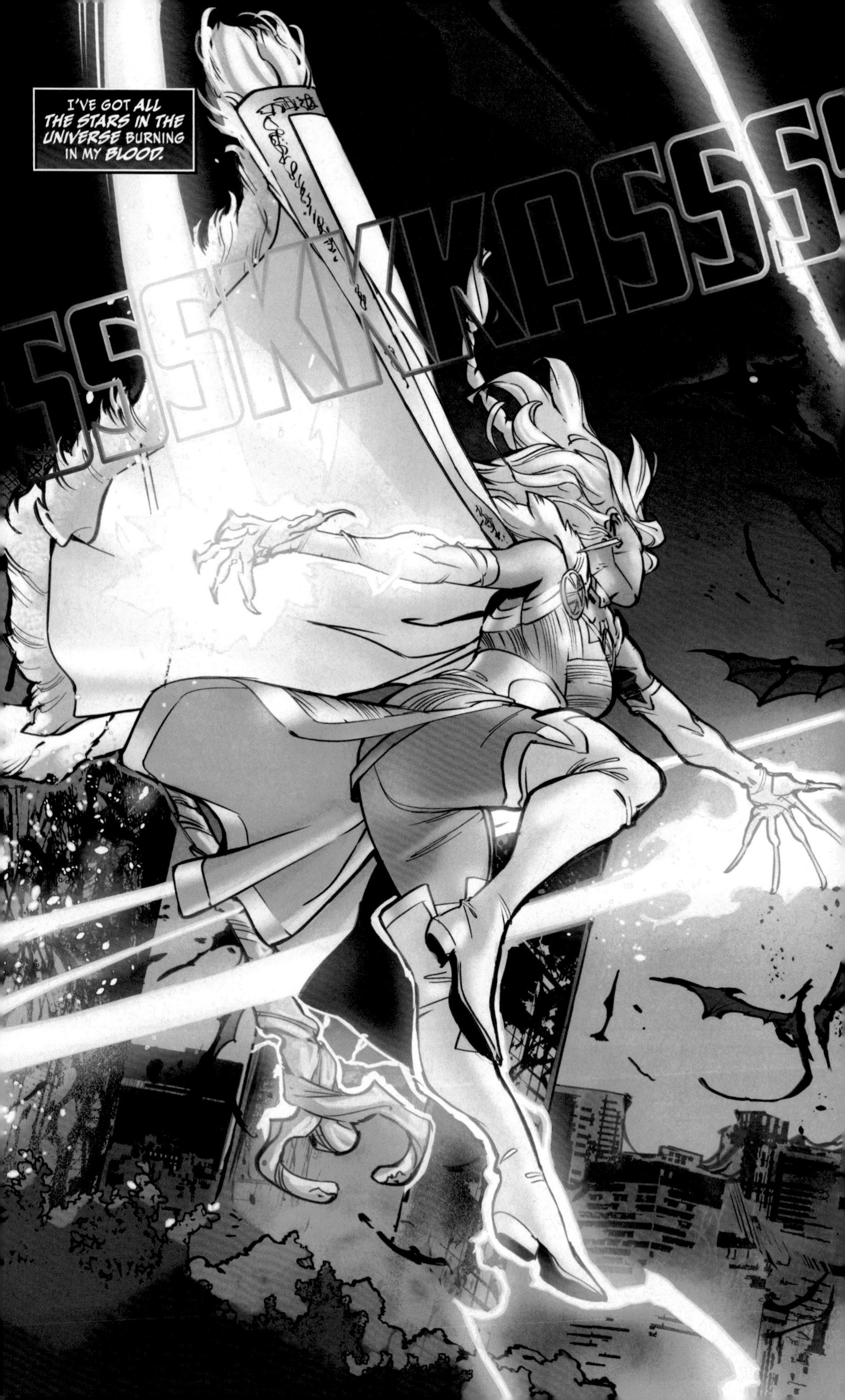
I'VE GOT ALL THE STARS IN THE UNIVERSE BURNING IN MY BLOOD.
SSSKKASSSS

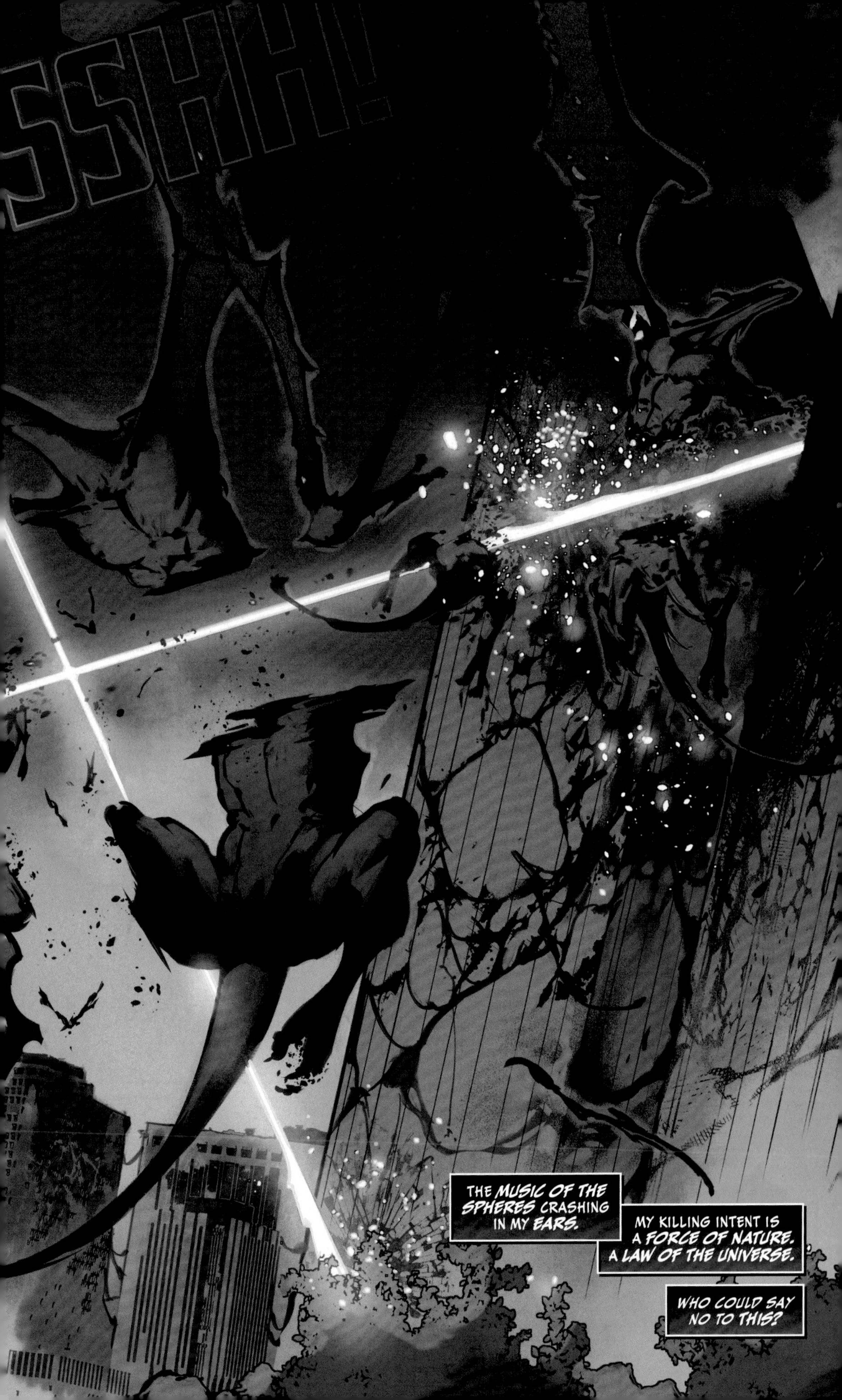
SSHH!
THE MUSIC OF THE SPHERES CRASHING IN MY EARS.
MY KILLING INTENT IS A FORCE OF NATURE. A LAW OF THE UNIVERSE.
WHO COULD SAY NO TO THIS?

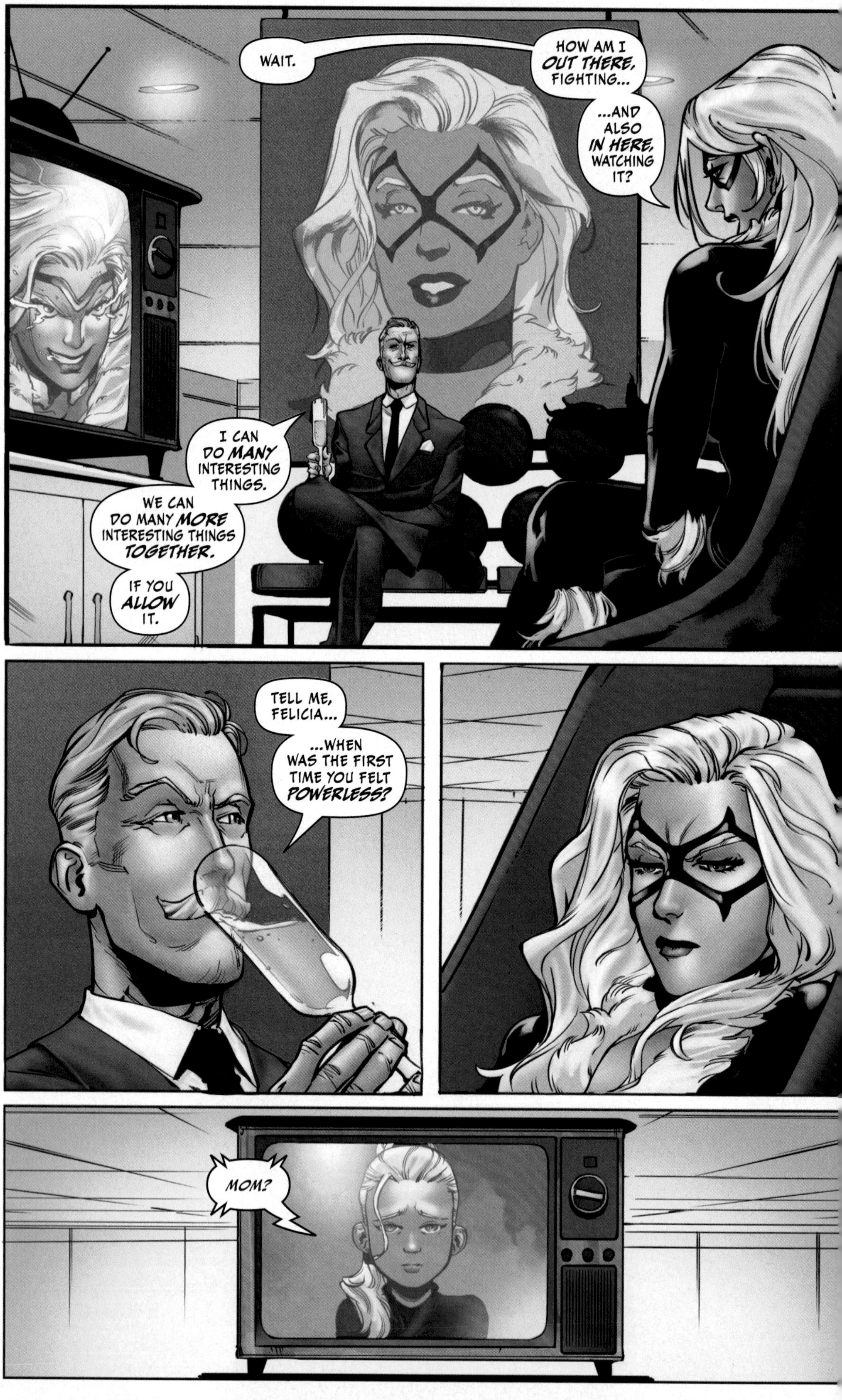
WAIT.
HOW AM I OUT THERE, FIGHTING...
...AND ALSO IN HERE, WATCHING IT?
I CAN DO MANY INTERESTING THINGS.
WE CAN DO MANY MORE INTERESTING THINGS TOGETHER.
IF YOU ALLOW IT.
TELL ME, FELICIA...
...WHEN WAS THE FIRST TIME YOU FELT POWERLESS?
MOM?

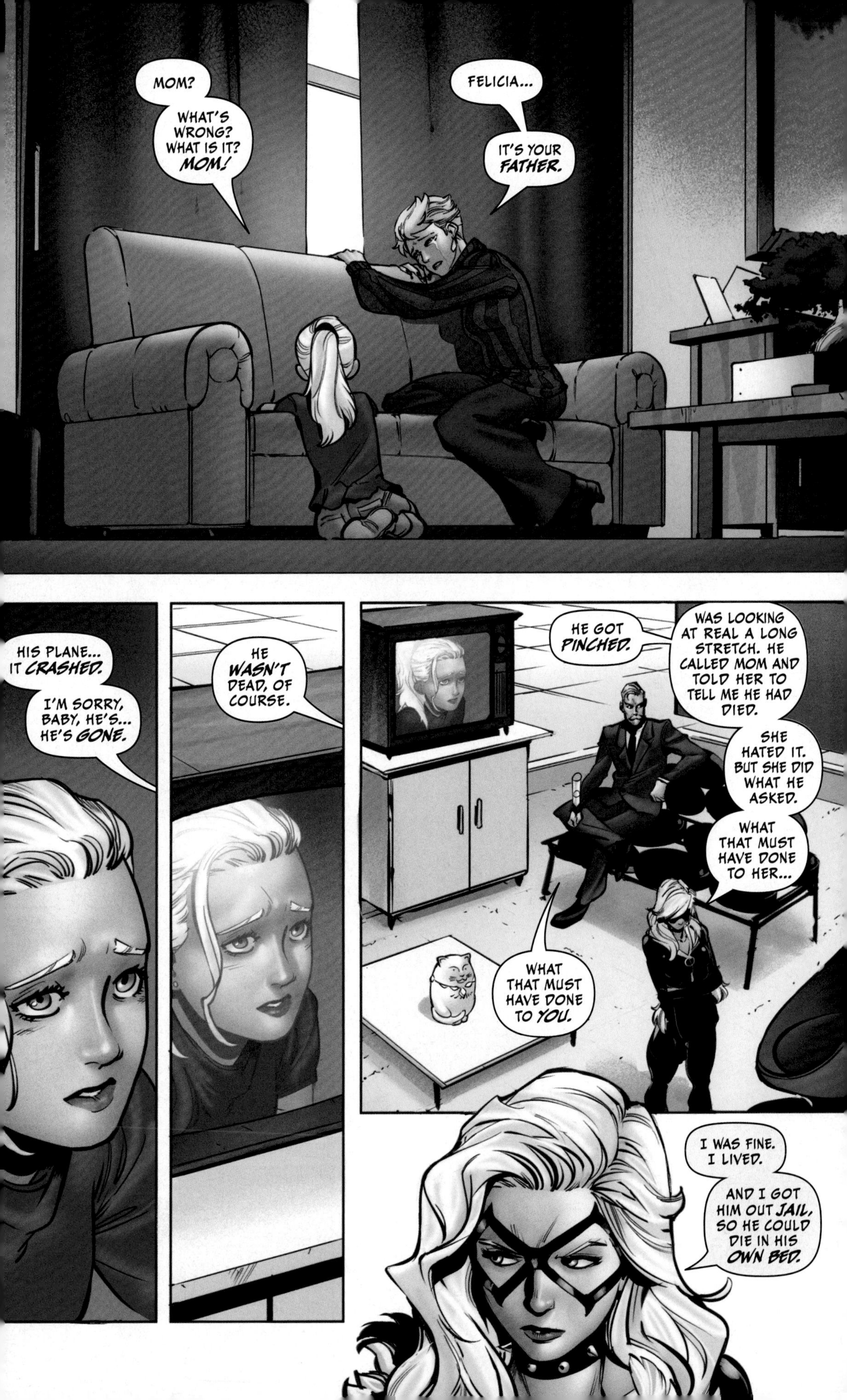

MOM?
WHAT'S WRONG? WHAT IS IT? MOM!
FELICIA...
IT'S YOUR FATHER.
HIS PLANE... IT CRASHED.
I'M SORRY, BABY, HE'S... HE'S GONE.
HE WASN'T DEAD, OF COURSE.
HE GOT PINCHED.
WAS LOOKING AT REAL A LONG STRETCH. HE CALLED MOM AND TOLD HER TO TELL ME HE HAD DIED.
SHE HATED IT. BUT SHE DID WHAT HE ASKED.
WHAT THAT MUST HAVE DONE TO HER...
WHAT THAT MUST HAVE DONE TO YOU.
I WAS FINE. I LIVED.
AND I GOT HIM OUT JAIL, SO HE COULD DIE IN HIS OWN BED.

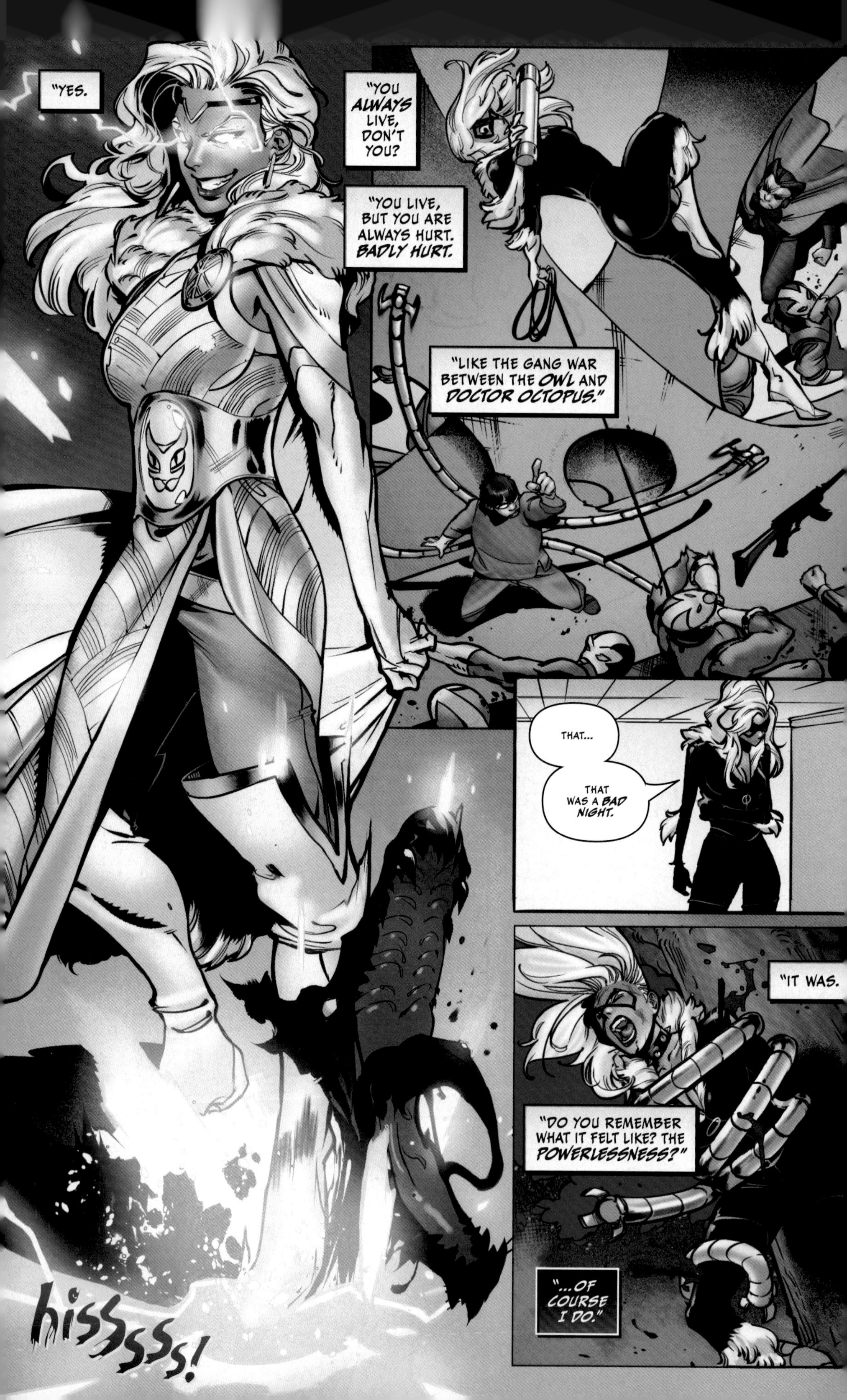
"YES.
"YOU ALWAYS LIVE, DON'T YOU?
"YOU LIVE, BUT YOU ARE ALWAYS HURT. BADLY HURT.
"LIKE THE GANG WAR BETWEEN THE OWL AND DOCTOR OCTOPUS."
THAT...
THAT WAS A BAD NIGHT.
"IT WAS.
"DO YOU REMEMBER WHAT IT FELT LIKE? THE POWERLESSNESS?"
"...OF COURSE I DO."
hissSSS!

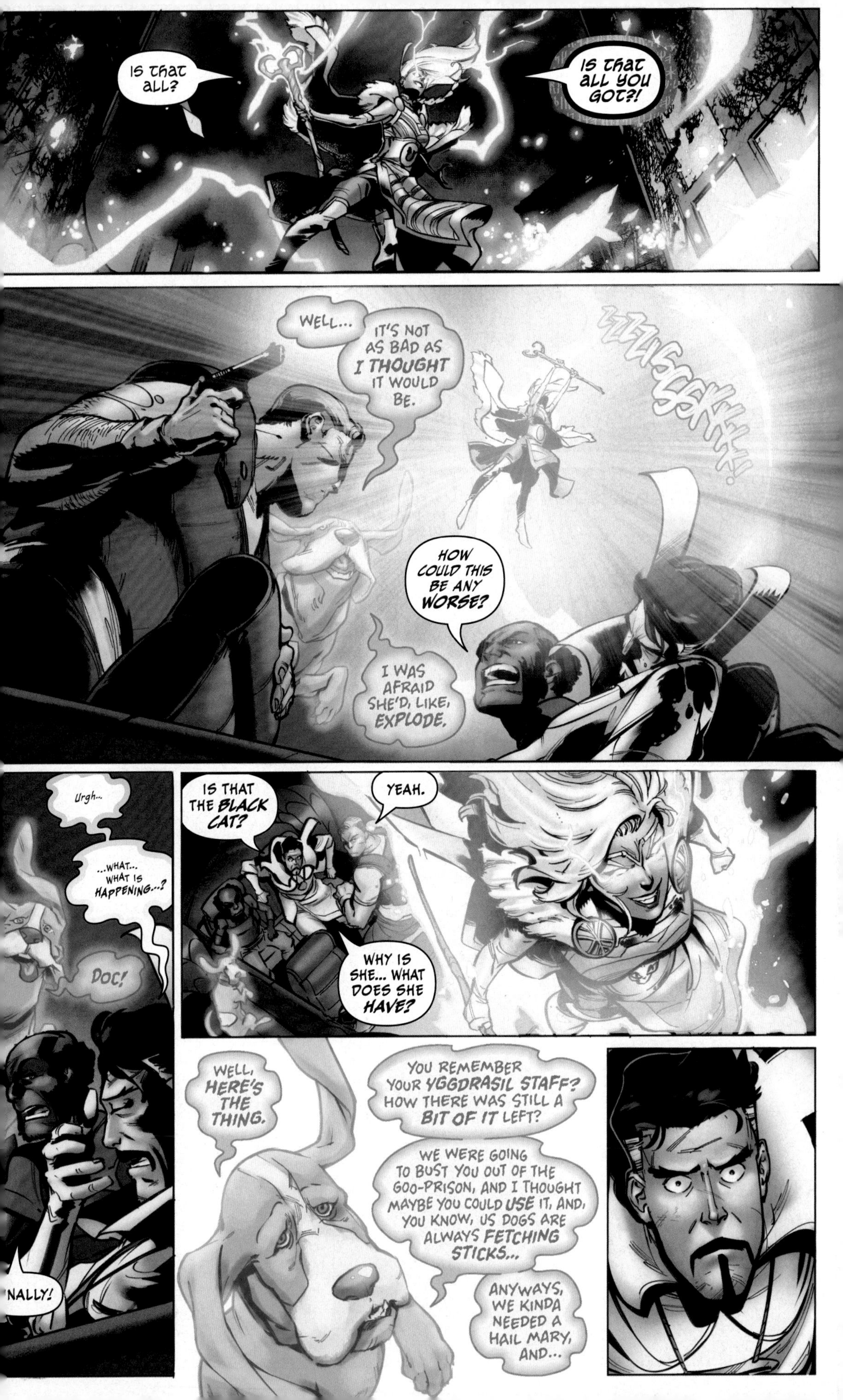

IS THAT ALL?
IS THAT ALL YOU GOT?!
WELL...
IT'S NOT AS BAD AS I THOUGHT IT WOULD BE.
ZZZISSSKKK!!
HOW COULD THIS BE ANY WORSE?
I WAS AFRAID SHE'D, LIKE, EXPLODE.
Urgh...
...WHAT... WHAT IS HAPPENING...?
DOC!
NALLY!
IS THAT THE BLACK CAT?
YEAH.
WHY IS SHE... WHAT DOES SHE HAVE?
WELL, HERE'S THE THING.
YOU REMEMBER YOUR YGGDRASIL STAFF? HOW THERE WAS STILL A BIT OF IT LEFT?
WE WERE GOING TO BUST YOU OUT OF THE GOO-PRISON, AND I THOUGHT MAYBE YOU COULD USE IT, AND, YOU KNOW, US DOGS ARE ALWAYS FETCHING STICKS...
ANYWAYS, WE KINDA NEEDED A HAIL MARY, AND...

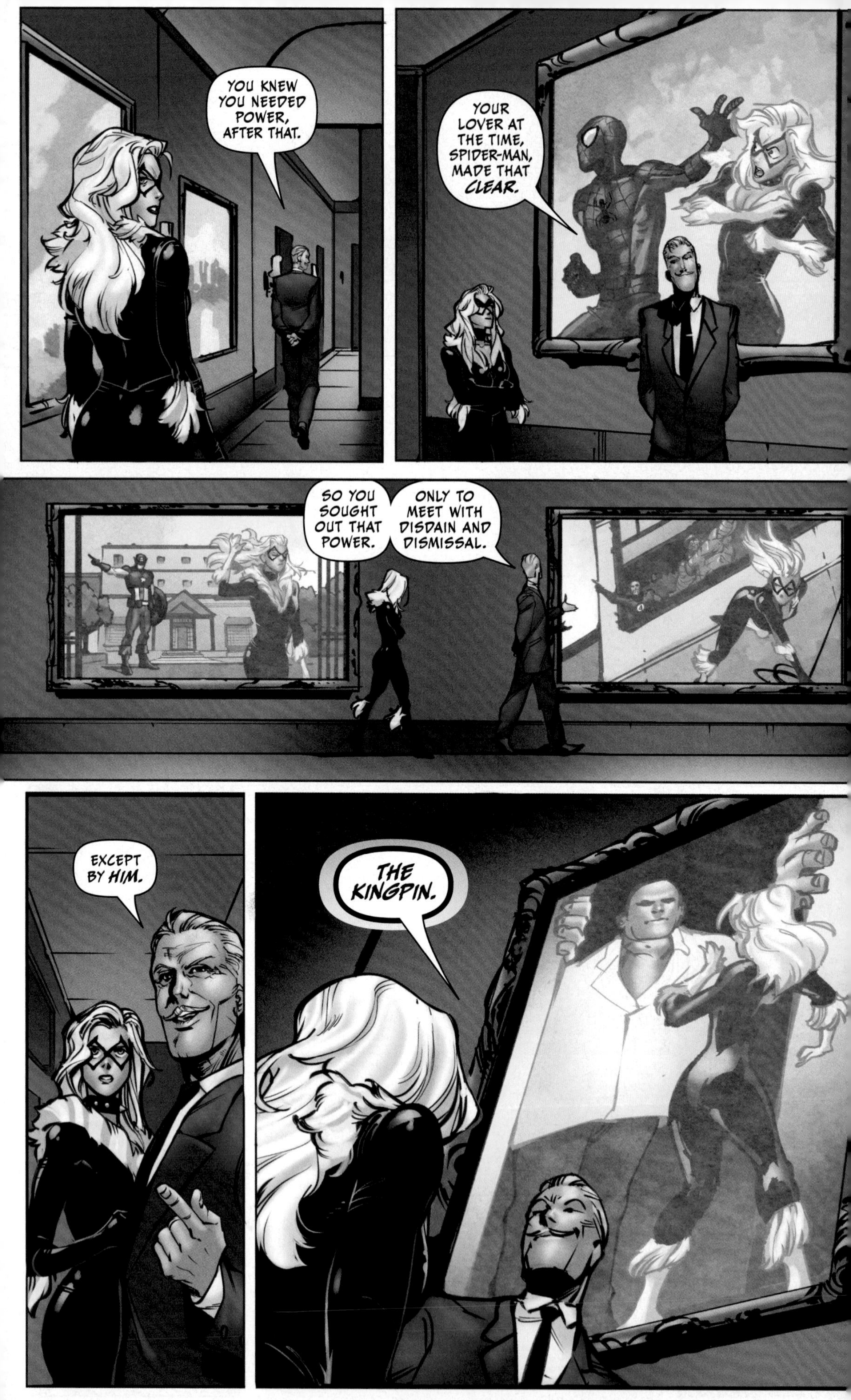

YOU KNEW YOU NEEDED POWER, AFTER THAT.
YOUR LOVER AT THE TIME, SPIDER-MAN, MADE THAT CLEAR.
SO YOU SOUGHT OUT THAT POWER.
ONLY TO MEET WITH DISDAIN AND DISMISSAL.
EXCEPT BY HIM.
THE KINGPIN.

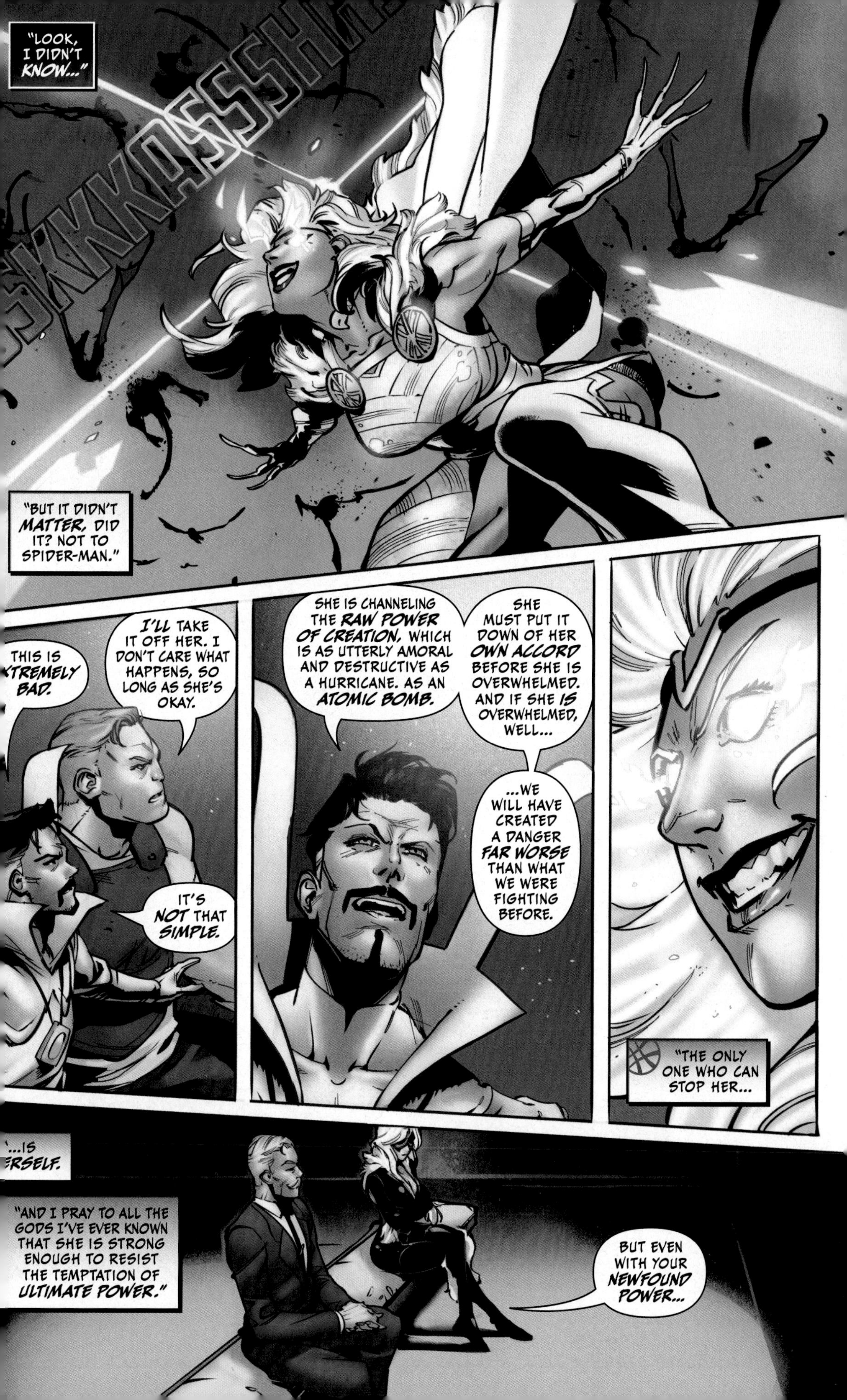
"LOOK, I DIDN'T KNOW..."
SKKKRASSSHH
"BUT IT DIDN'T MATTER, DID IT? NOT TO SPIDER-MAN."
THIS IS XTREMELY BAD.
I'LL TAKE IT OFF HER. I DON'T CARE WHAT HAPPENS, SO LONG AS SHE'S OKAY.
IT'S NOT THAT SIMPLE.
SHE IS CHANNELING THE RAW POWER OF CREATION, WHICH IS AS UTTERLY AMORAL AND DESTRUCTIVE AS A HURRICANE. AS AN ATOMIC BOMB.
SHE MUST PUT IT DOWN OF HER OWN ACCORD BEFORE SHE IS OVERWHELMED. AND IF SHE IS OVERWHELMED, WELL...
...WE WILL HAVE CREATED A DANGER FAR WORSE THAN WHAT WE WERE FIGHTING BEFORE.
"THE ONLY ONE WHO CAN STOP HER...
...IS ERSELF.
"AND I PRAY TO ALL THE GODS I'VE EVER KNOWN THAT SHE IS STRONG ENOUGH TO RESIST THE TEMPTATION OF ULTIMATE POWER."
BUT EVEN WITH YOUR NEWFOUND POWER...

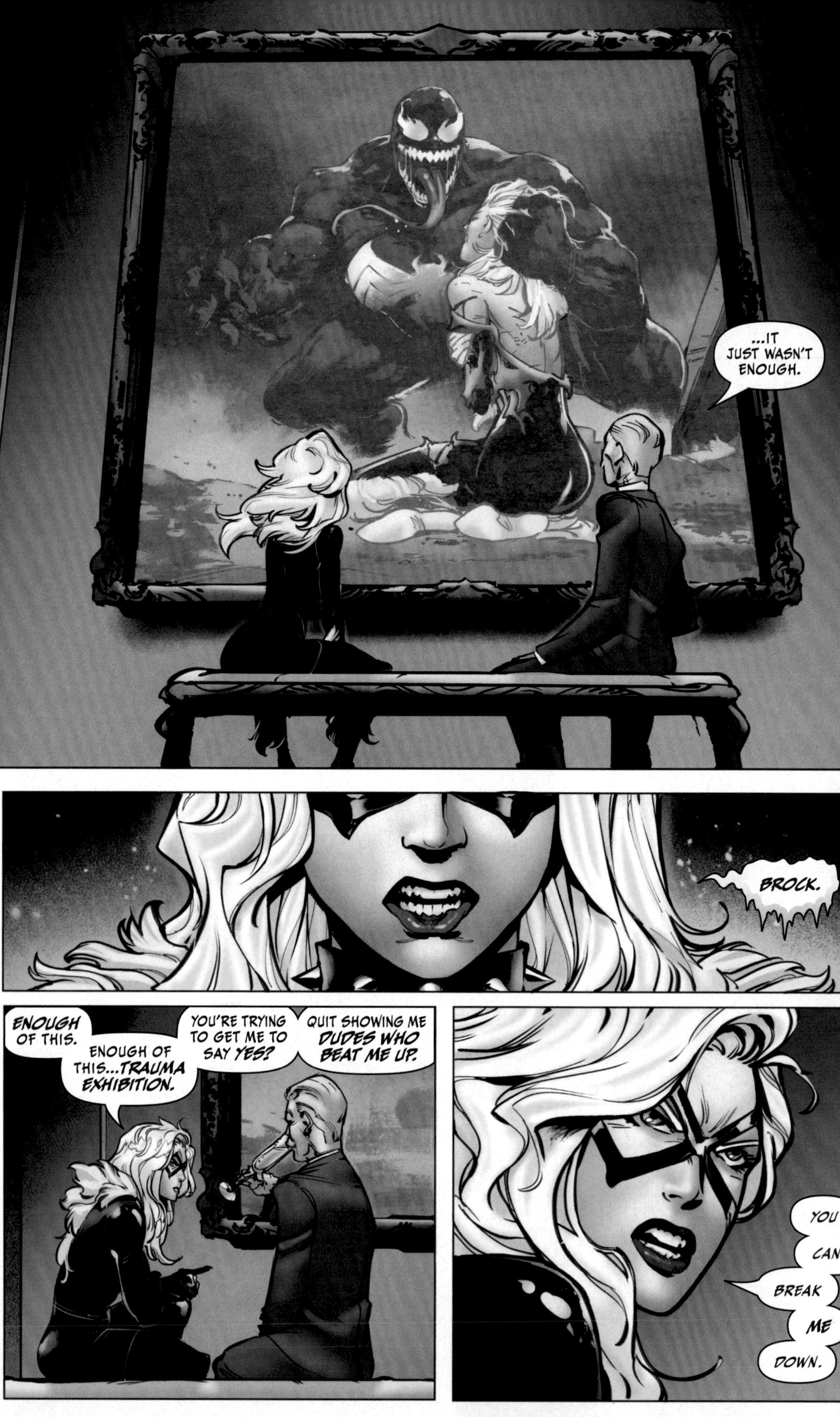
...IT JUST WASN'T ENOUGH.
BROCK.
ENOUGH OF THIS.
ENOUGH OF THIS...TRAUMA EXHIBITION.
YOU'RE TRYING TO GET ME TO SAY YES?
QUIT SHOWING ME DUDES WHO BEAT ME UP.
YOU CAN' BREAK ME DOWN.

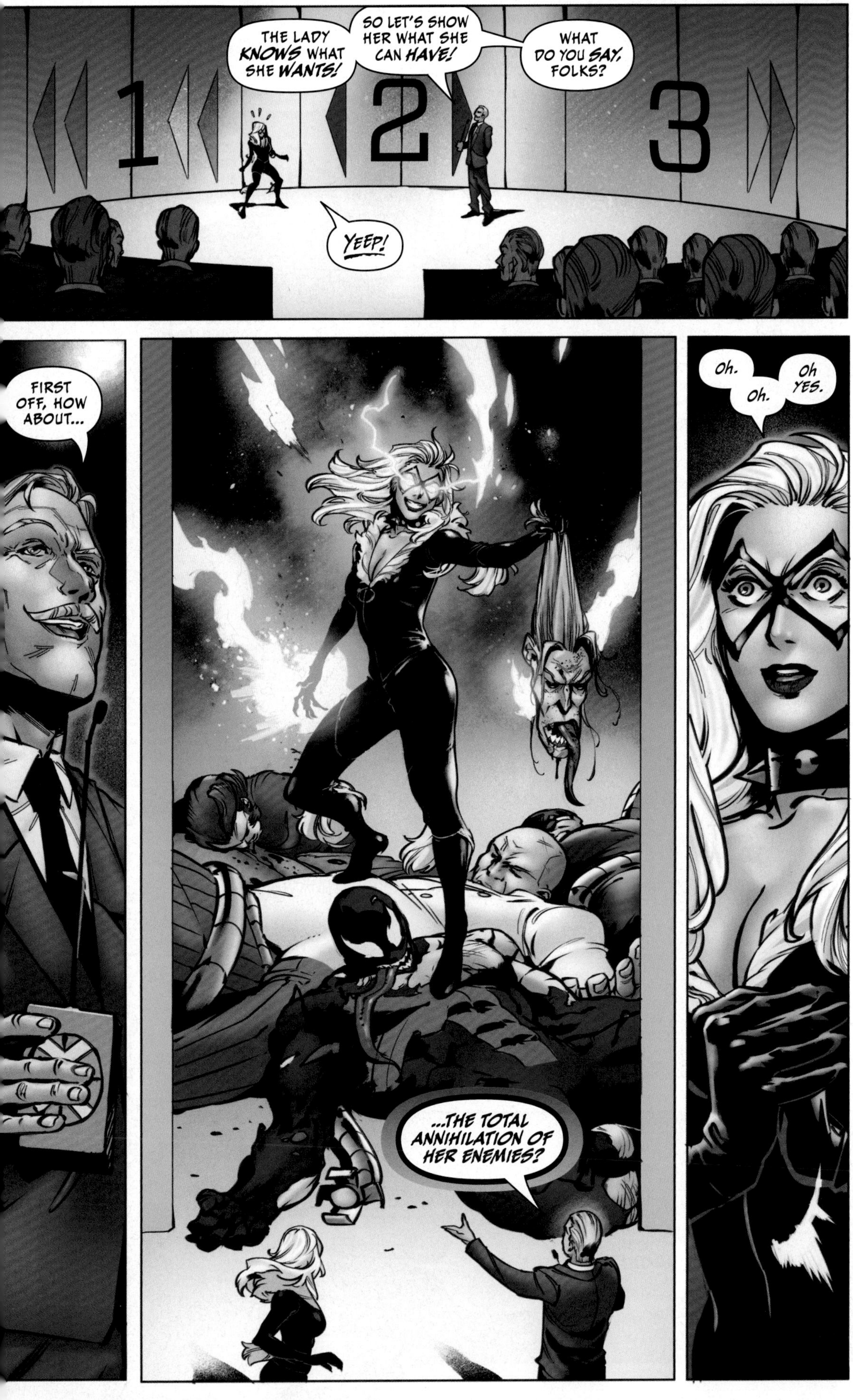
THE LADY KNOWS WHAT SHE WANTS!
SO LET'S SHOW HER WHAT SHE CAN HAVE!
WHAT DO YOU SAY, FOLKS?
1
2
3
YEEP!
FIRST OFF, HOW ABOUT...
...THE TOTAL ANNIHILATION OF HER ENEMIES?
Oh.
Oh.
Oh YES.

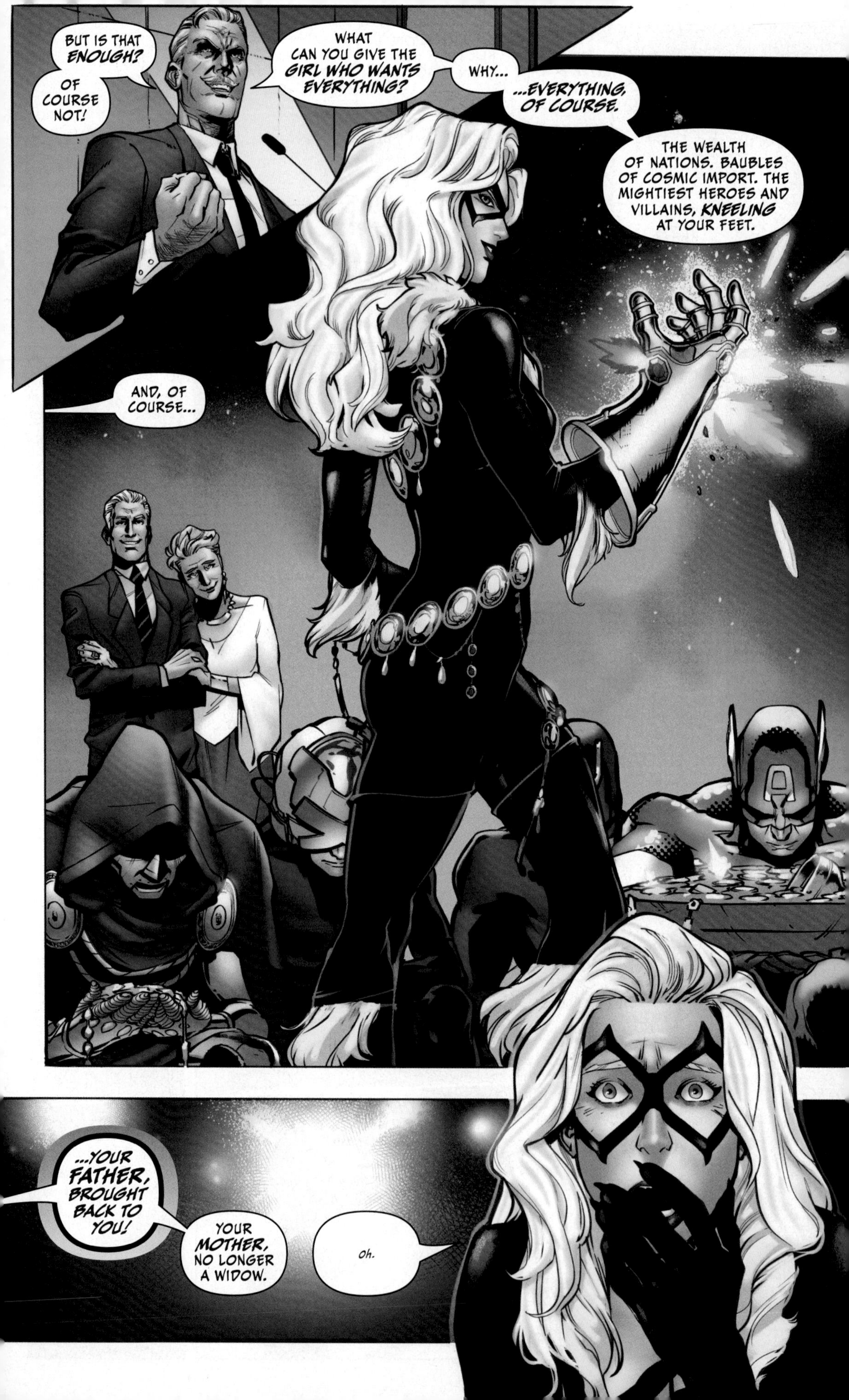
BUT IS THAT ENOUGH?
OF COURSE NOT!
WHAT CAN YOU GIVE THE GIRL WHO WANTS EVERYTHING?
WHY...
...EVERYTHING, OF COURSE.
THE WEALTH OF NATIONS. BAUBLES OF COSMIC IMPORT. THE MIGHTIEST HEROES AND VILLAINS, KNEELING AT YOUR FEET.
AND, OF COURSE...
...YOUR FATHER, BROUGHT BACK TO YOU!
YOUR MOTHER, NO LONGER A WIDOW.
Oh.

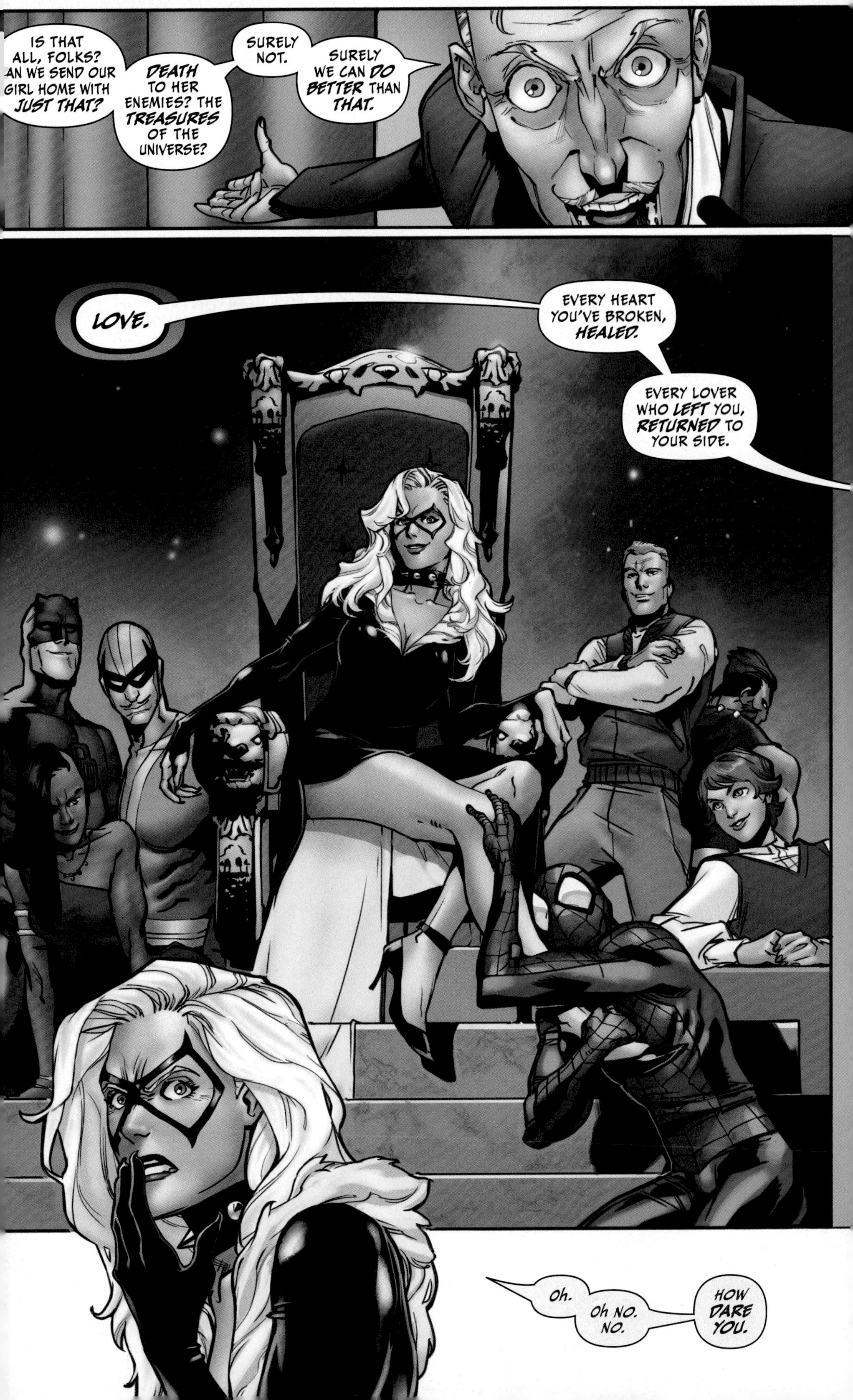
IS THAT ALL, FOLKS? CAN WE SEND OUR GIRL HOME WITH JUST THAT?
DEATH TO HER ENEMIES? THE TREASURES OF THE UNIVERSE?
SURELY NOT.
SURELY WE CAN DO BETTER THAN THAT.
LOVE.
EVERY HEART YOU'VE BROKEN, HEALED.
EVERY LOVER WHO LEFT YOU, RETURNED TO YOUR SIDE.
Oh.
Oh NO. NO.
HOW DARE YOU.

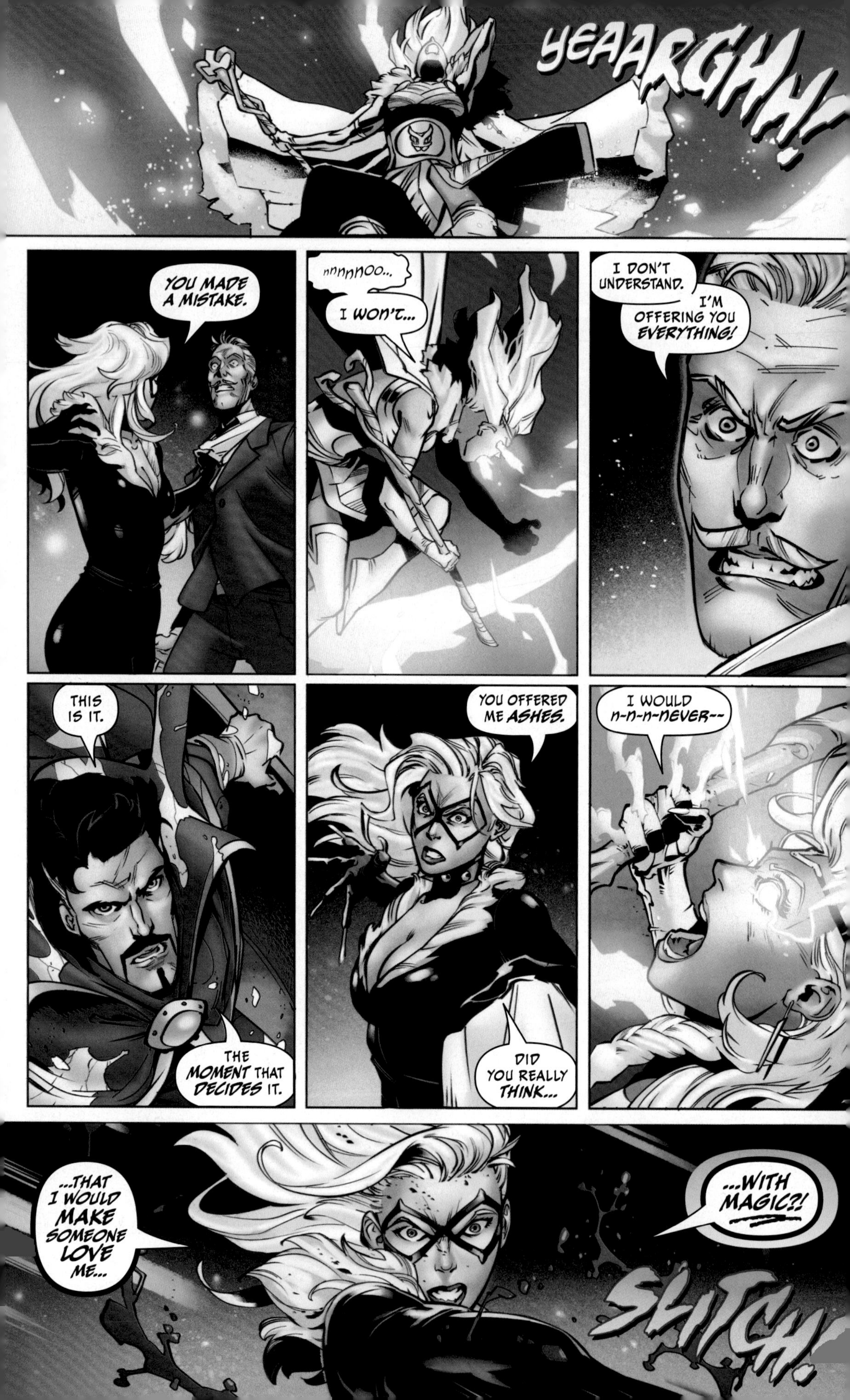
YEAARGHH!
YOU MADE A MISTAKE.
nnnnnoo...
I WON'T...
I DON'T UNDERSTAND.
I'M OFFERING YOU EVERYTHING!
THIS IS IT.
THE MOMENT THAT DECIDES IT.
YOU OFFERED ME ASHES.
DID YOU REALLY THINK...
I WOULD n-n-n-NEVER--
...THAT I WOULD MAKE SOMEONE LOVE ME...
...WITH MAGIC?!
SLITCH!

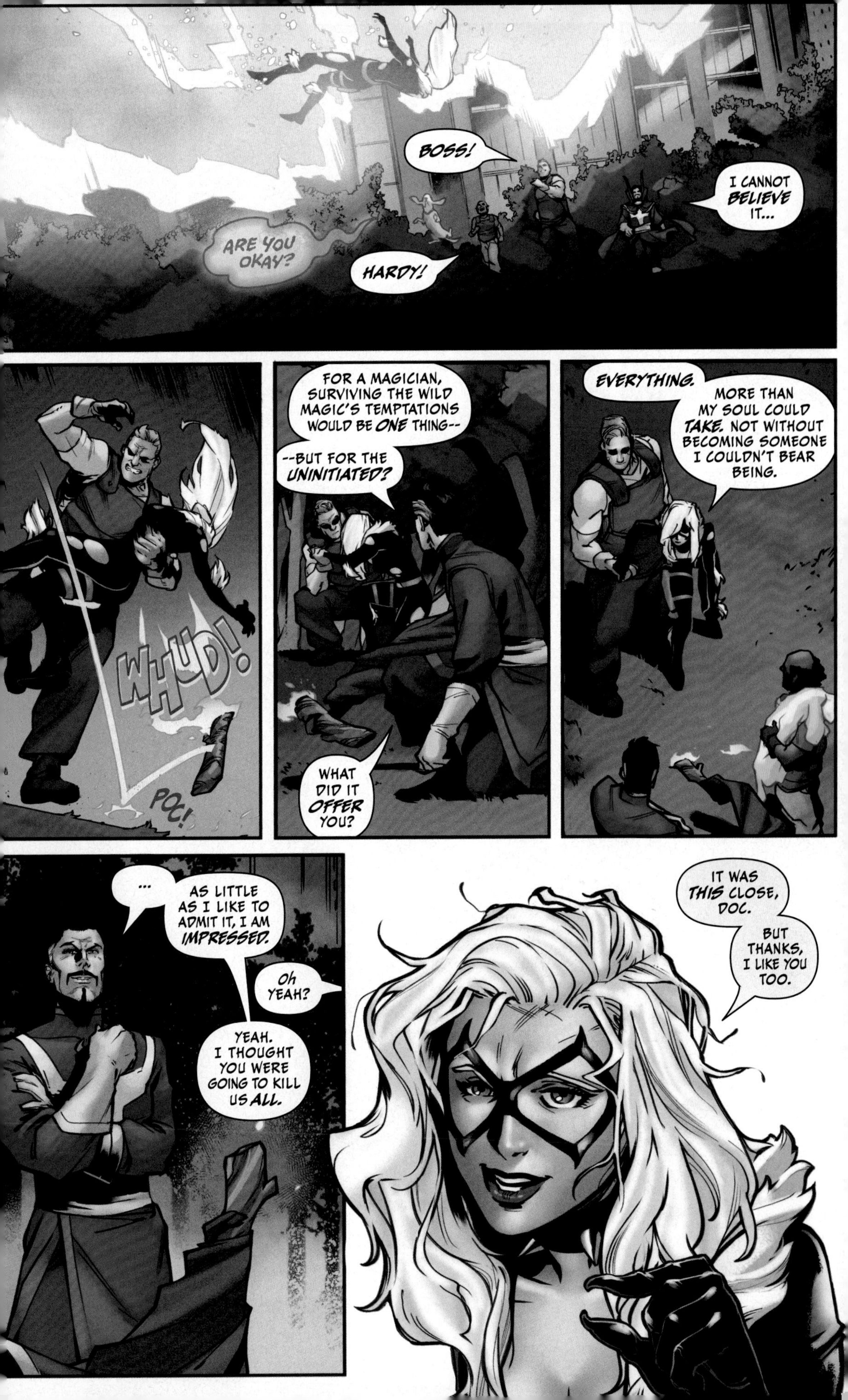
BOSS!
I CANNOT BELIEVE IT...
ARE YOU OKAY?
HARDY!
WHUD!
POC!
FOR A MAGICIAN, SURVIVING THE WILD MAGIC'S TEMPTATIONS WOULD BE ONE THING--
--BUT FOR THE UNINITIATED?
WHAT DID IT OFFER YOU?
EVERYTHING.
MORE THAN MY SOUL COULD TAKE. NOT WITHOUT BECOMING SOMEONE I COULDN'T BEAR BEING.
...
AS LITTLE AS I LIKE TO ADMIT IT, I AM IMPRESSED.
Oh YEAH?
YEAH. I THOUGHT YOU WERE GOING TO KILL US ALL.
IT WAS THIS CLOSE, DOC.
BUT THANKS, I LIKE YOU TOO.

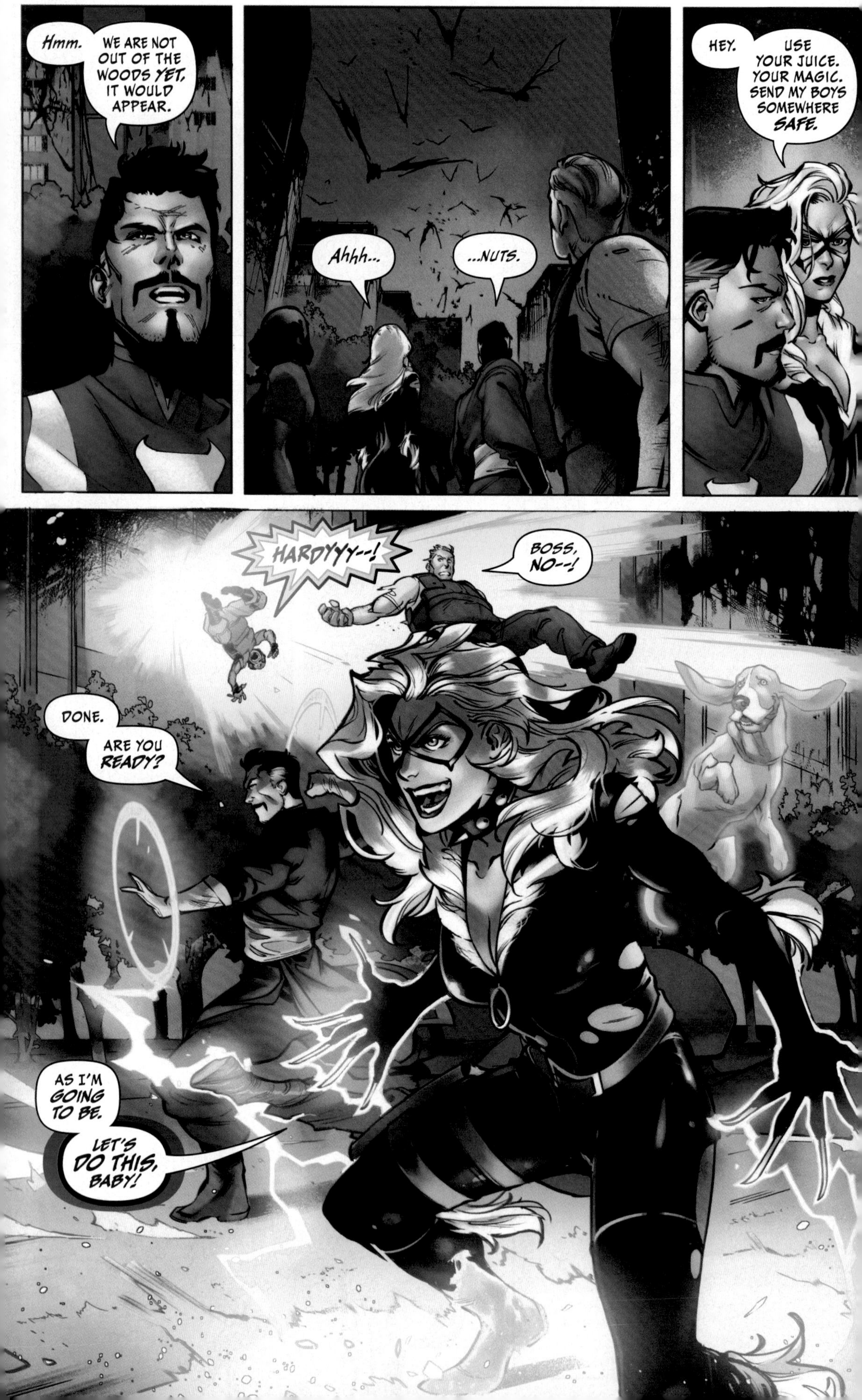
Hmm.
WE ARE NOT OUT OF THE WOODS YET, IT WOULD APPEAR.
Ahhh...
...NUTS.
HEY.
USE YOUR JUICE. YOUR MAGIC. SEND MY BOYS SOMEWHERE SAFE.
HARDYYY--!
BOSS, NO--!
DONE.
ARE YOU READY?
AS I'M GOING TO BE.
LET'S DO THIS, BABY!

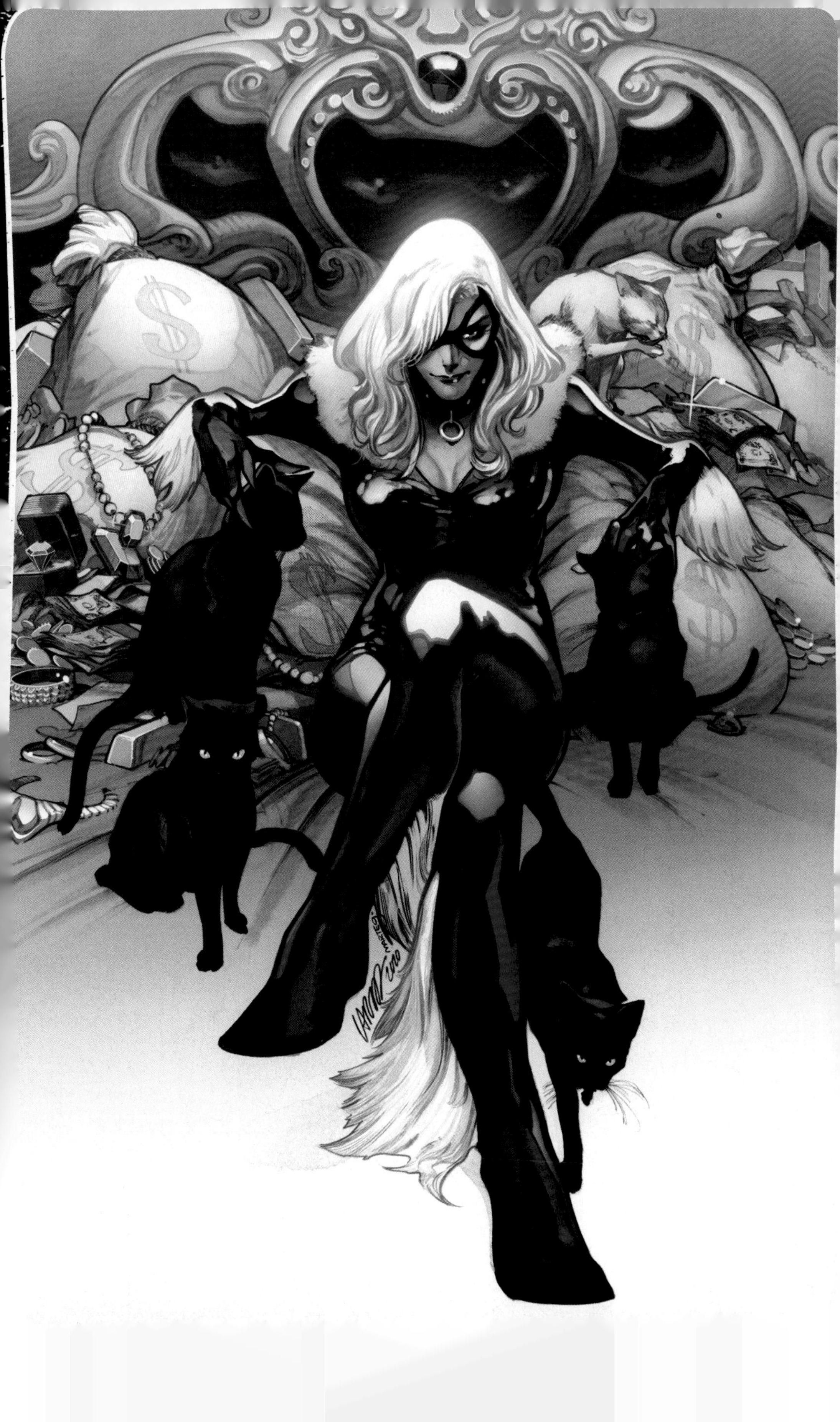

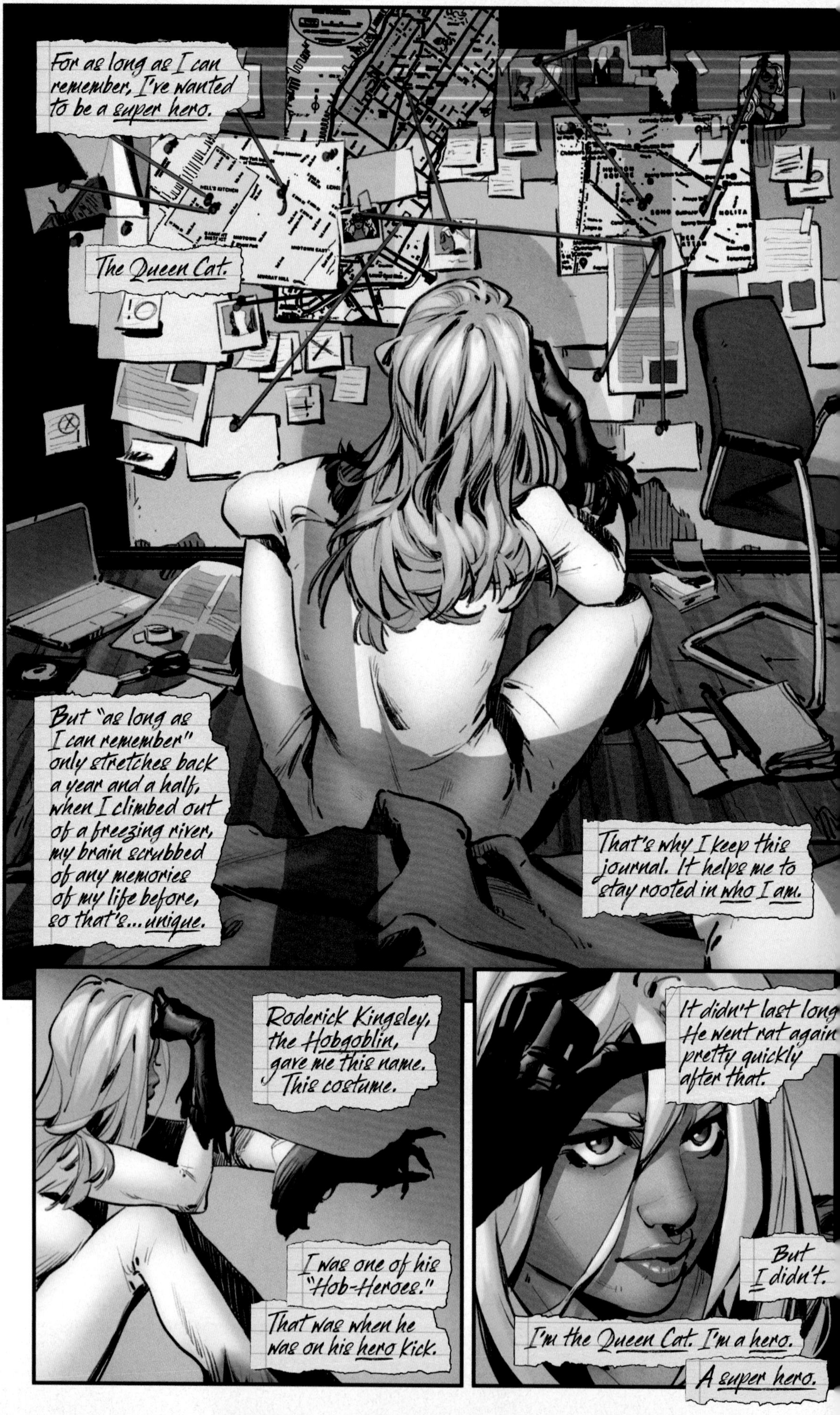
For as long as I can remember, I've wanted to be a super hero.
The Queen Cat.
But "as long as I can remember" only stretches back a year and a half, when I climbed out of a freezing river, my brain scrubbed of any memories of my life before, so that's... unique.
That's why I keep this journal. It helps me to stay rooted in who I am.
Roderick Kingsley, the Hobgoblin, gave me this name. This costume.
I was one of his "Hob-Heroes."
That was when he was on his hero kick.
It didn't last long. He went rat again pretty quickly after that.
But I didn't.
I'm the Queen Cat. I'm a hero.
A super hero.

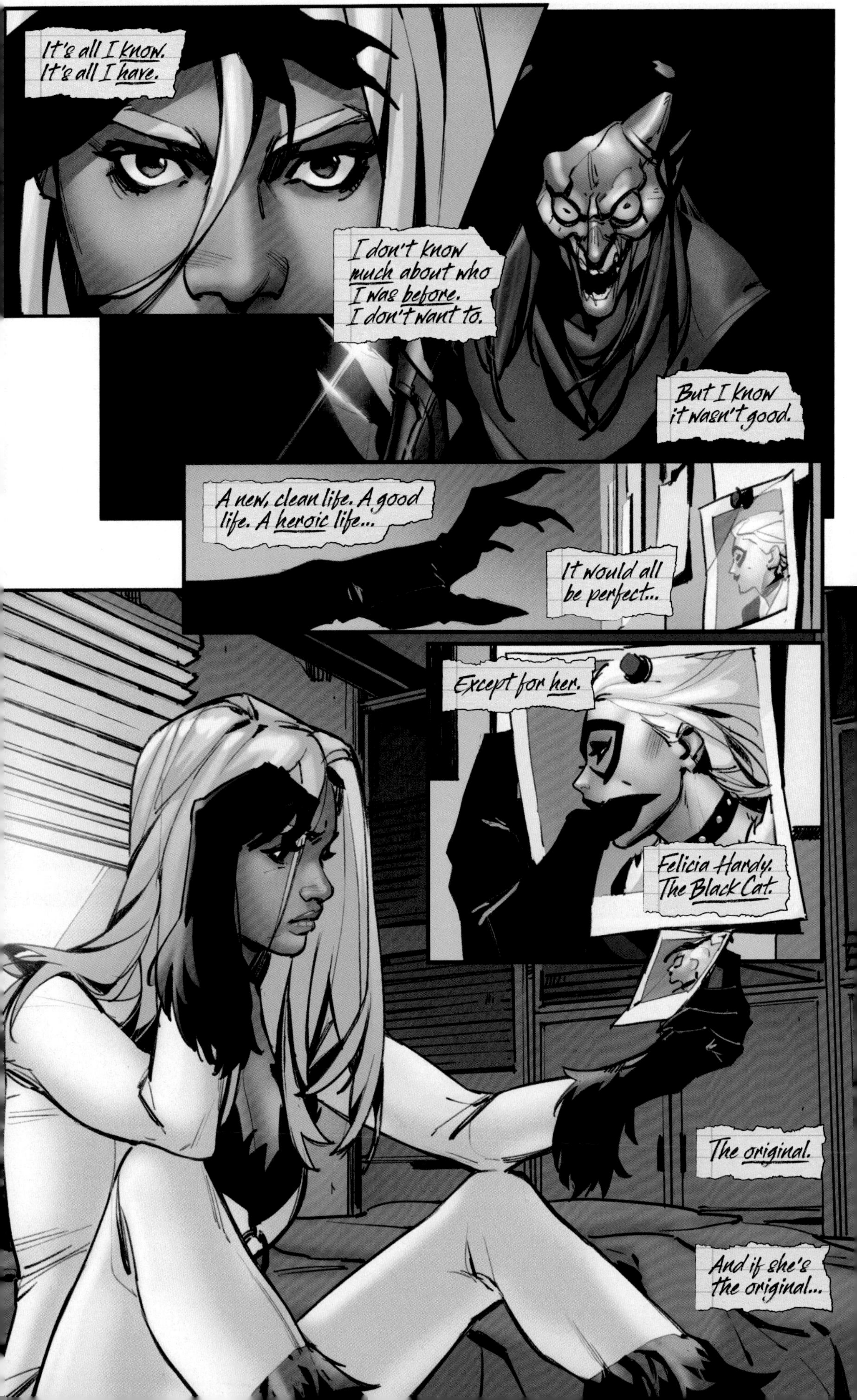
It's all I know.
It's all I have.
I don't know much about who I was before.
I don't want to.
But I know it wasn't good.
A new, clean life. A good life. A heroic life...
It would all be perfect...
Except for her.
Felicia Hardy. The Black Cat.
The original.
And if she's the original...

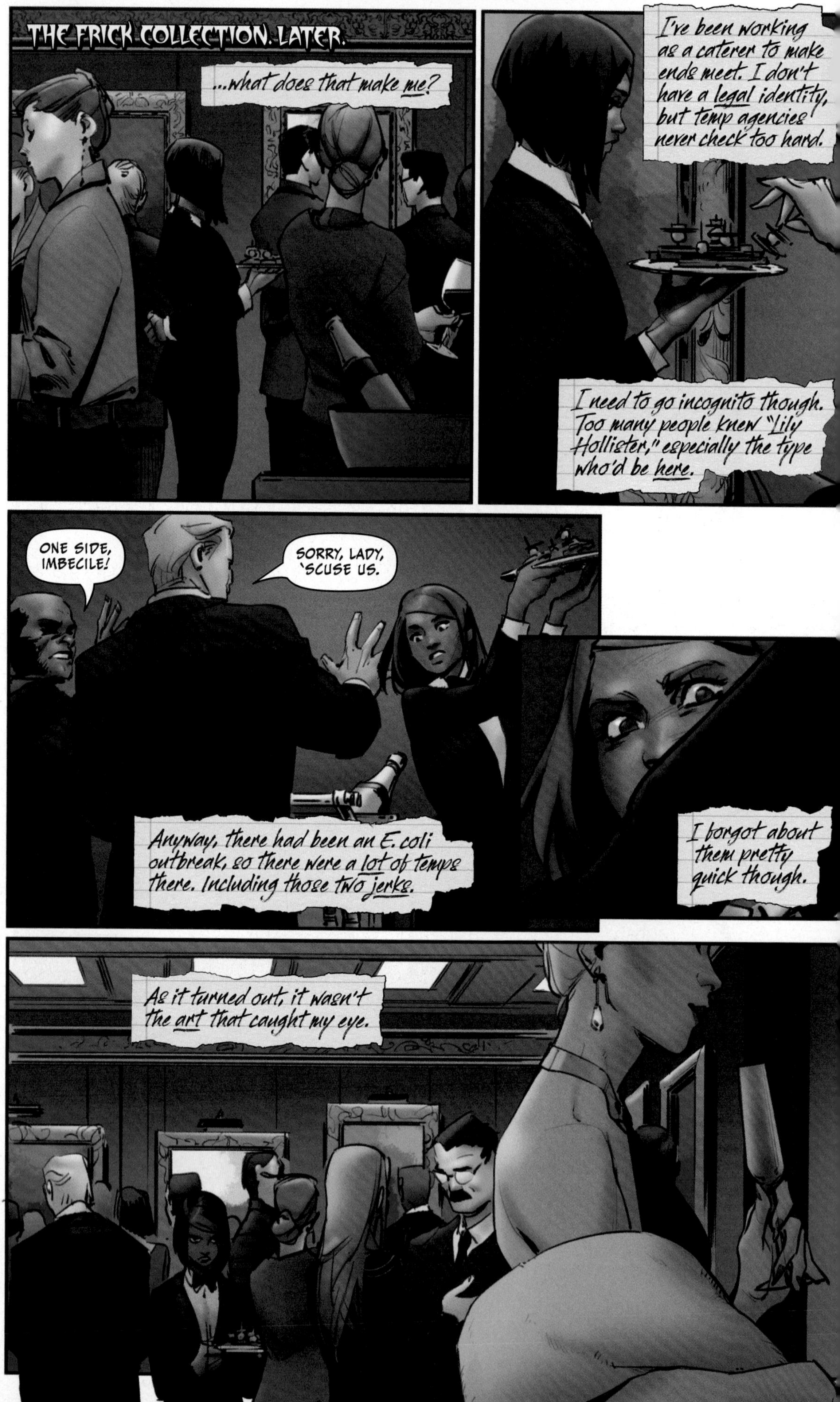
THE FRICK COLLECTION. LATER.
...what does that make me?
I've been working as a caterer to make ends meet. I don't have a legal identity, but temp agencies never check too hard.
I need to go incognito though. Too many people knew "Lily Hollister," especially the type who'd be here.
ONE SIDE, IMBECILE!
SORRY, LADY, 'SCUSE US.
Anyway, there had been an E. coli outbreak, so there were a lot of temps there. Including those two jerks.
I forgot about them pretty quick though.
As it turned out, it wasn't the art that caught my eye.

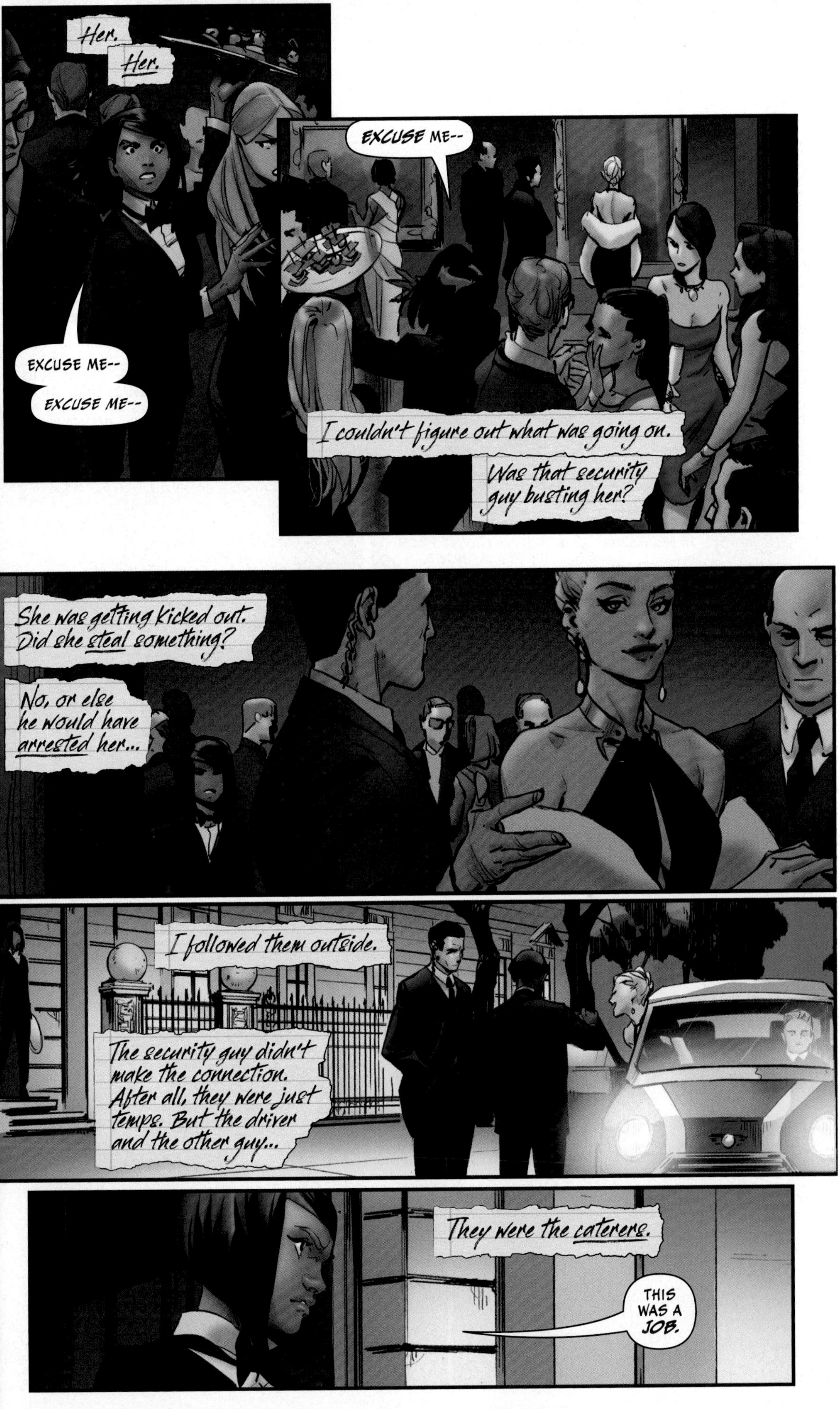
Her.
Her.
EXCUSE ME--
EXCUSE ME--
EXCUSE ME--
I couldn't figure out what was going on.
Was that security guy busting her?
She was getting kicked out. Did she steal something?
No, or else he would have arrested her...
I followed them outside.
The security guy didn't make the connection. After all, they were just temps. But the driver and the other guy...
They were the caterers.
THIS WAS A JOB.

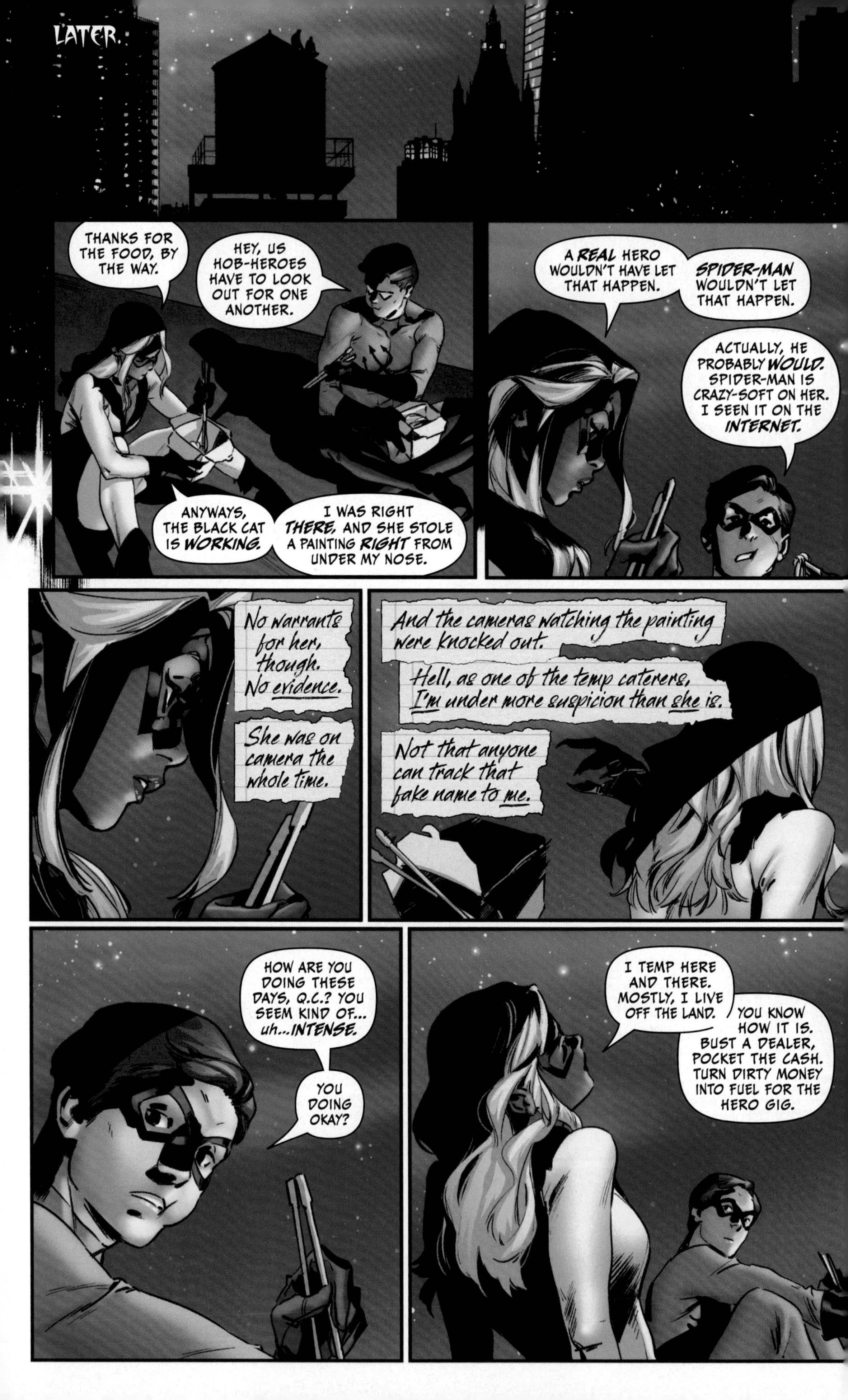
LATER.
THANKS FOR THE FOOD, BY THE WAY.
HEY, US HOB-HEROES HAVE TO LOOK OUT FOR ONE ANOTHER.
ANYWAYS, THE BLACK CAT IS WORKING.
I WAS RIGHT THERE, AND SHE STOLE A PAINTING RIGHT FROM UNDER MY NOSE.
A REAL HERO WOULDN'T HAVE LET THAT HAPPEN.
SPIDER-MAN WOULDN'T LET THAT HAPPEN.
ACTUALLY, HE PROBABLY WOULD. SPIDER-MAN IS CRAZY-SOFT ON HER. I SEEN IT ON THE INTERNET.
No warrants for her, though. No evidence.
She was on camera the whole time.
And the cameras watching the painting were knocked out.
Hell, as one of the temp caterers, I'm under more suspicion than she is.
Not that anyone can track that fake name to me.
HOW ARE YOU DOING THESE DAYS, Q.C.? YOU SEEM KIND OF... uh...INTENSE.
YOU DOING OKAY?
I TEMP HERE AND THERE. MOSTLY, I LIVE OFF THE LAND.
YOU KNOW HOW IT IS. BUST A DEALER, POCKET THE CASH. TURN DIRTY MONEY INTO FUEL FOR THE HERO GIG.

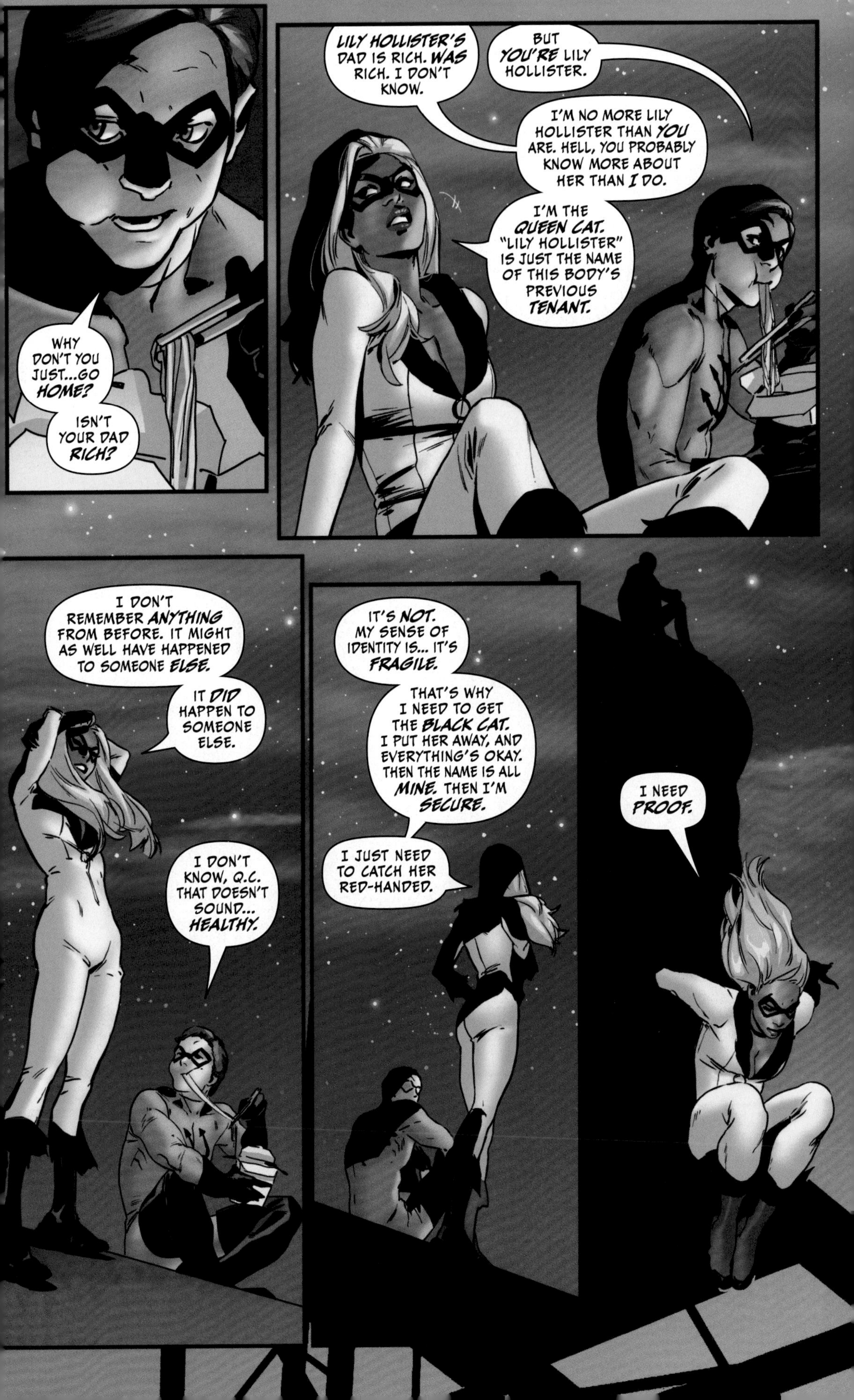
WHY DON'T YOU JUST...GO HOME?
ISN'T YOUR DAD RICH?
LILY HOLLISTER'S DAD IS RICH. WAS RICH. I DON'T KNOW.
BUT YOU'RE LILY HOLLISTER.
I'M NO MORE LILY HOLLISTER THAN YOU ARE. HELL, YOU PROBABLY KNOW MORE ABOUT HER THAN I DO.
I'M THE QUEEN CAT. "LILY HOLLISTER" IS JUST THE NAME OF THIS BODY'S PREVIOUS TENANT.
I DON'T REMEMBER ANYTHING FROM BEFORE. IT MIGHT AS WELL HAVE HAPPENED TO SOMEONE ELSE.
IT DID HAPPEN TO SOMEONE ELSE.
I DON'T KNOW, Q.C. THAT DOESN'T SOUND... HEALTHY.
IT'S NOT. MY SENSE OF IDENTITY IS... IT'S FRAGILE.
THAT'S WHY I NEED TO GET THE BLACK CAT. I PUT HER AWAY, AND EVERYTHING'S OKAY. THEN THE NAME IS ALL MINE. THEN I'M SECURE.
I JUST NEED TO CATCH HER RED-HANDED.
I NEED PROOF.

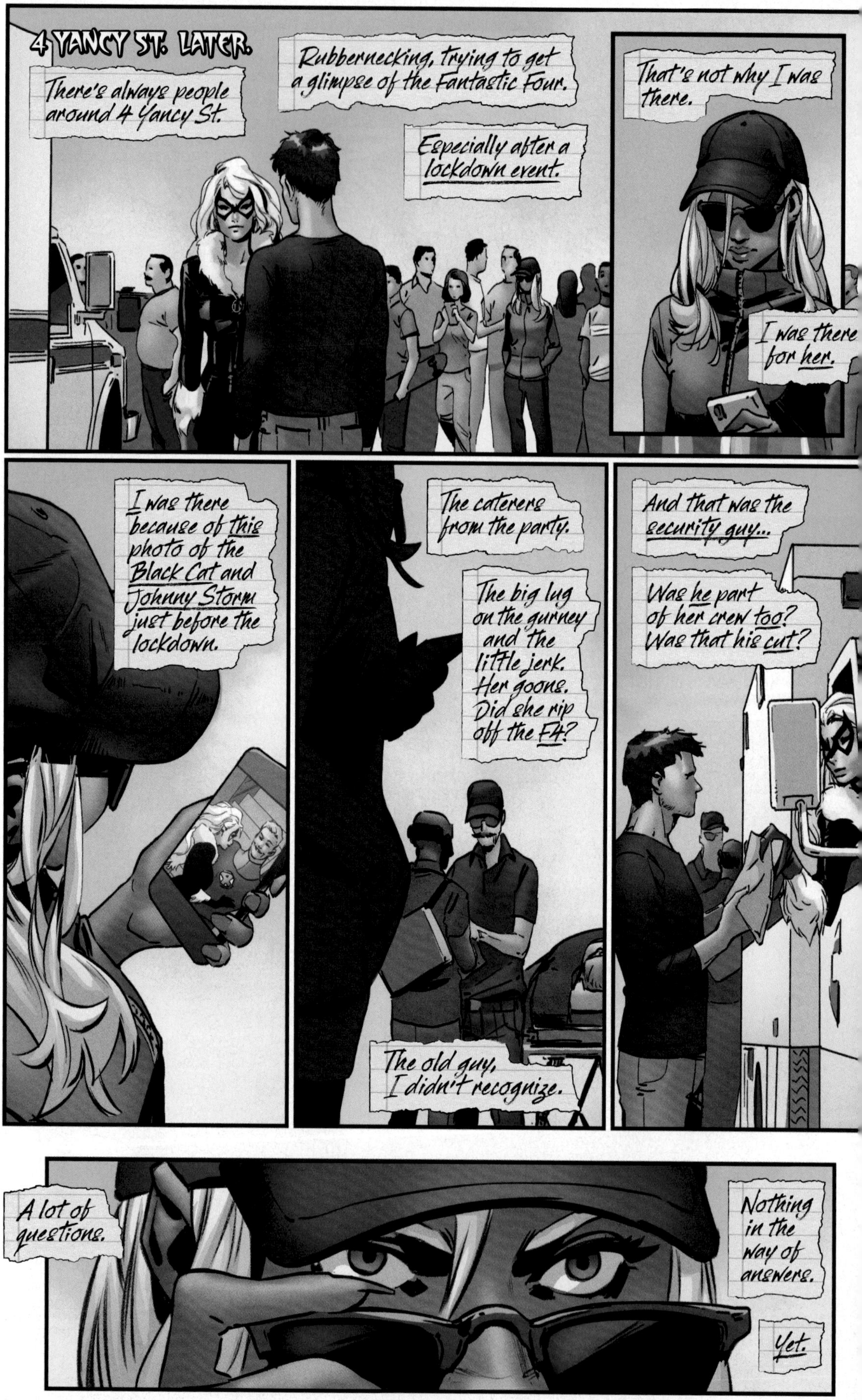
4 YANCY ST. LATER.
There's always people around 4 Yancy St.
Rubbernecking, trying to get a glimpse of the Fantastic Four.
Especially after a lockdown event.
That's not why I was there.
I was there for her.
I was there because of this photo of the Black Cat and Johnny Storm just before the lockdown.
The caterers from the party.
The big lug on the gurney and the little jerk. Her goons. Did she rip off the F4?
The old guy, I didn't recognize.
And that was the security guy...
Was he part of her crew too? Was that his cut?
A lot of questions.
Nothing in the way of answers.
Yet.

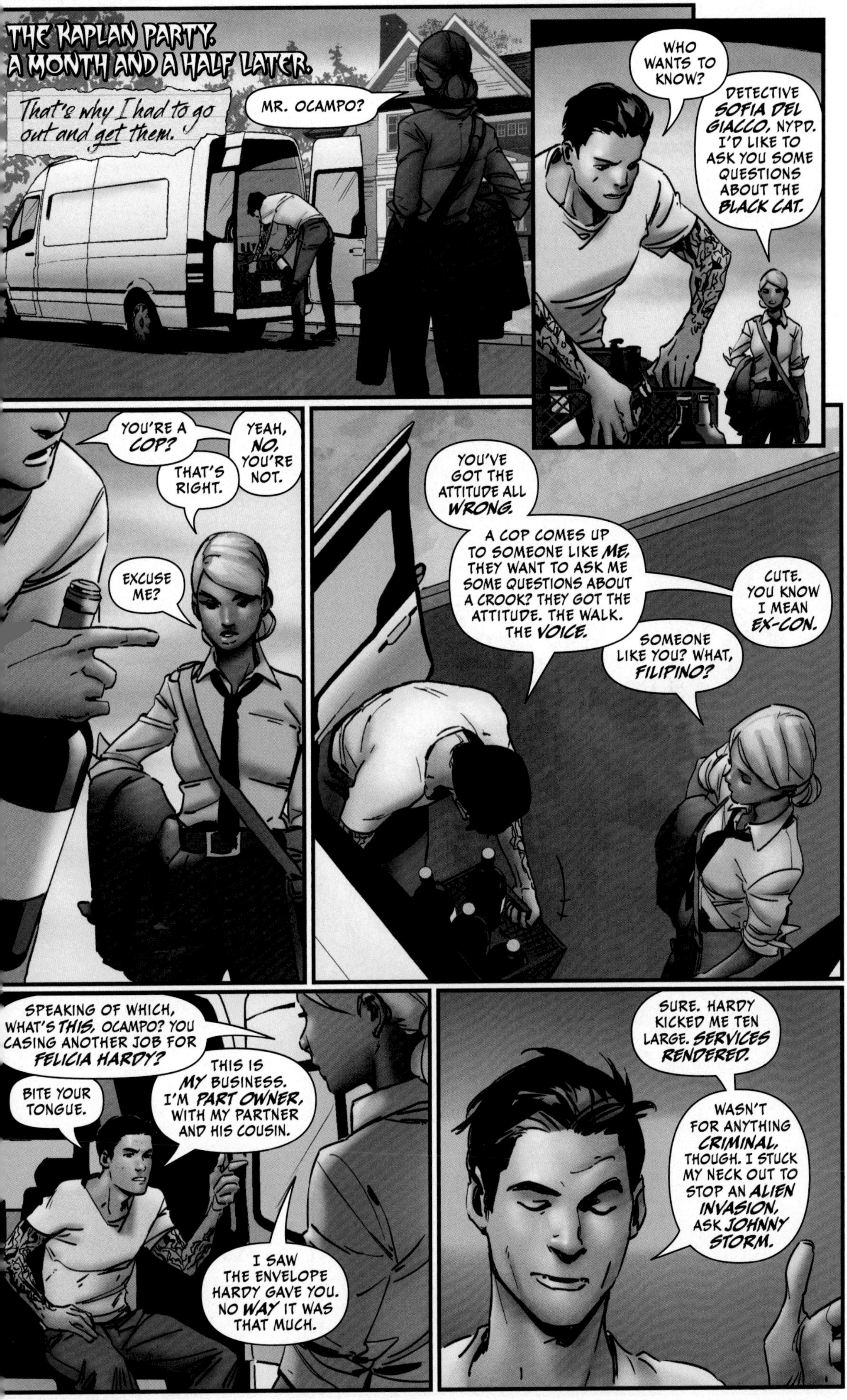
THE KAPLAN PARTY.
A MONTH AND A HALF LATER.
That's why I had to go out and get them.
MR. OCAMPO?
WHO WANTS TO KNOW?
DETECTIVE SOFIA DEL GIACCO, NYPD. I'D LIKE TO ASK YOU SOME QUESTIONS ABOUT THE BLACK CAT.
YOU'RE A COP?
THAT'S RIGHT.
YEAH, NO, YOU'RE NOT.
EXCUSE ME?
YOU'VE GOT THE ATTITUDE ALL WRONG.
A COP COMES UP TO SOMEONE LIKE ME, THEY WANT TO ASK ME SOME QUESTIONS ABOUT A CROOK? THEY GOT THE ATTITUDE. THE WALK. THE VOICE.
SOMEONE LIKE YOU? WHAT, FILIPINO?
CUTE. YOU KNOW I MEAN EX-CON.
SPEAKING OF WHICH, WHAT'S THIS, OCAMPO? YOU CASING ANOTHER JOB FOR FELICIA HARDY?
BITE YOUR TONGUE.
THIS IS MY BUSINESS. I'M PART OWNER, WITH MY PARTNER AND HIS COUSIN.
I SAW THE ENVELOPE HARDY GAVE YOU. NO WAY IT WAS THAT MUCH.
SURE. HARDY KICKED ME TEN LARGE. SERVICES RENDERED.
WASN'T FOR ANYTHING CRIMINAL, THOUGH. I STUCK MY NECK OUT TO STOP AN ALIEN INVASION, ASK JOHNNY STORM.

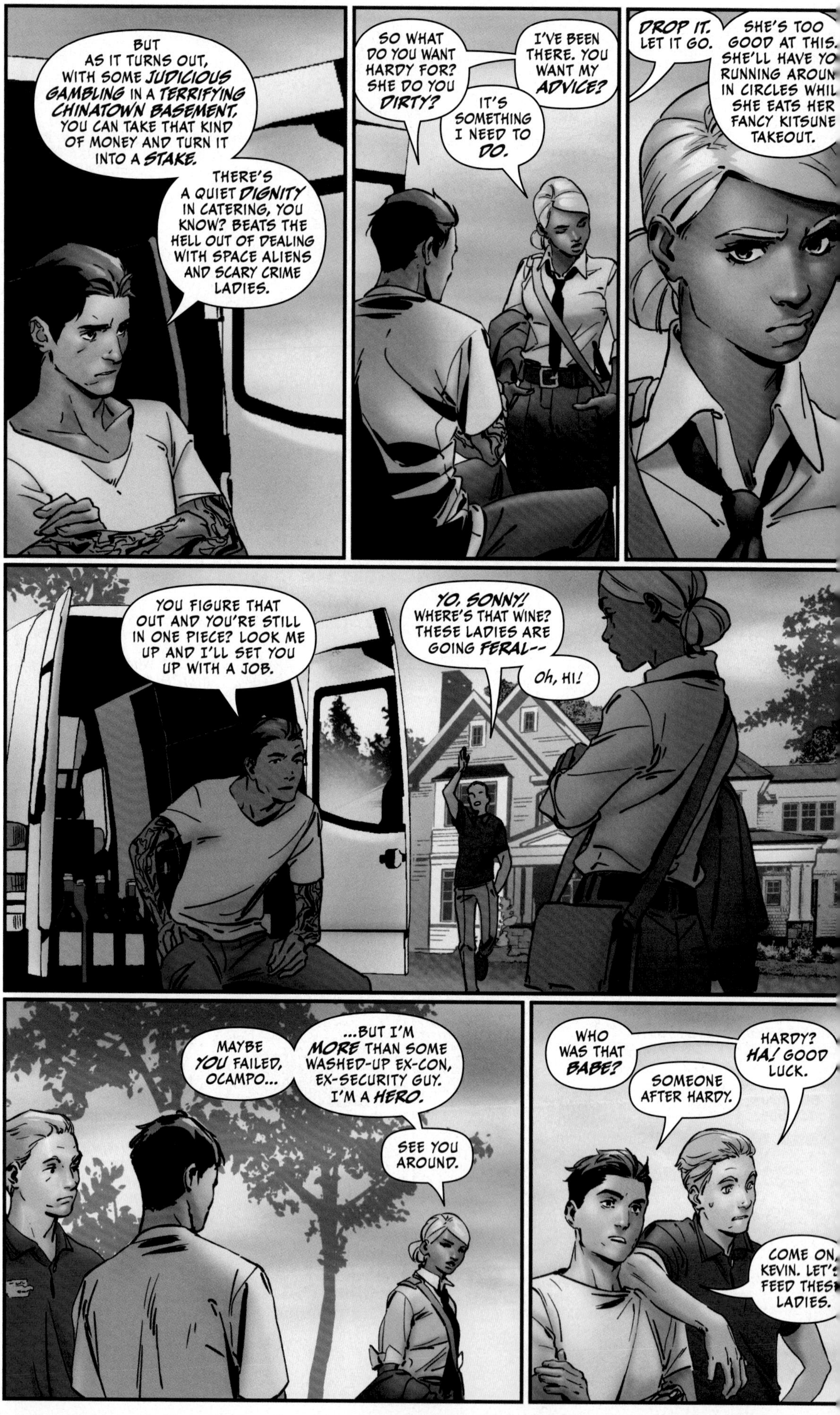
BUT AS IT TURNS OUT, WITH SOME JUDICIOUS GAMBLING IN A TERRIFYING CHINATOWN BASEMENT, YOU CAN TAKE THAT KIND OF MONEY AND TURN IT INTO A STAKE.
THERE'S A QUIET DIGNITY IN CATERING, YOU KNOW? BEATS THE HELL OUT OF DEALING WITH SPACE ALIENS AND SCARY CRIME LADIES.
SO WHAT DO YOU WANT HARDY FOR? SHE DO YOU DIRTY?
I'VE BEEN THERE. YOU WANT MY ADVICE?
IT'S SOMETHING I NEED TO DO.
DROP IT. LET IT GO.
SHE'S TOO GOOD AT THIS. SHE'LL HAVE YO RUNNING AROUN IN CIRCLES WHIL SHE EATS HER FANCY KITSUNE TAKEOUT.
YOU FIGURE THAT OUT AND YOU'RE STILL IN ONE PIECE? LOOK ME UP AND I'LL SET YOU UP WITH A JOB.
YO, SONNY! WHERE'S THAT WINE? THESE LADIES ARE GOING FERAL--
Oh, HI!
MAYBE YOU FAILED, OCAMPO...
...BUT I'M MORE THAN SOME WASHED-UP EX-CON, EX-SECURITY GUY. I'M A HERO.
SEE YOU AROUND.
WHO WAS THAT BABE?
SOMEONE AFTER HARDY.
HARDY? HA! GOOD LUCK.
COME ON, KEVIN. LET' FEED THES LADIES.

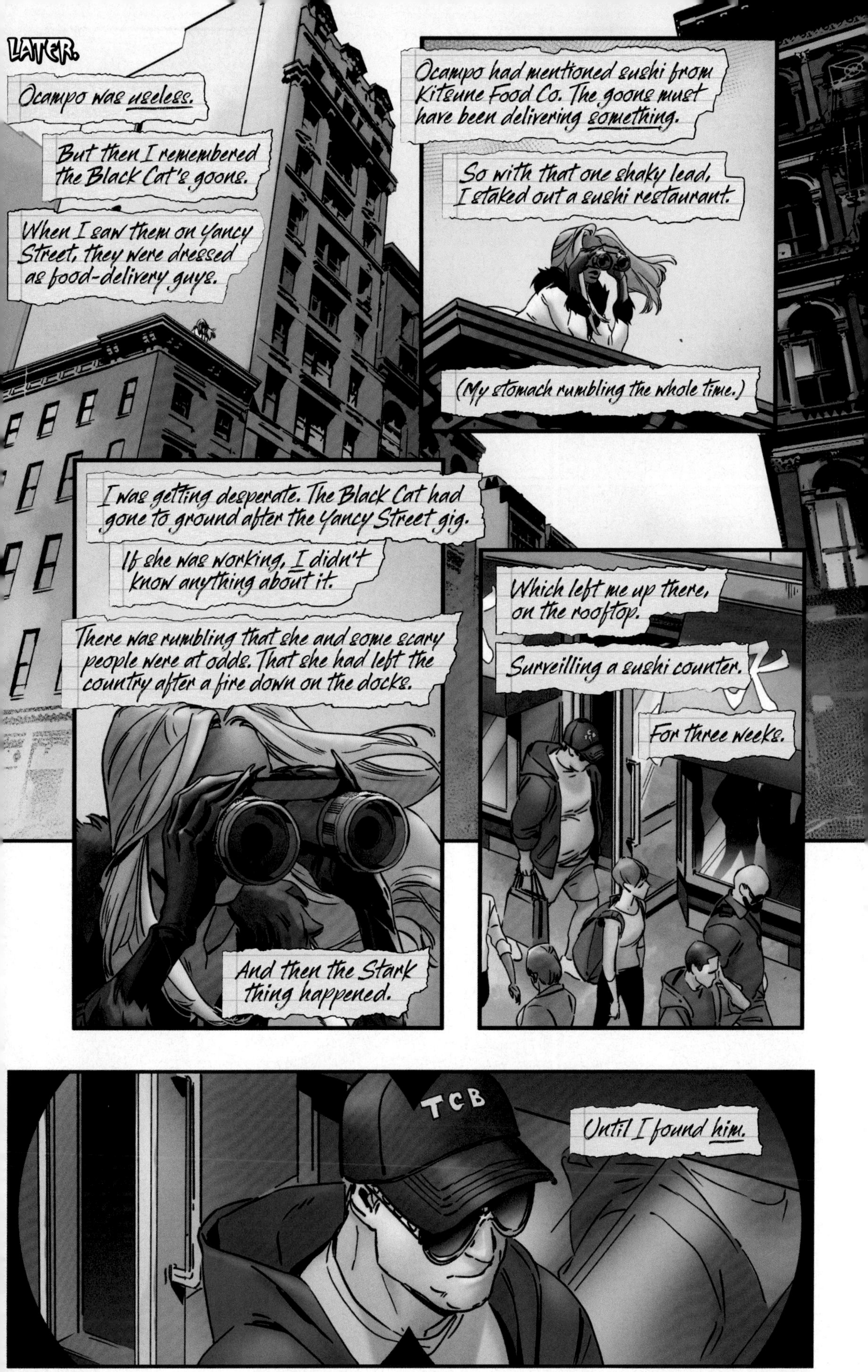
LATER.
Ocampo was useless.
But then I remembered the Black Cat's goons.
When I saw them on Yancy Street, they were dressed as food-delivery guys.
Ocampo had mentioned sushi from Kitsune Food Co. The goons must have been delivering something.
So with that one shaky lead, I staked out a sushi restaurant.
(My stomach rumbling the whole time.)
I was getting desperate. The Black Cat had gone to ground after the Yancy Street gig.
If she was working, I didn't know anything about it.
There was rumbling that she and some scary people were at odds. That she had left the country after a fire down on the docks.
And then the Stark thing happened.
Which left me up there, on the rooftop.
Surveilling a sushi counter.
For three weeks.
TCB
Until I found him.

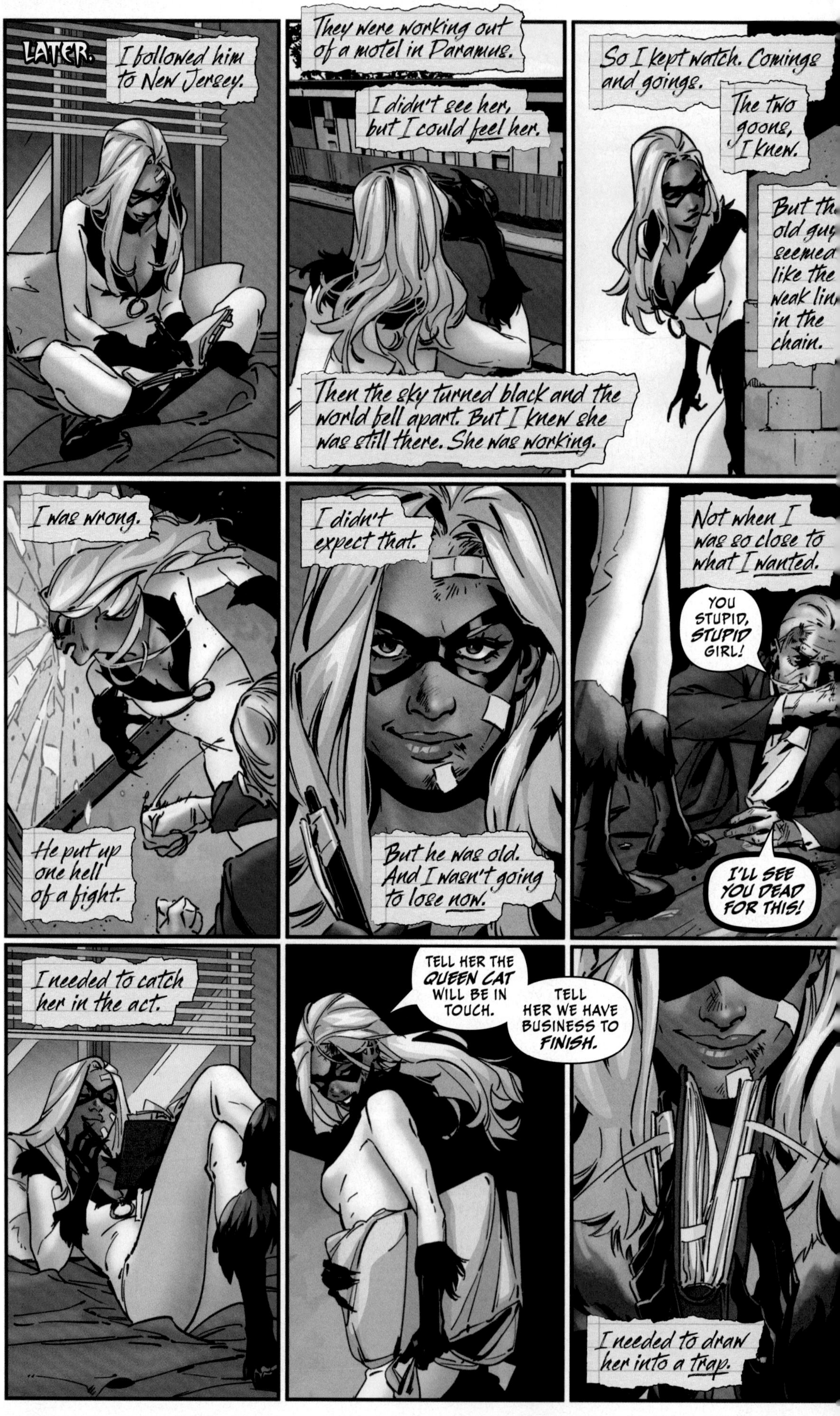
LATER.
I followed him to New Jersey.
They were working out of a motel in Paramus.
I didn't see her, but I could feel her.
Then the sky turned black and the world fell apart. But I knew she was still there. She was working.
So I kept watch. Comings and goings.
The two goons, I knew.
But th
old gu
seemed
like the
weak lin
in the
chain.
I was wrong.
He put up one hell of a fight.
I didn't expect that.
But he was old. And I wasn't going to lose now.
Not when I was so close to what I wanted.
YOU STUPID, STUPID GIRL!
I'LL SEE YOU DEAD FOR THIS!
I needed to catch her in the act.
TELL HER THE QUEEN CAT WILL BE IN TOUCH.
TELL HER WE HAVE BUSINESS TO FINISH.
I needed to draw her into a trap.

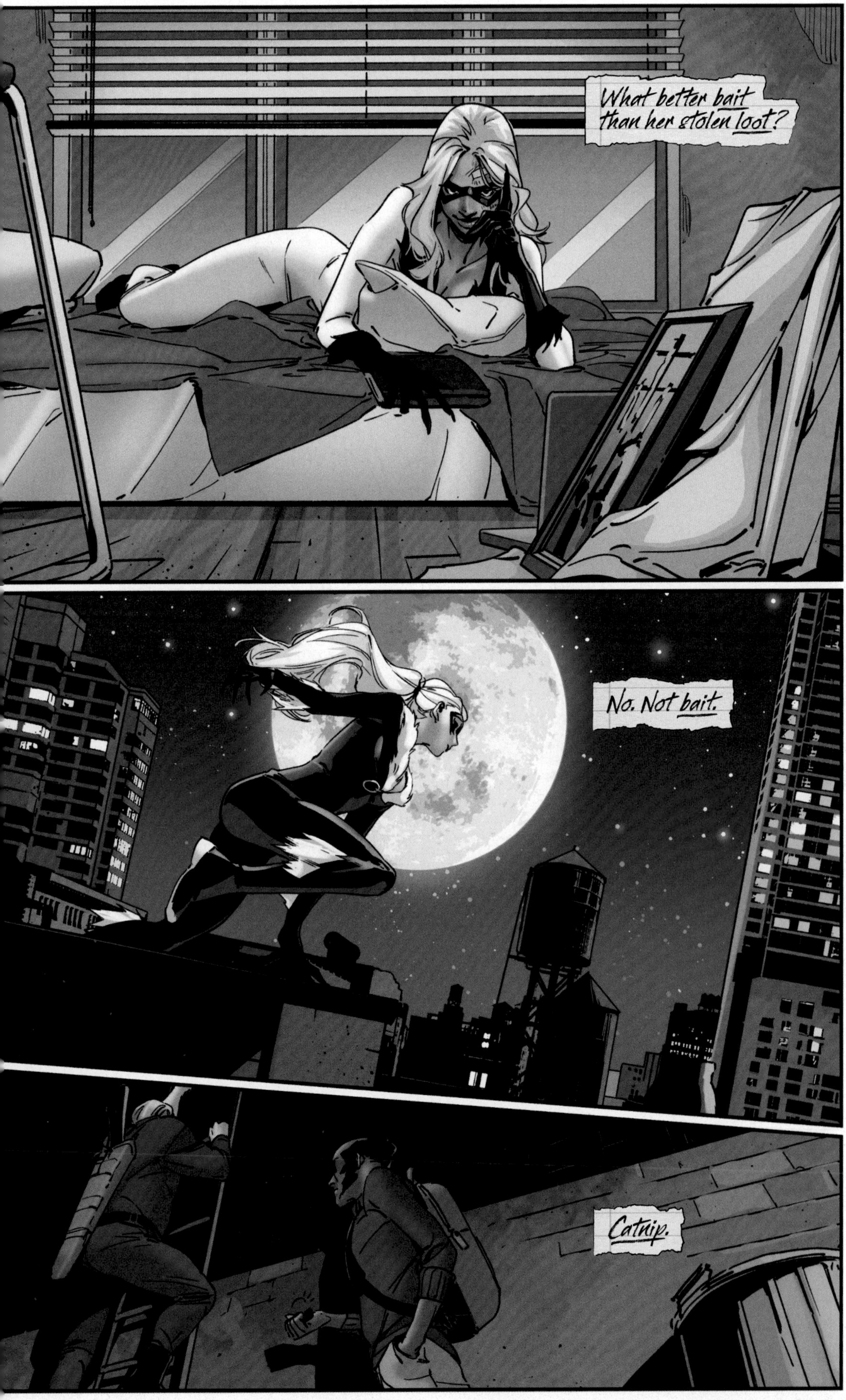
What better bait than her stolen loot?
No. Not bait.
Catnip.

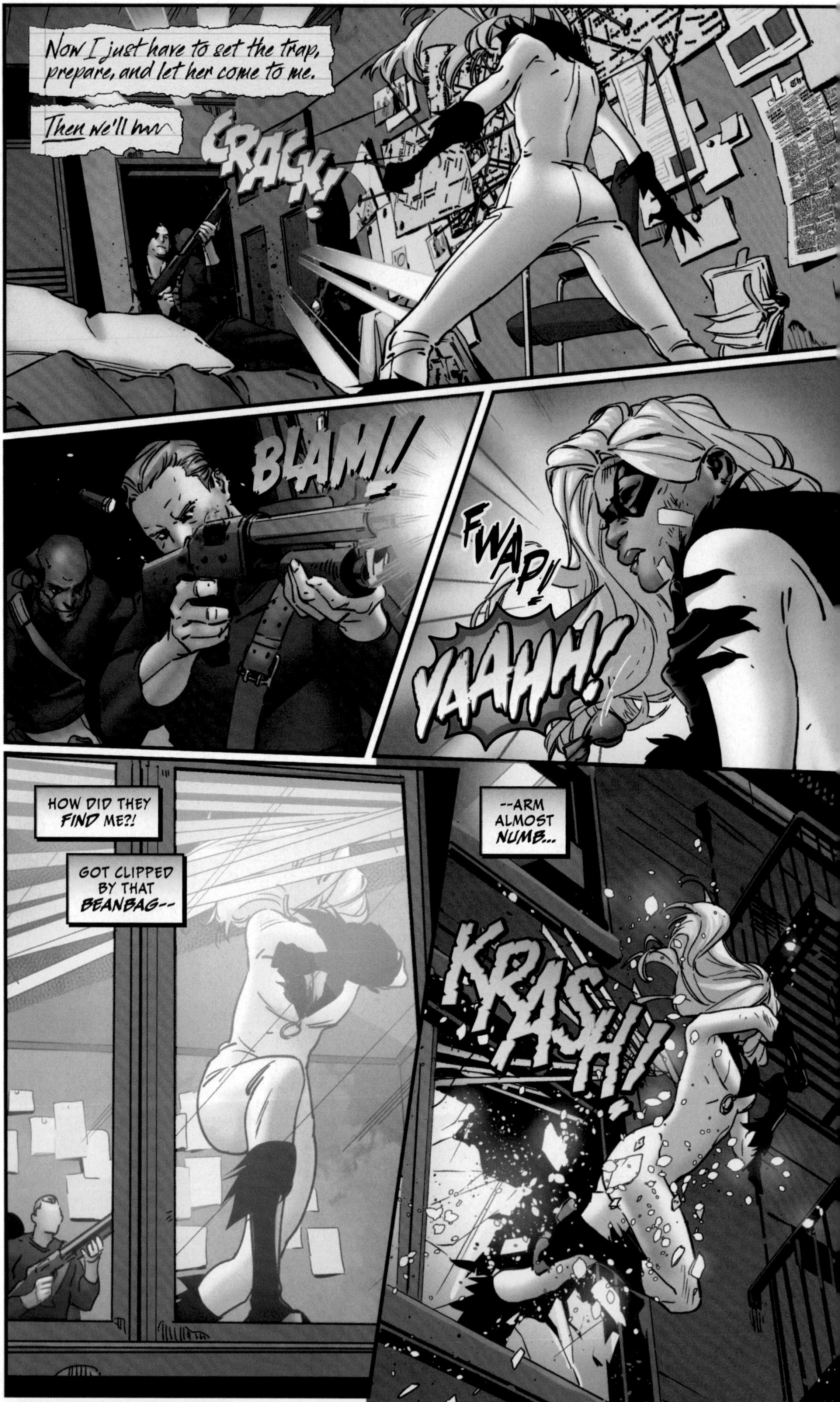
Now I just have to set the trap, prepare, and let her come to me.
Then we'll
CRACK!
BLAM!!
FWAP!
YAAHH!
HOW DID THEY FIND ME?!
GOT CLIPPED BY THAT BEANBAG--
--ARM ALMOST NUMB...
KRASH!

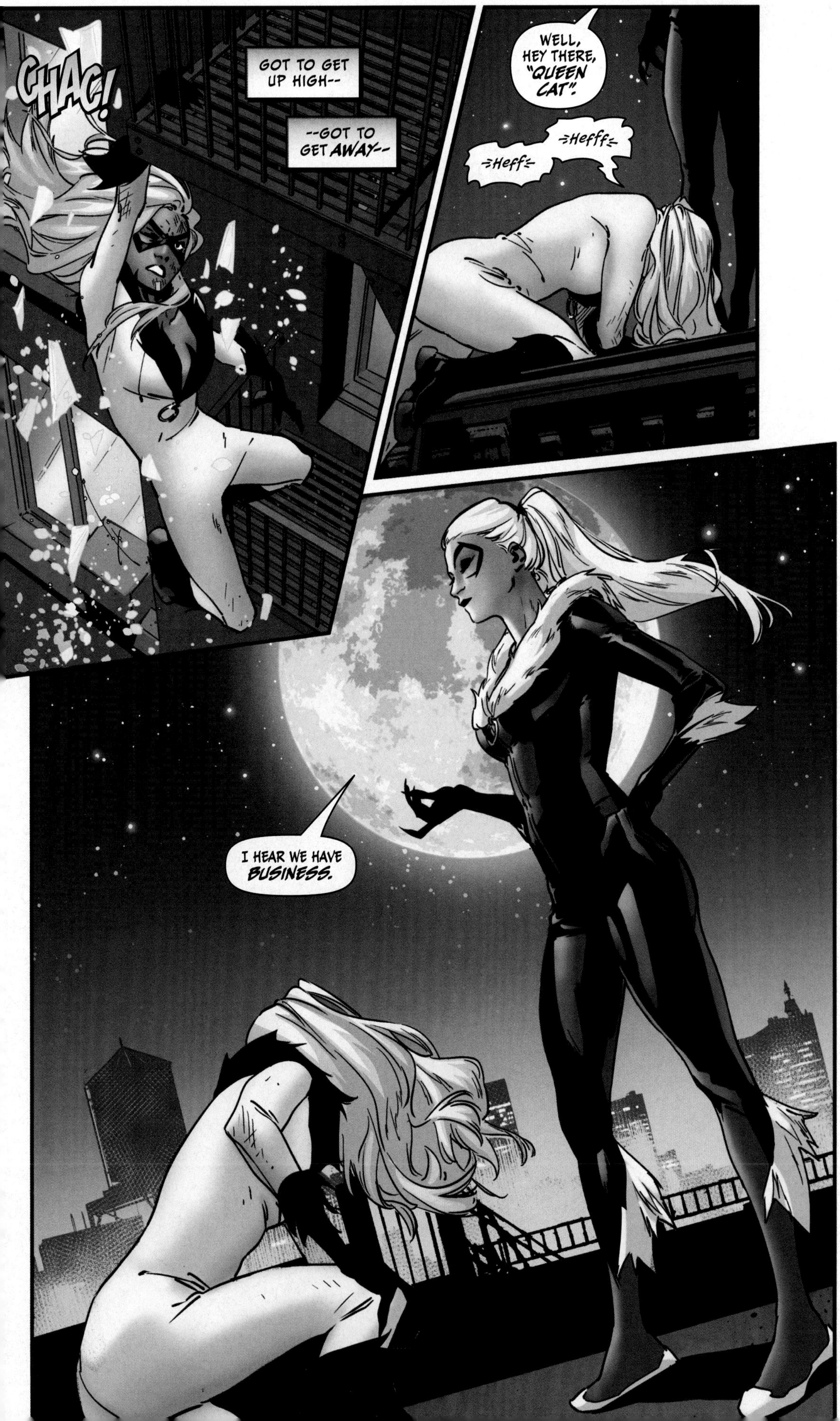
CHAC!
GOT TO GET UP HIGH--
--GOT TO GET AWAY--
WELL, HEY THERE, "QUEEN CAT".
=Heff=
=Hefff=
I HEAR WE HAVE BUSINESS.

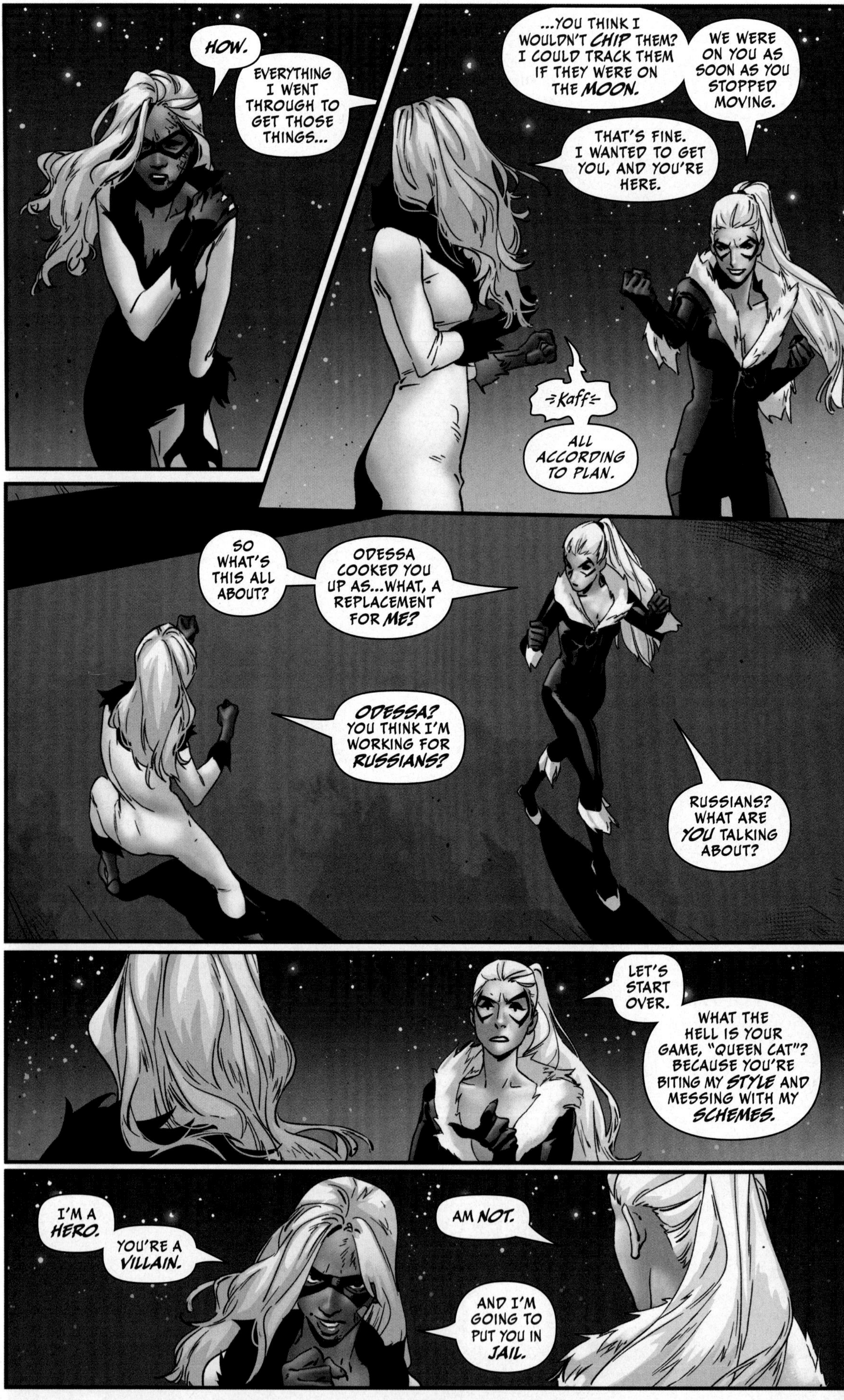
HOW.
EVERYTHING I WENT THROUGH TO GET THOSE THINGS...
...YOU THINK I WOULDN'T CHIP THEM? I COULD TRACK THEM IF THEY WERE ON THE MOON.
WE WERE ON YOU AS SOON AS YOU STOPPED MOVING.
THAT'S FINE. I WANTED TO GET YOU, AND YOU'RE HERE.
Kaff
ALL ACCORDING TO PLAN.
SO WHAT'S THIS ALL ABOUT?
ODESSA COOKED YOU UP AS...WHAT, A REPLACEMENT FOR ME?
ODESSA? YOU THINK I'M WORKING FOR RUSSIANS?
RUSSIANS? WHAT ARE YOU TALKING ABOUT?
LET'S START OVER.
WHAT THE HELL IS YOUR GAME, "QUEEN CAT"? BECAUSE YOU'RE BITING MY STYLE AND MESSING WITH MY SCHEMES.
I'M A HERO.
YOU'RE A VILLAIN.
AM NOT.
AND I'M GOING TO PUT YOU IN JAIL.

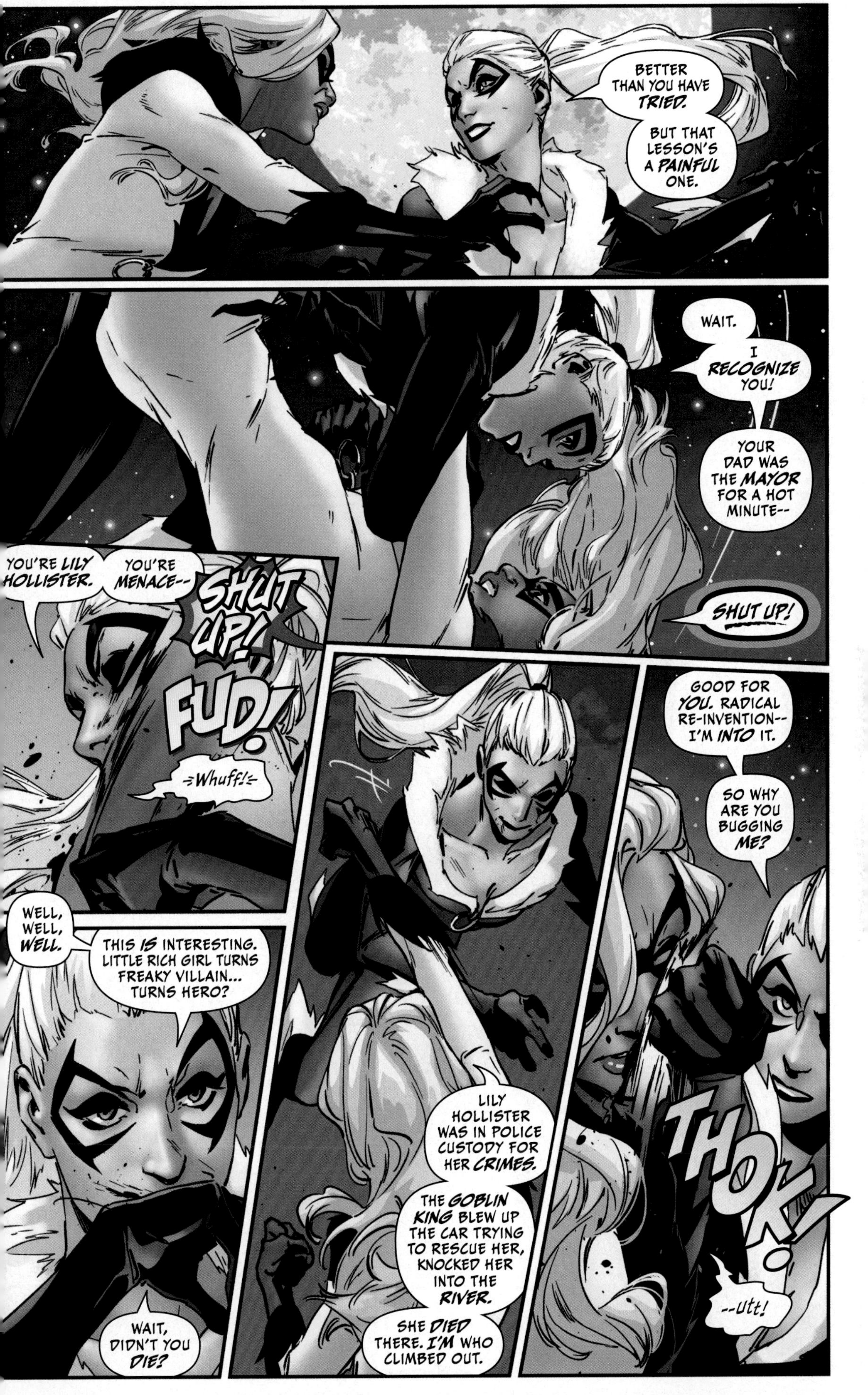
BETTER THAN YOU HAVE TRIED.
BUT THAT LESSON'S A PAINFUL ONE.
WAIT.
I RECOGNIZE YOU!
YOUR DAD WAS THE MAYOR FOR A HOT MINUTE--
YOU'RE LILY HOLLISTER.
YOU'RE MENACE--
SHUT UP!
SHUT UP!
FUD!
Whuff!
GOOD FOR YOU. RADICAL RE-INVENTION-- I'M INTO IT.
SO WHY ARE YOU BUGGING ME?
WELL, WELL, WELL.
THIS IS INTERESTING. LITTLE RICH GIRL TURNS FREAKY VILLAIN... TURNS HERO?
WAIT, DIDN'T YOU DIE?
LILY HOLLISTER WAS IN POLICE CUSTODY FOR HER CRIMES.
THE GOBLIN KING BLEW UP THE CAR TRYING TO RESCUE HER, KNOCKED HER INTO THE RIVER.
SHE DIED THERE. I'M WHO CLIMBED OUT.
THOK!
--utt!

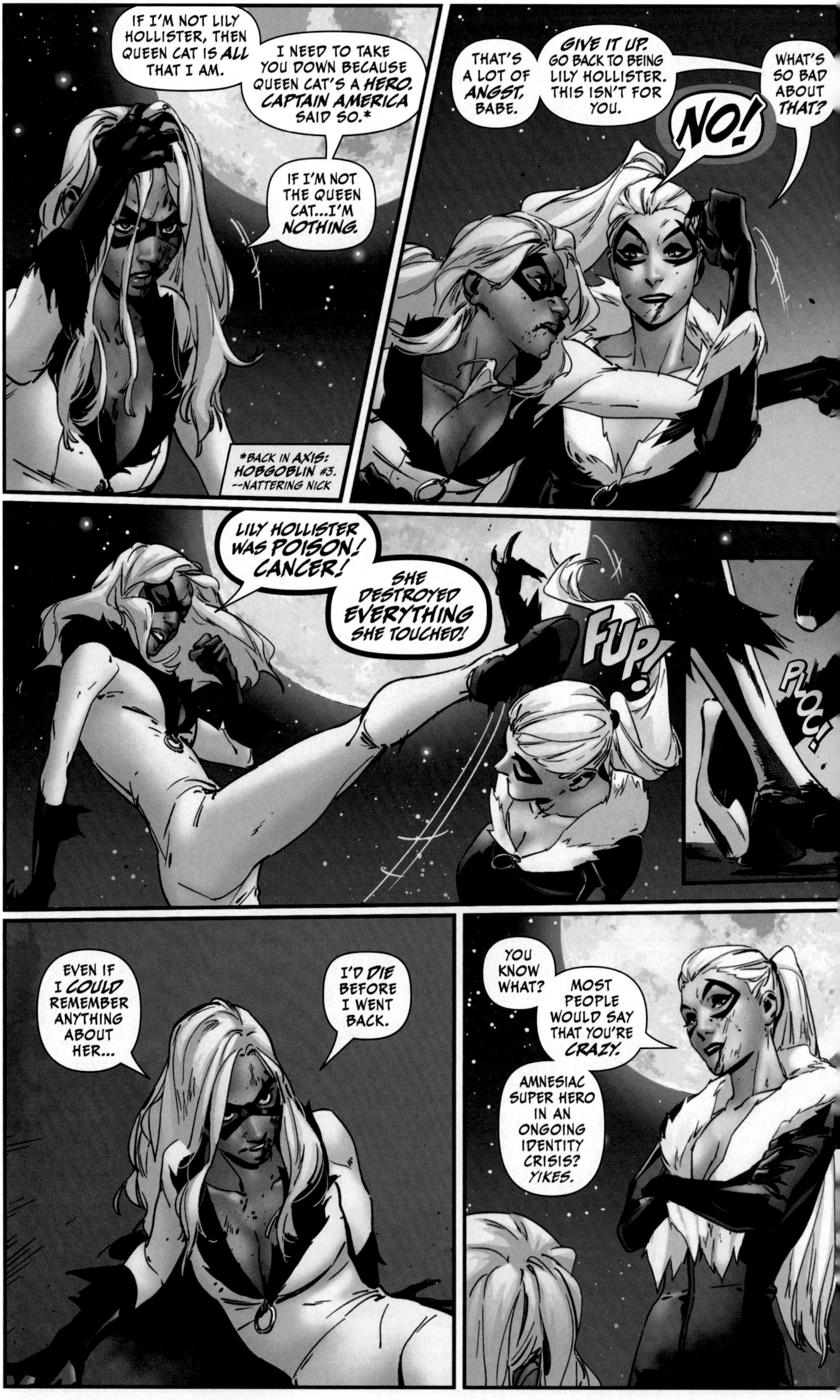
IF I'M NOT LILY HOLLISTER, THEN QUEEN CAT IS ALL THAT I AM.
I NEED TO TAKE YOU DOWN BECAUSE QUEEN CAT'S A HERO. CAPTAIN AMERICA SAID SO.*
IF I'M NOT THE QUEEN CAT...I'M NOTHING.
*BACK IN AXIS: HOBGOBLIN #3. --NATTERING NICK
THAT'S A LOT OF ANGST, BABE.
GIVE IT UP. GO BACK TO BEING LILY HOLLISTER. THIS ISN'T FOR YOU.
NO!
WHAT'S SO BAD ABOUT THAT?
LILY HOLLISTER WAS POISON! CANCER!
SHE DESTROYED EVERYTHING SHE TOUCHED!
FUP!
PLOC!
EVEN IF I COULD REMEMBER ANYTHING ABOUT HER...
I'D DIE BEFORE I WENT BACK.
YOU KNOW WHAT?
MOST PEOPLE WOULD SAY THAT YOU'RE CRAZY.
AMNESIAC SUPER HERO IN AN ONGOING IDENTITY CRISIS? YIKES.

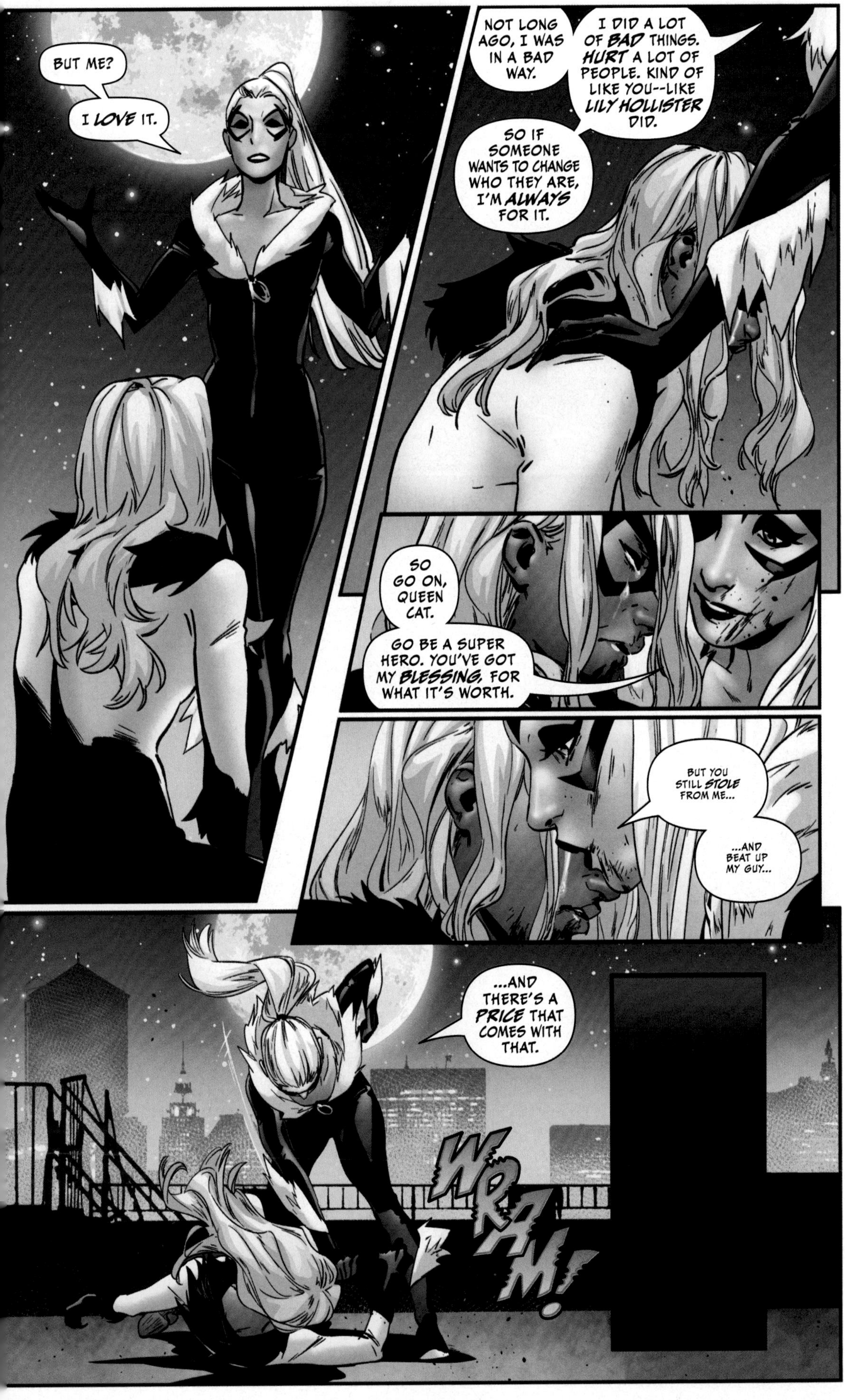
BUT ME?
I LOVE IT.
NOT LONG AGO, I WAS IN A BAD WAY.
I DID A LOT OF BAD THINGS. HURT A LOT OF PEOPLE. KIND OF LIKE YOU--LIKE LILY HOLLISTER DID.
SO IF SOMEONE WANTS TO CHANGE WHO THEY ARE, I'M ALWAYS FOR IT.
SO GO ON, QUEEN CAT.
GO BE A SUPER HERO. YOU'VE GOT MY BLESSING, FOR WHAT IT'S WORTH.
BUT YOU STILL STOLE FROM ME...
...AND BEAT UP MY GUY...
...AND THERE'S A PRICE THAT COMES WITH THAT.
WRAM!

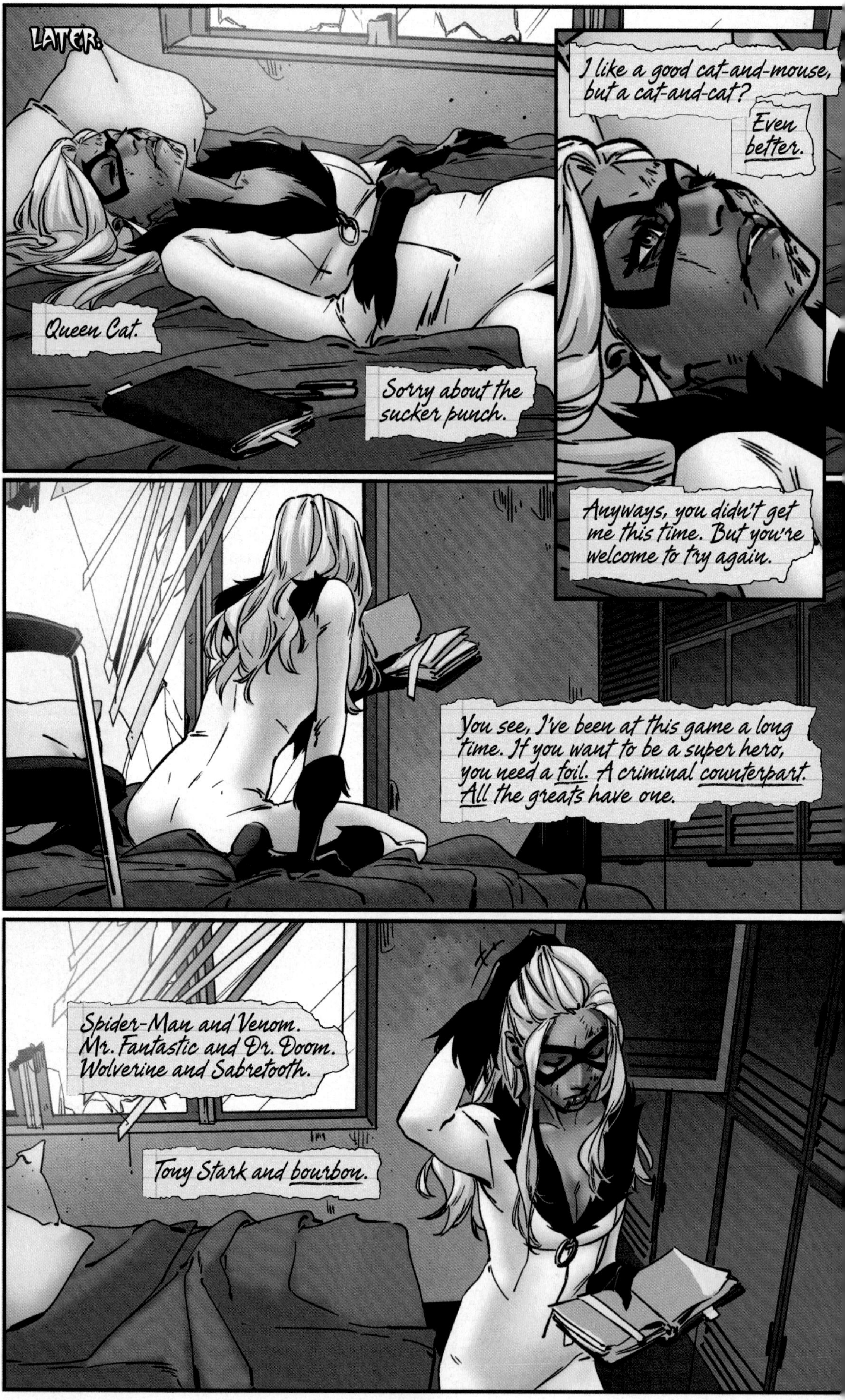
LATER.
I like a good cat-and-mouse, but a cat-and-cat?
Even better.
Queen Cat.
Sorry about the sucker punch.
Anyways, you didn't get me this time. But you're welcome to try again.
You see, I've been at this game a long time. If you want to be a super hero, you need a foil. A criminal counterpart. All the greats have one.
Spider-Man and Venom. Mr. Fantastic and Dr. Doom. Wolverine and Sabretooth.
Tony Stark and bourbon.

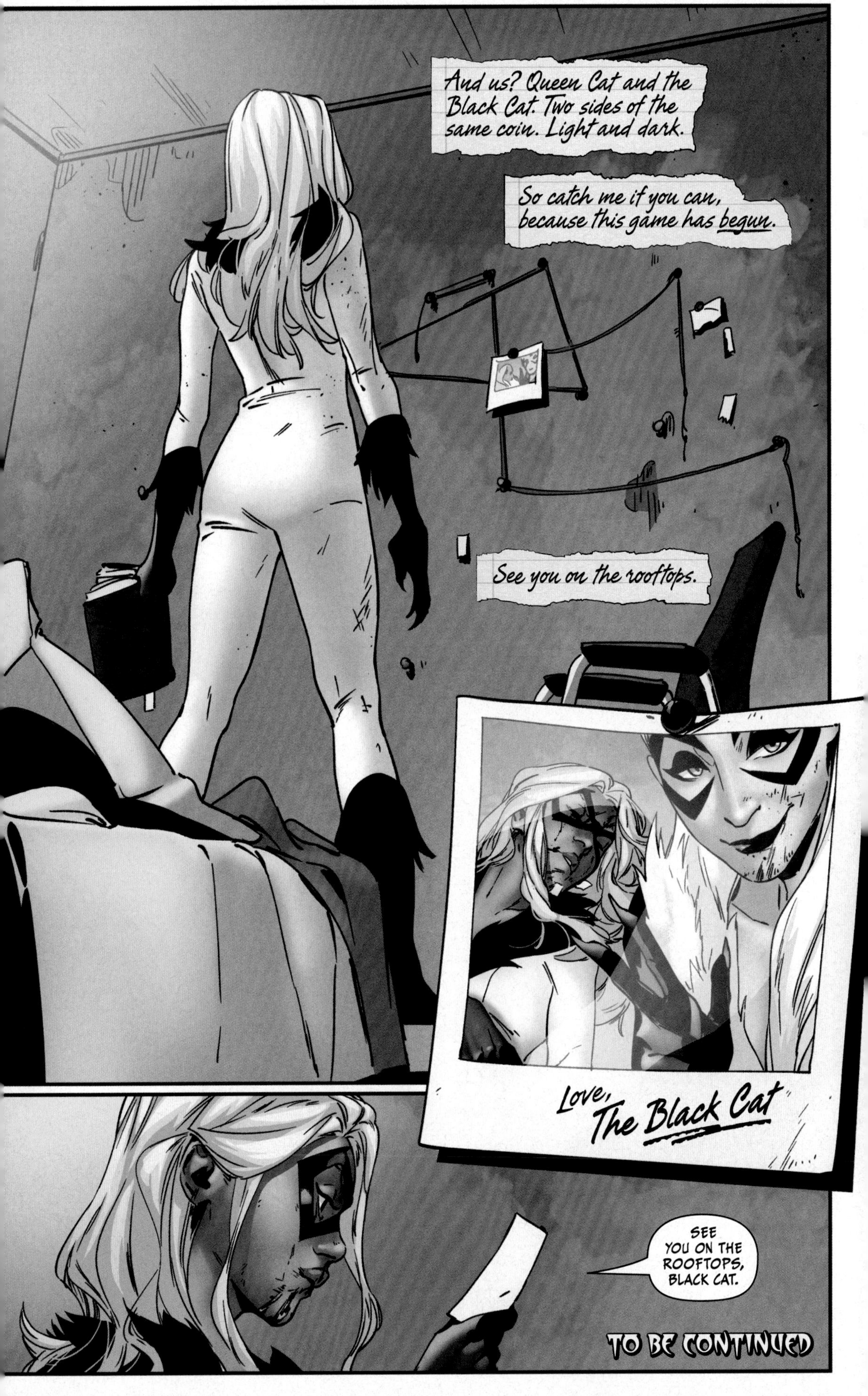

And us? Queen Cat and the Black Cat. Two sides of the same coin. Light and dark.
So catch me if you can, because this game has begun.
See you on the rooftops.
Love, The Black Cat
SEE YOU ON THE ROOFTOPS, BLACK CAT.
TO BE CONTINUED

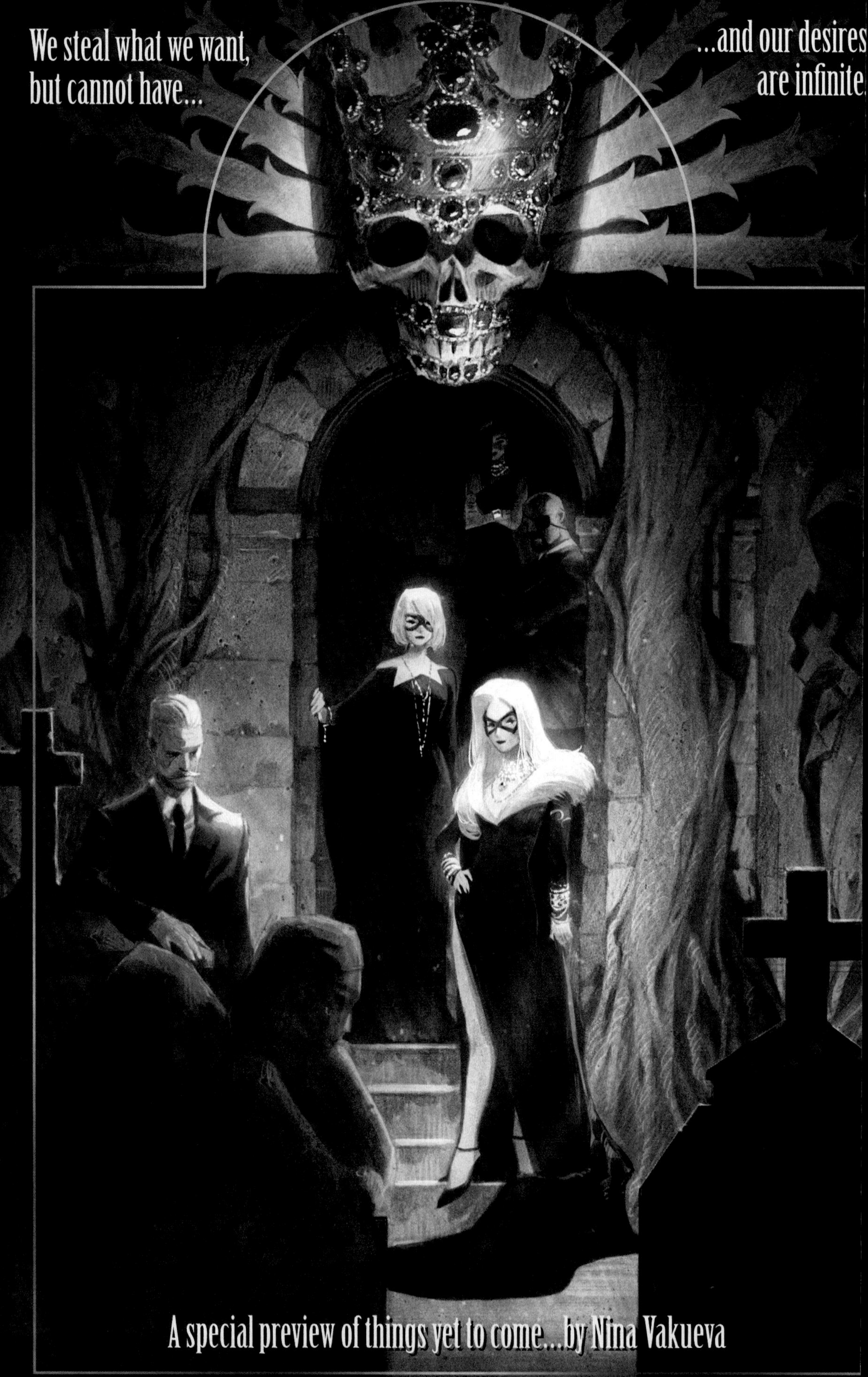

We steal what we want, but cannot have...
...and our desires are infinite.
A special preview of things yet to come...by Nina Vakueva

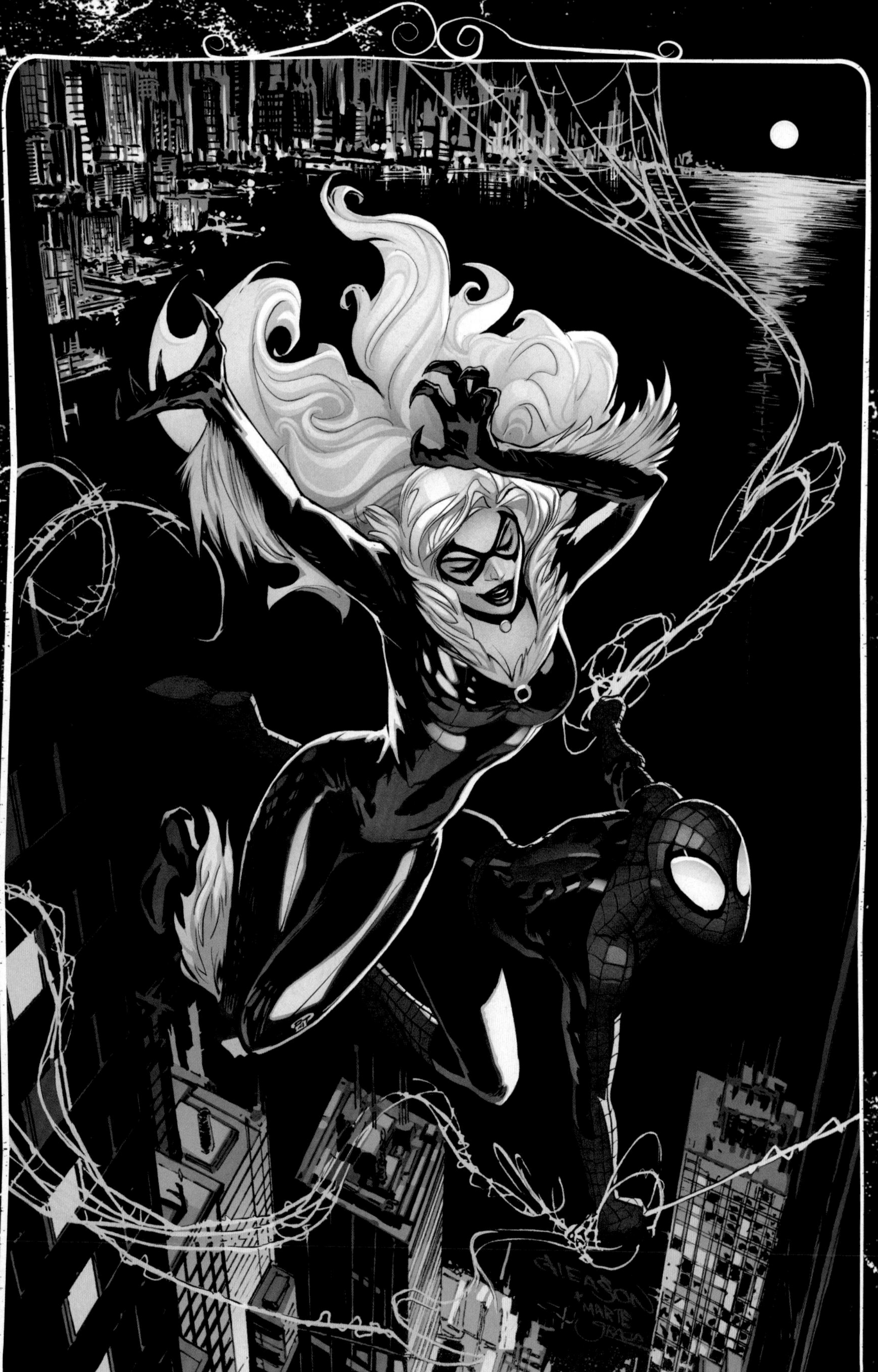

#1 variant by **PATRICK GLEASON** & **MARTE GRACIA**

#1 Headshot variant by **TODD NAUCK** & **RACHELLE ROSENBERG**

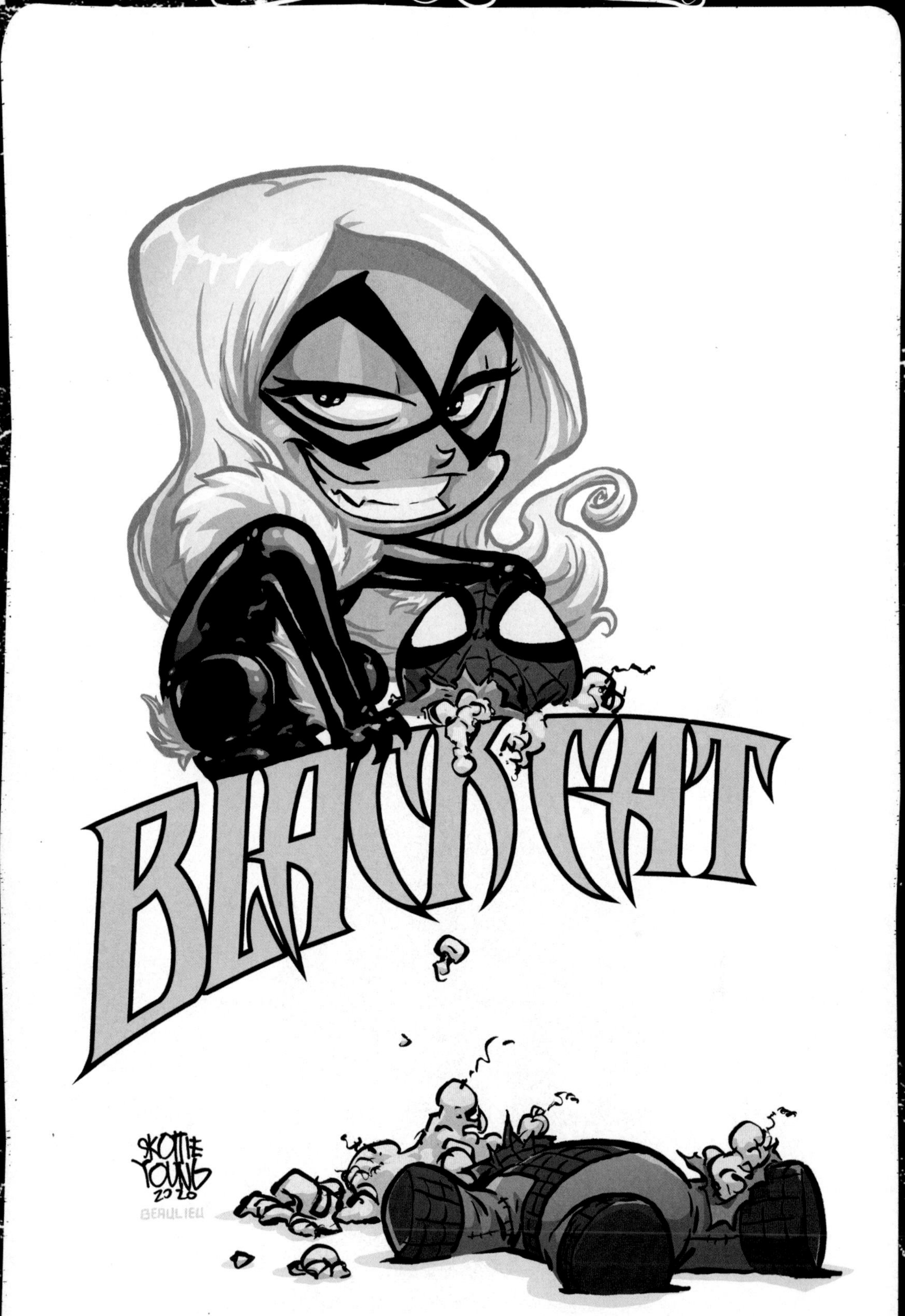
BLACK CAT
SKOTTIE YOUNG 2020
BEAULIEU

#1 variant by **SKOTTIE YOUNG**

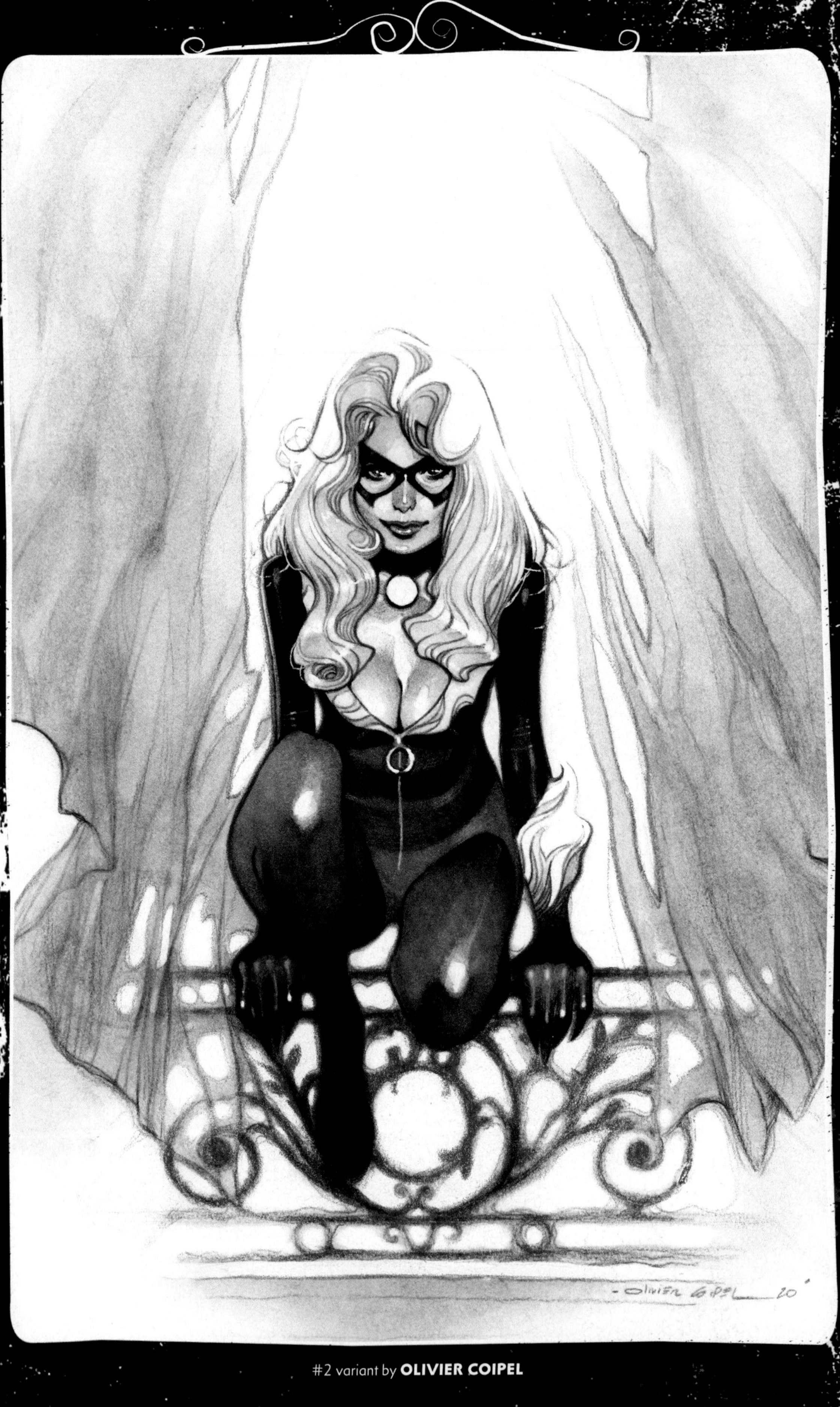

#2 variant by **OLIVIER COIPEL**

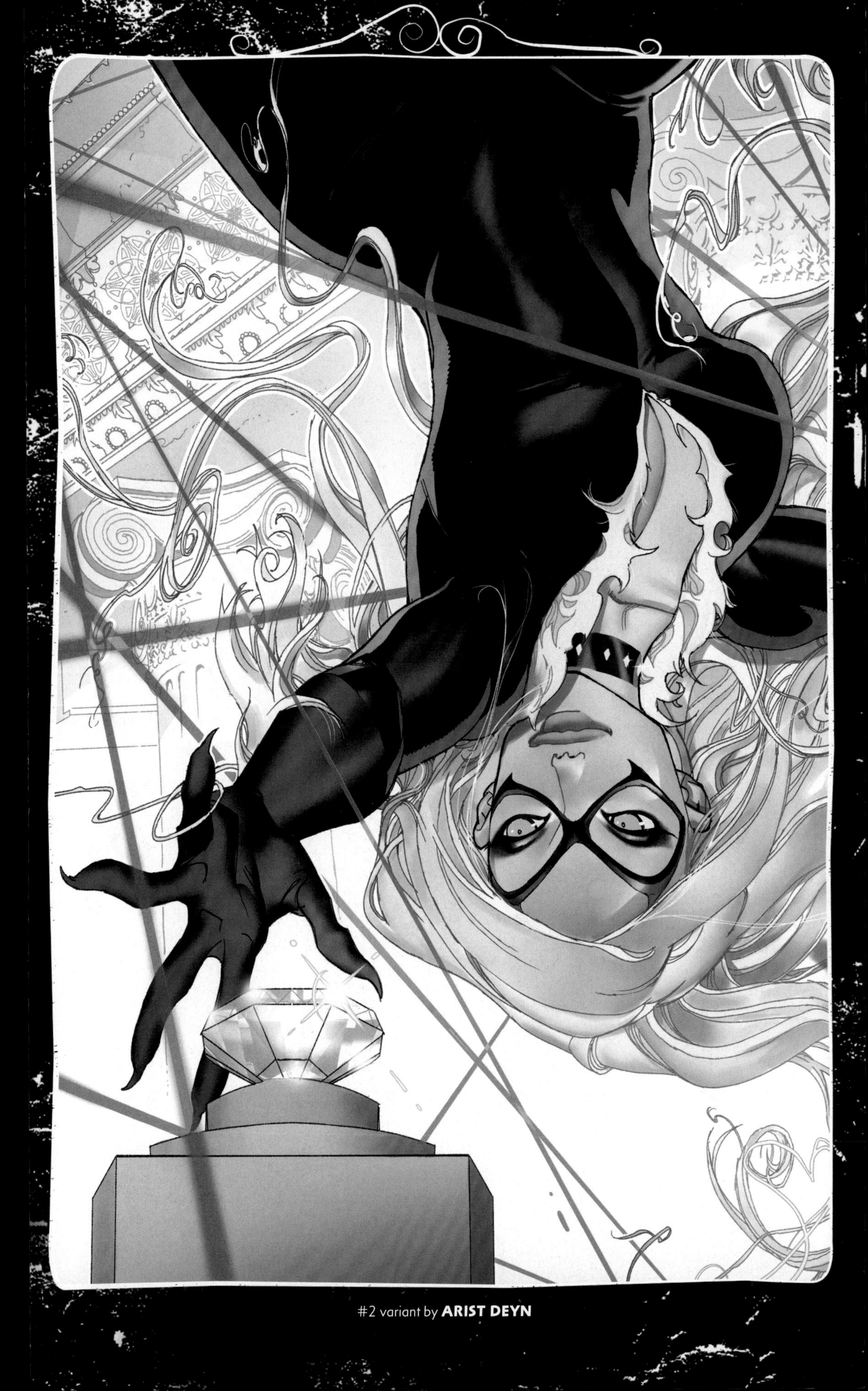

#2 variant by **ARIST DEYN**

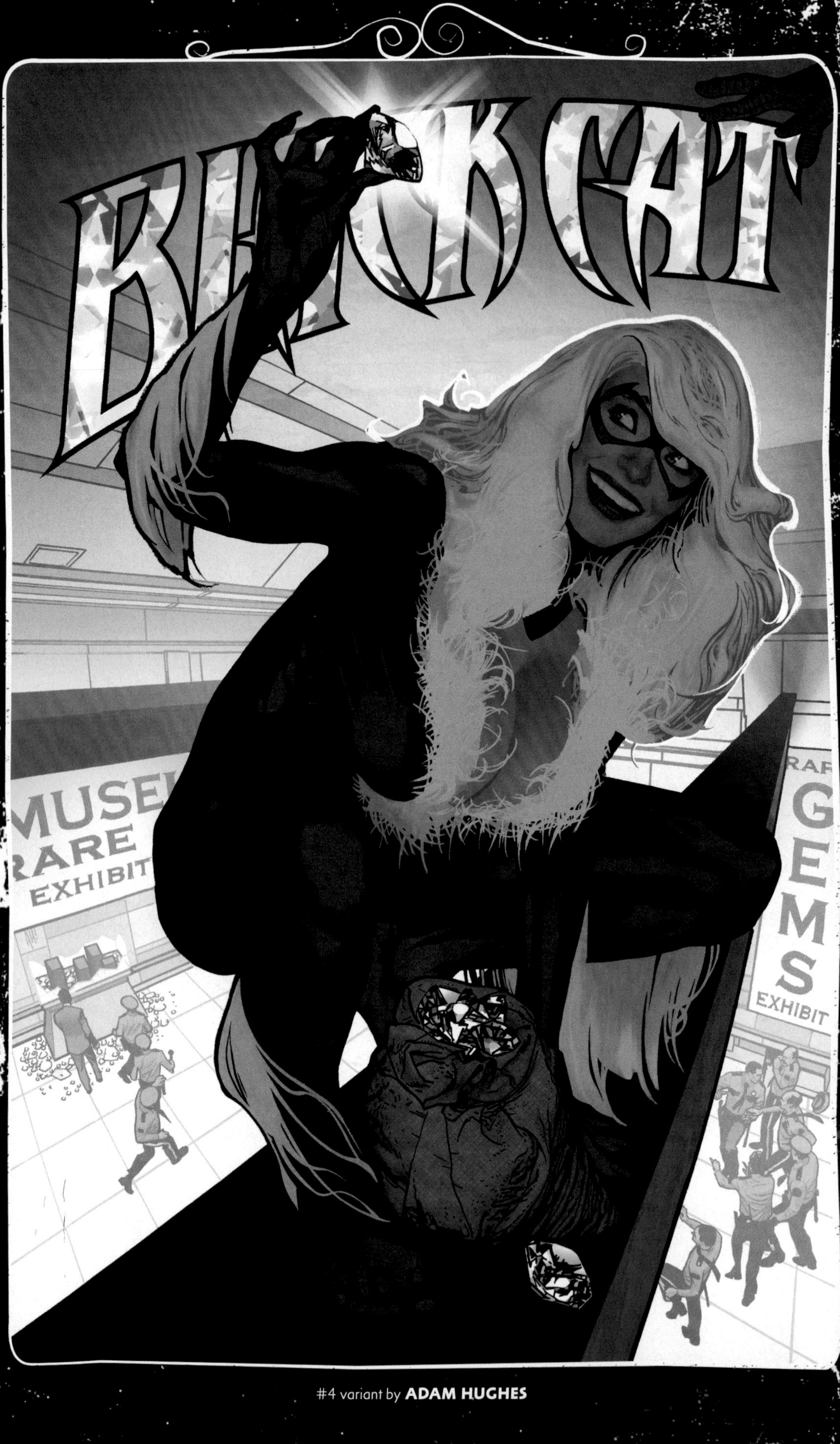
BLACK CAT
MUSE
RARE
EXHIBIT
RAR
GEMS
EXHIBIT

#4 variant by **ADAM HUGHES**

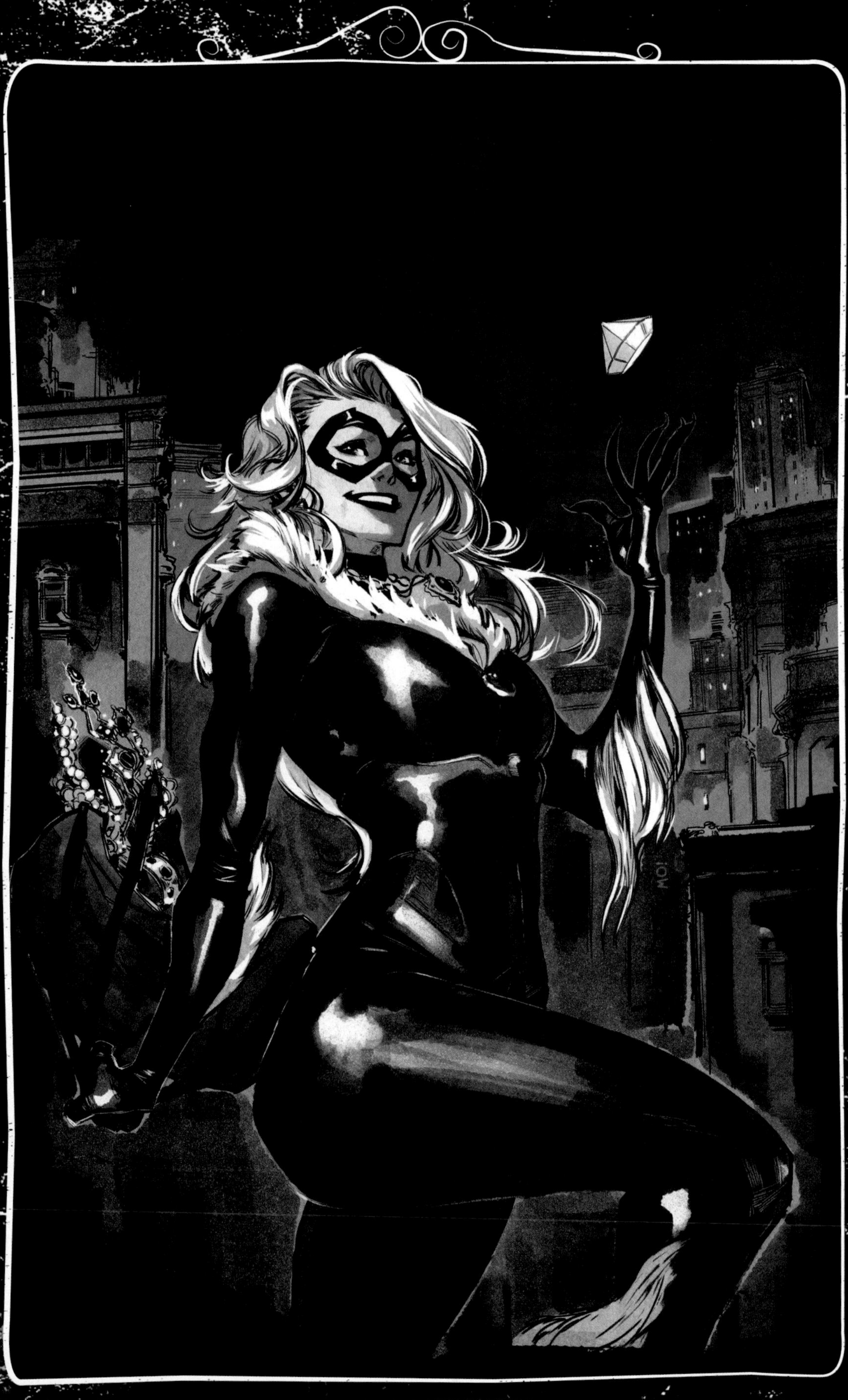

#3 variant by **NABETSE ZITRO**

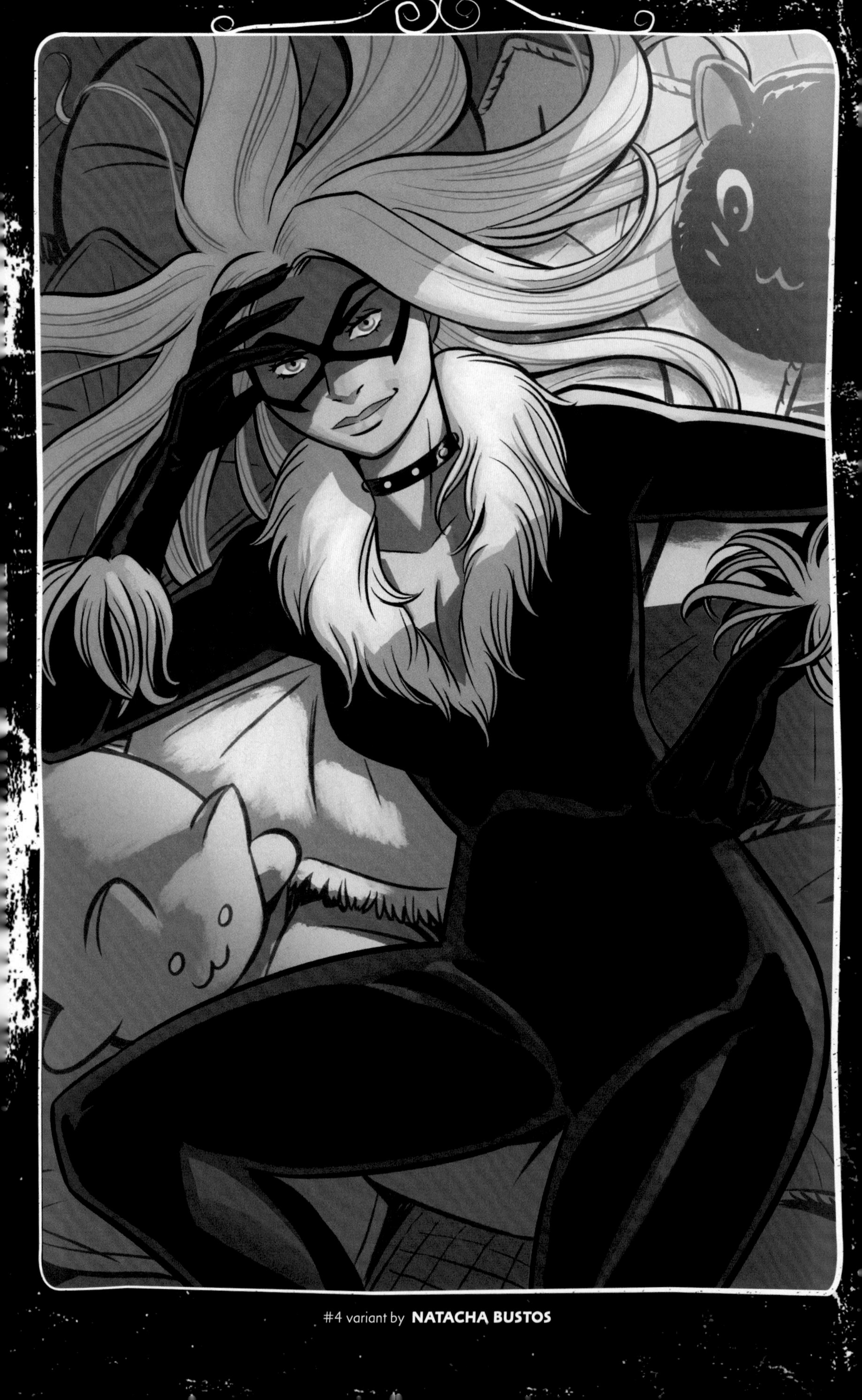

#4 variant by **NATACHA BUSTOS**

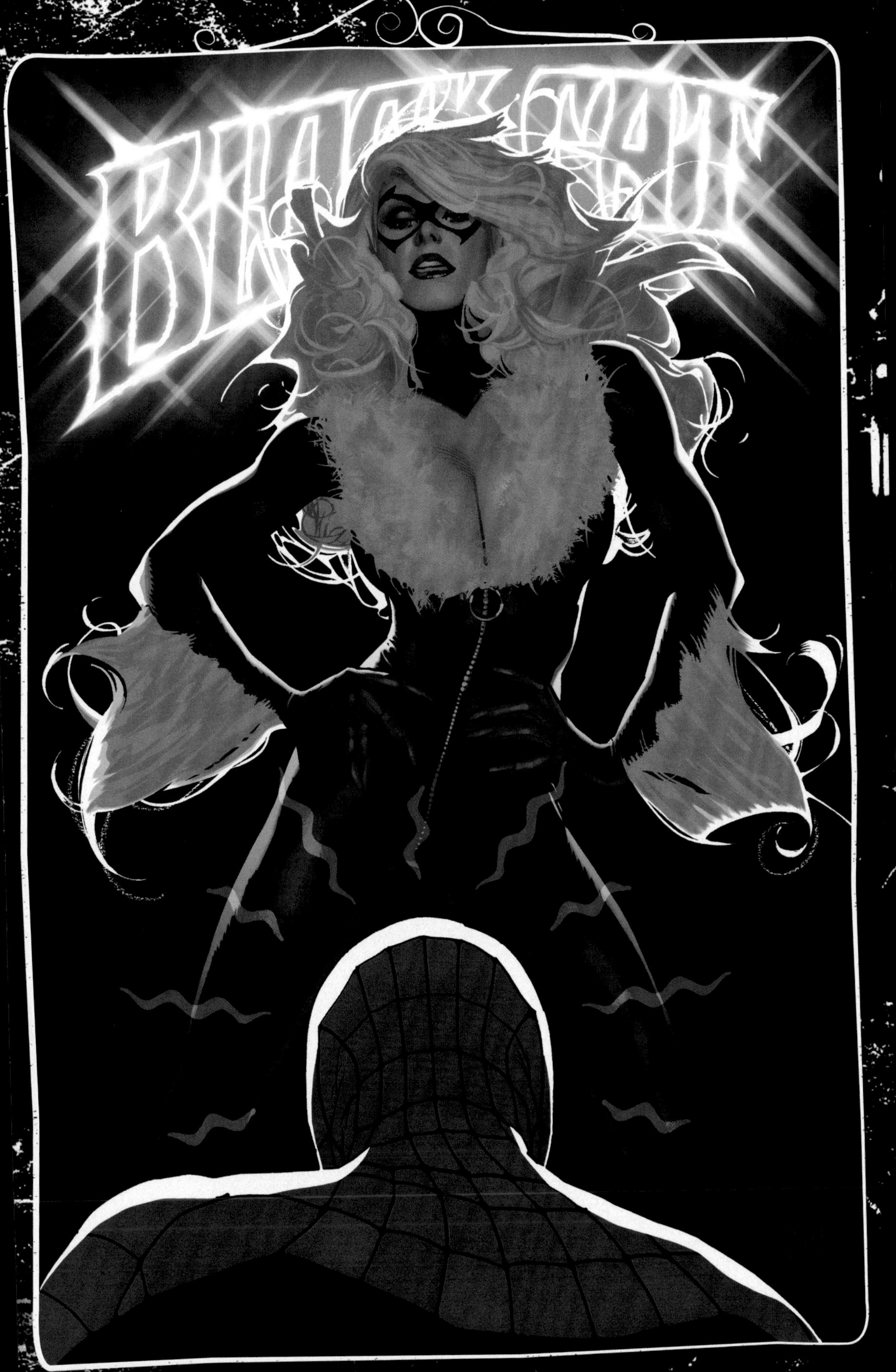

#4 variant by **ADAM HUGHES**

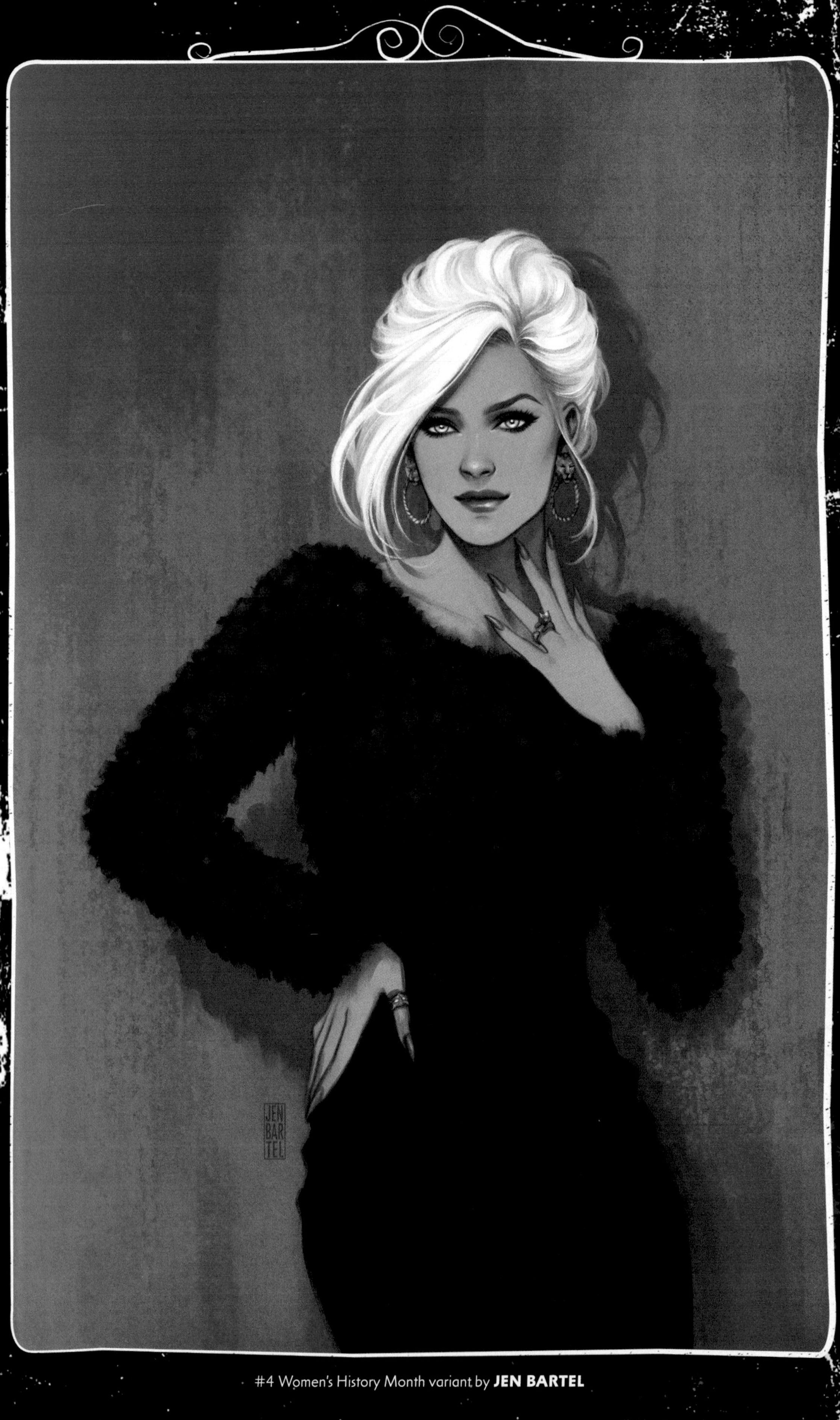
JEN
BAR
TEL

#4 Women's History Month variant by **JEN BARTEL**

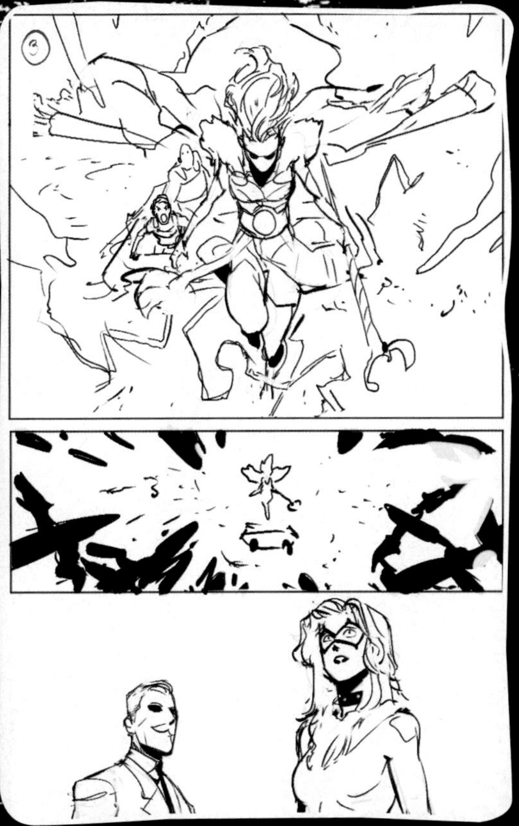
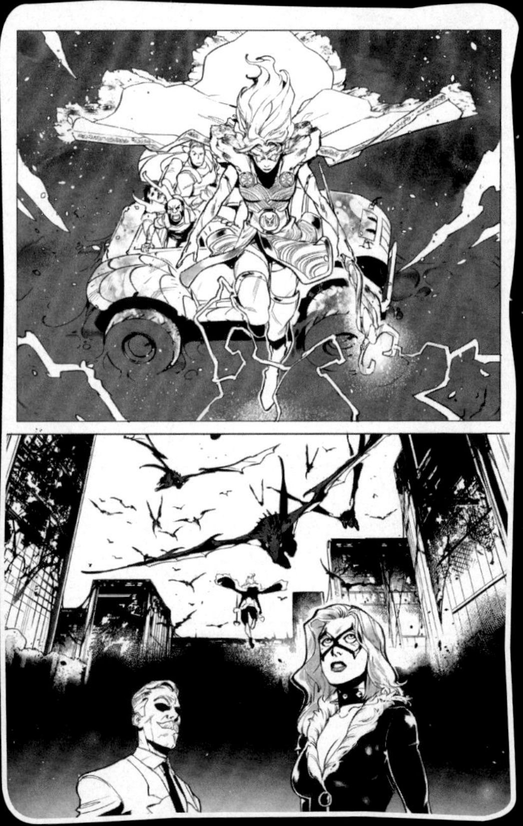
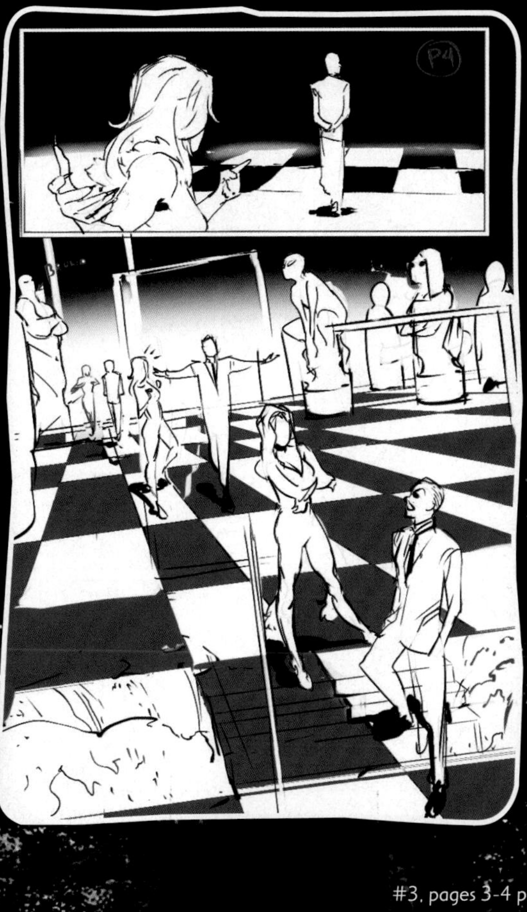
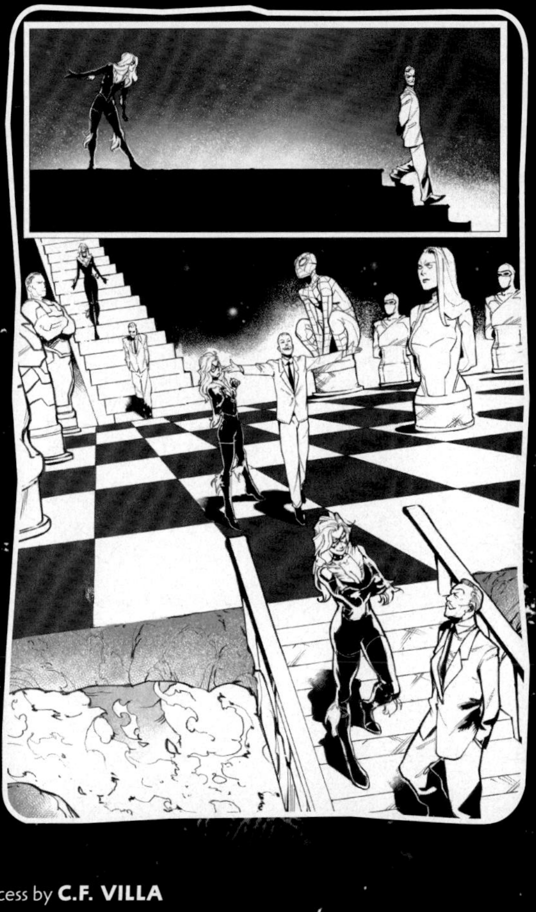

#3, pages 3-4 process by **C.F. VILLA**

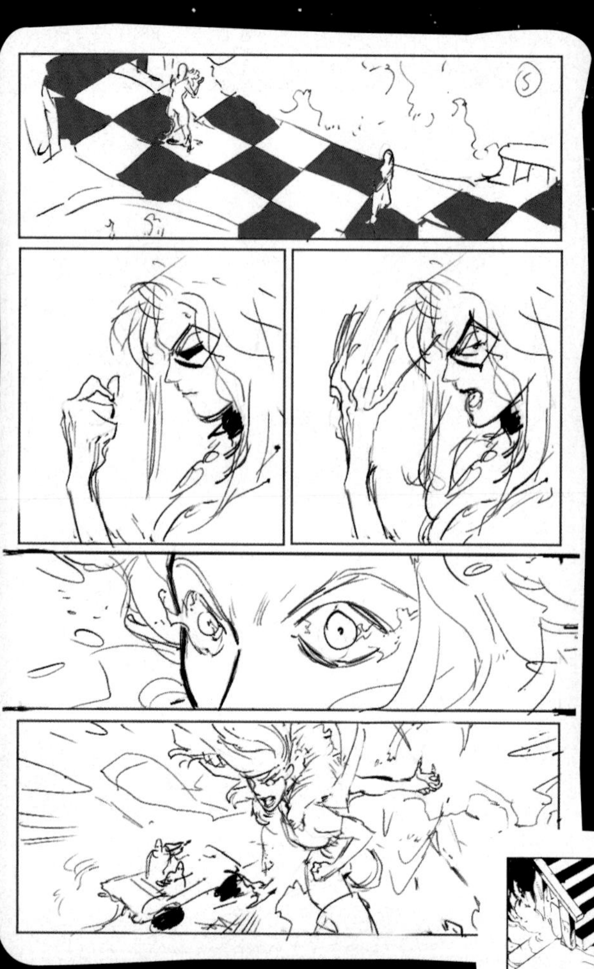
5

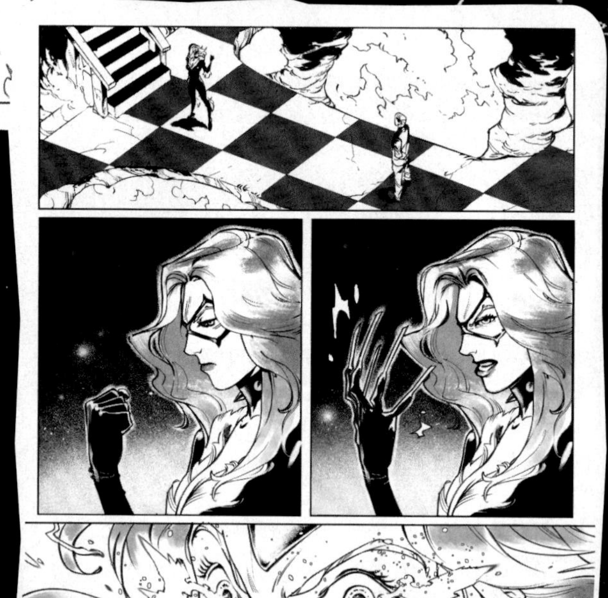

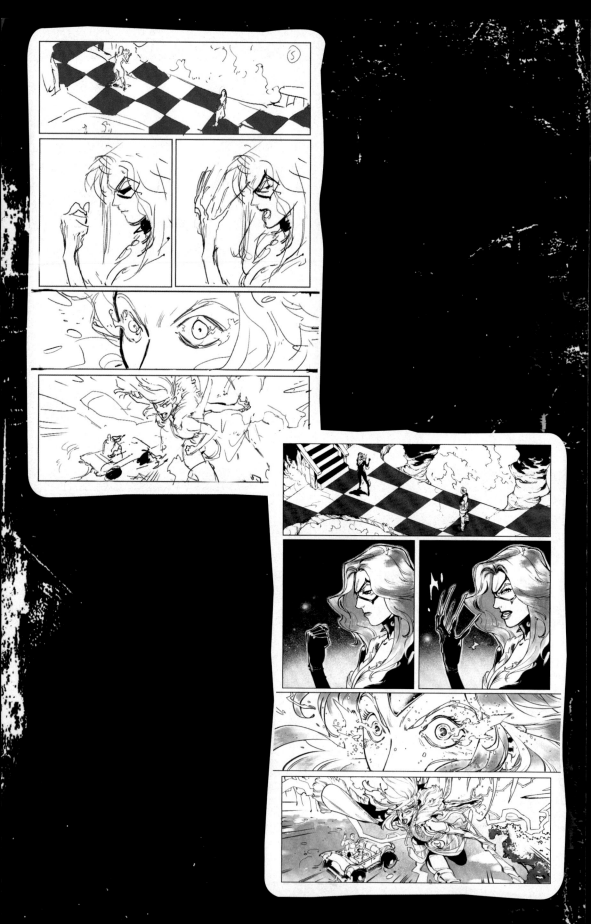

#3, page 5 process by **C.F. VILLA**

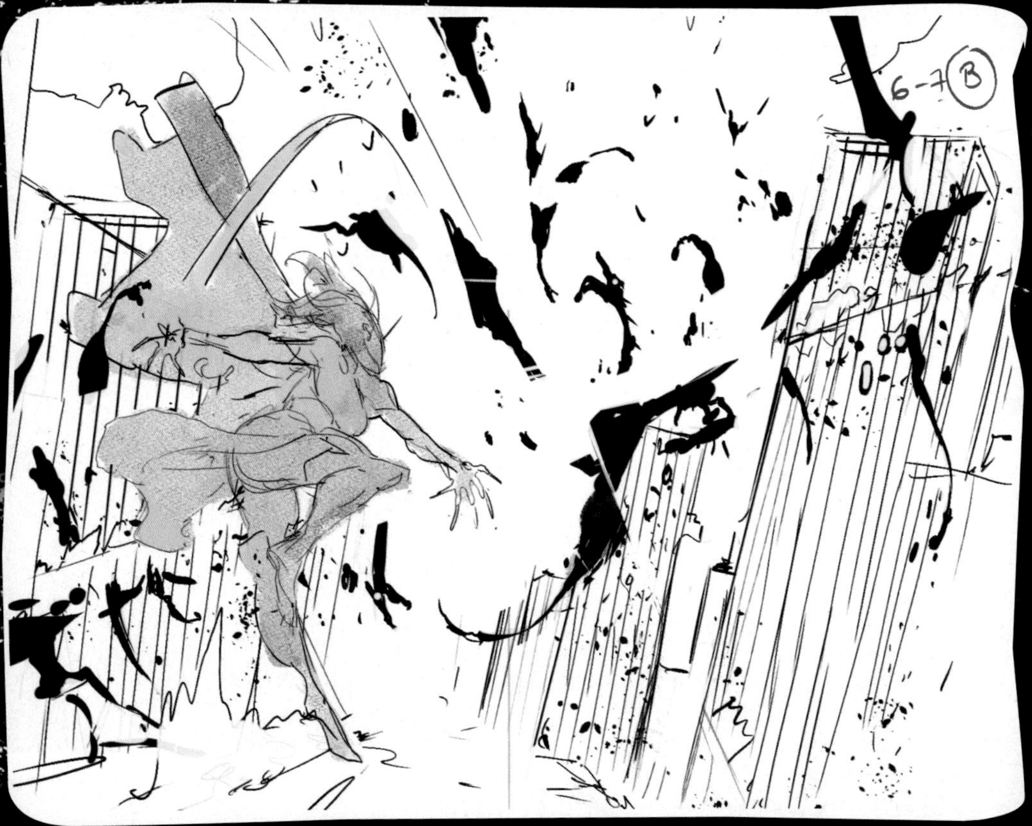
6-7 B

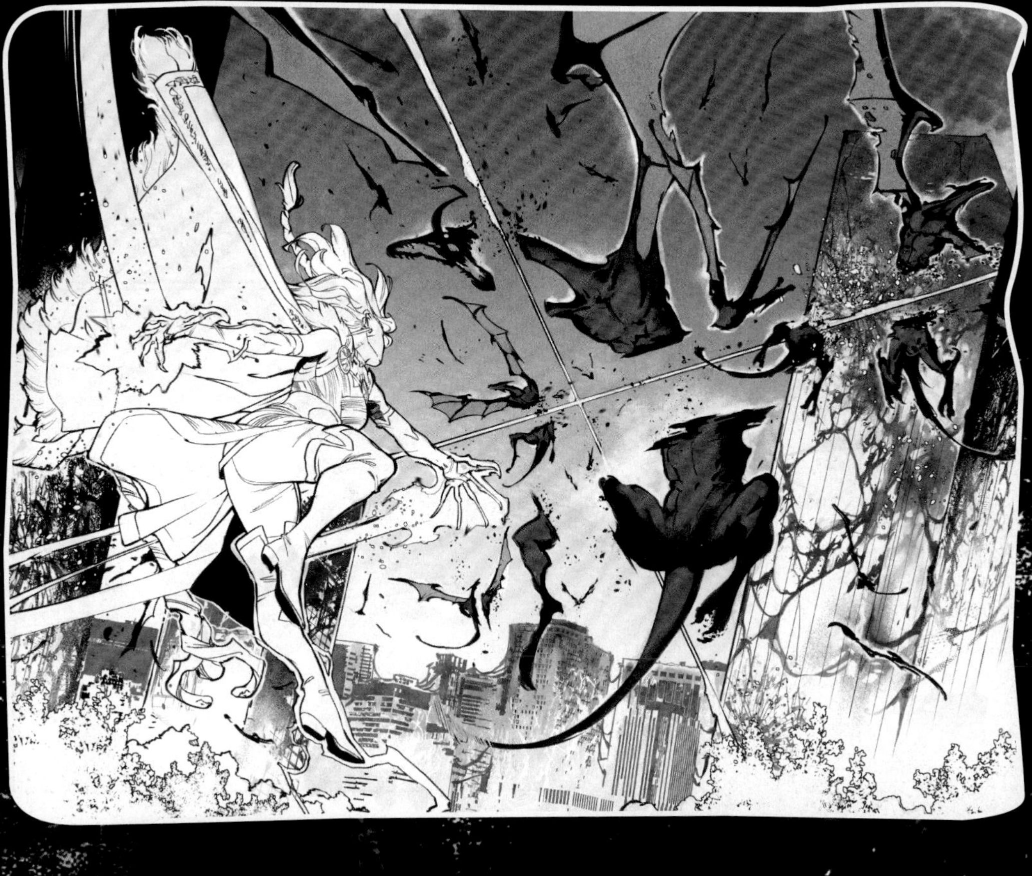

#3, pages 6-7 process by **C.F. VILLA**

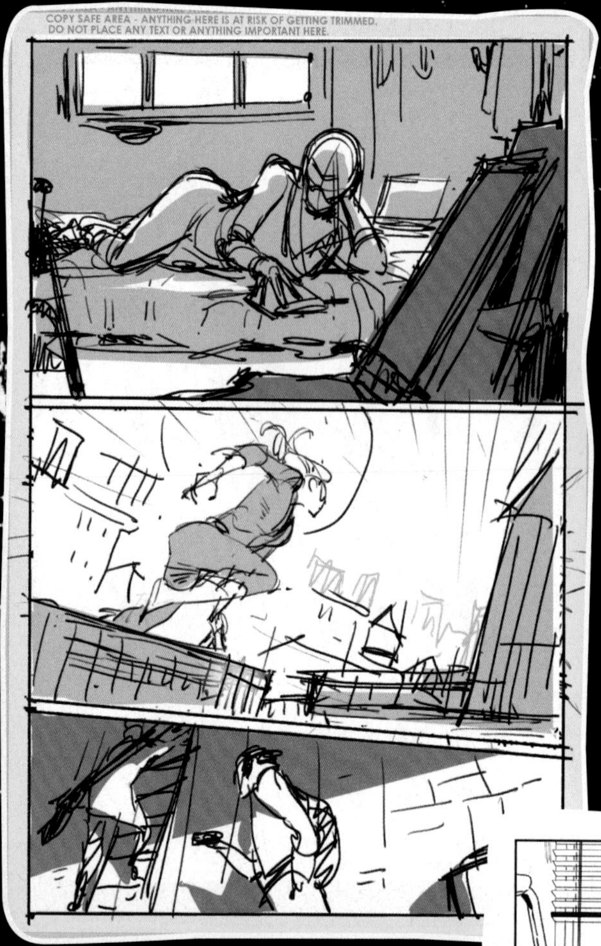
COPY SAFE AREA - ANYTHING HERE IS AT RISK OF GETTING TRIMMED.
DO NOT PLACE ANY TEXT OR ANYTHING IMPORTANT HERE.

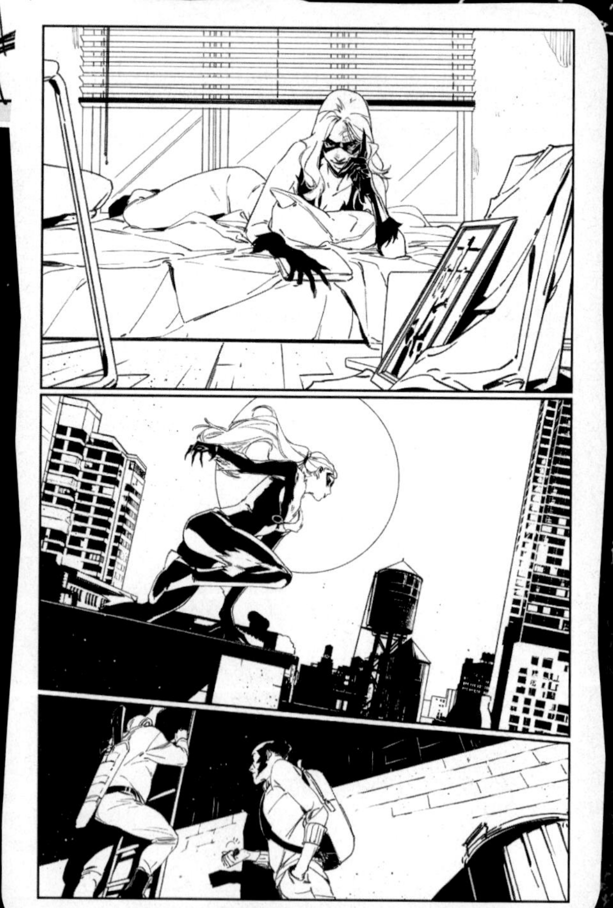

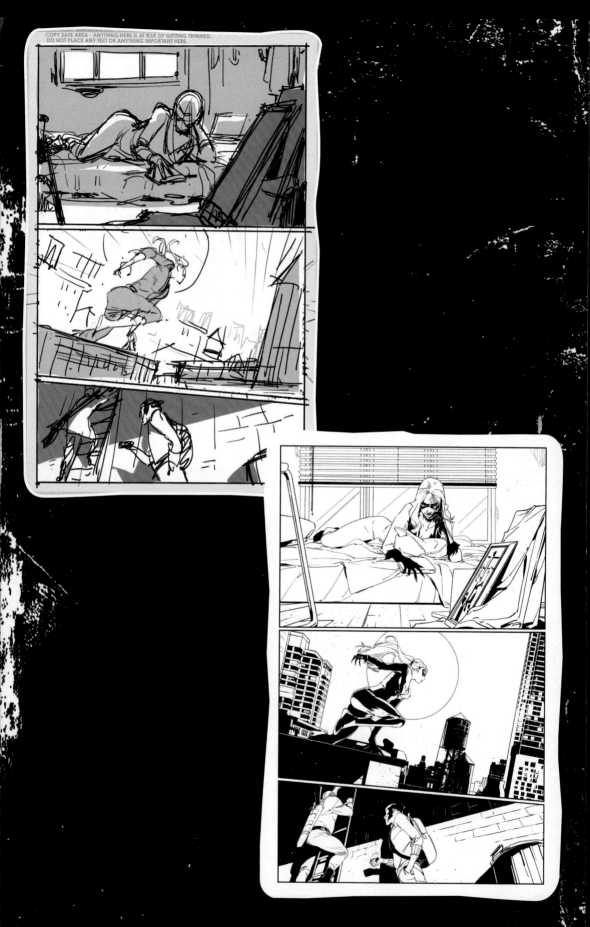

#4, page 12 process by **NINA VAKUEVA**

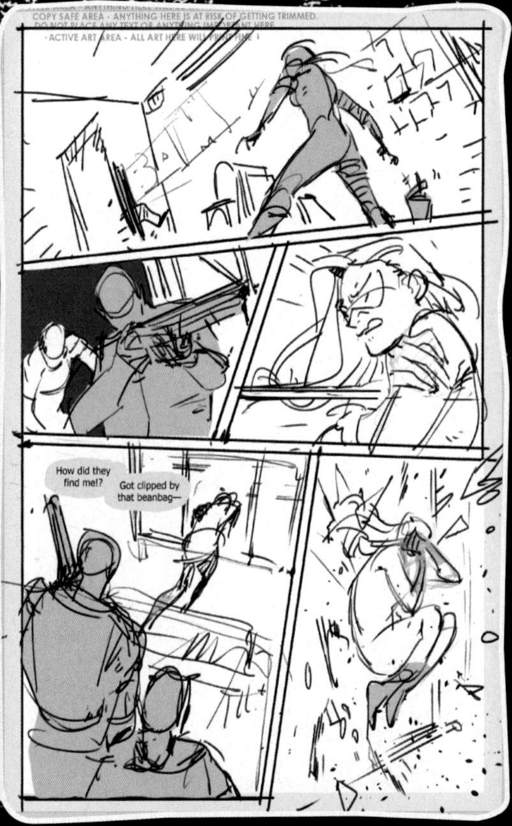
COPY SAFE AREA - ANYTHING HERE IS AT RISK OF GETTING TRIMMED.
How did they find me?
Got clipped by that beanbag—

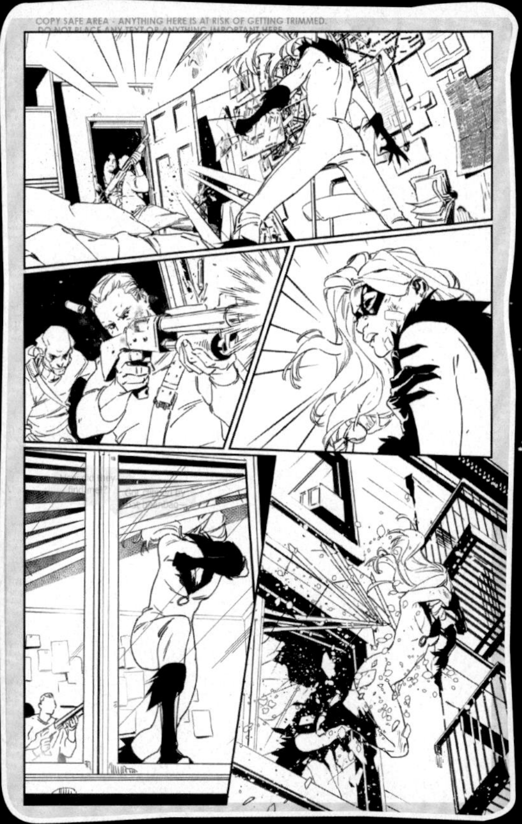
COPY SAFE AREA - ANYTHING HERE IS AT RISK OF GETTING TRIMMED.

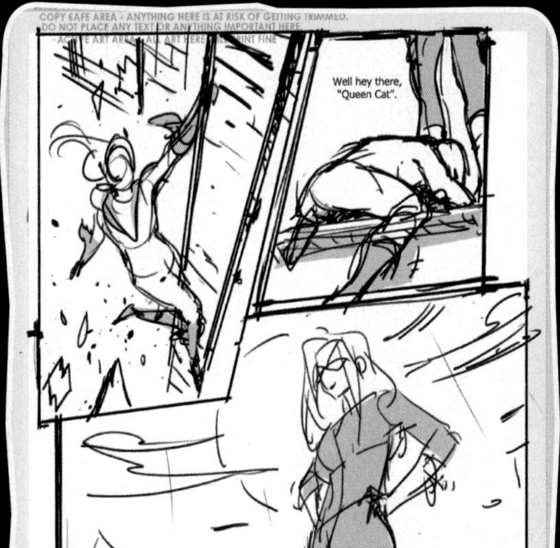
COPY SAFE AREA - ANYTHING HERE IS AT RISK OF GETTING TRIMMED.
DO NOT PLACE ANY TEXT OR ANYTHING IMPORTANT HERE.
Well hey there, "Queen Cat".

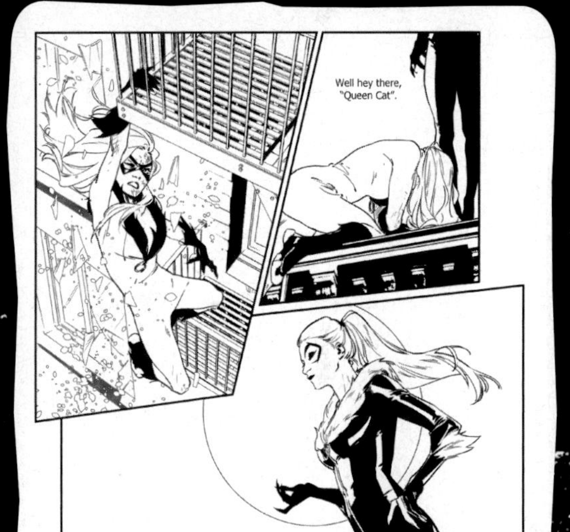
Well hey there, "Queen Cat".

#4, pages 13-14 process by **NINA VAKUEVA**

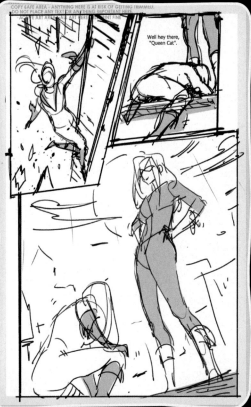

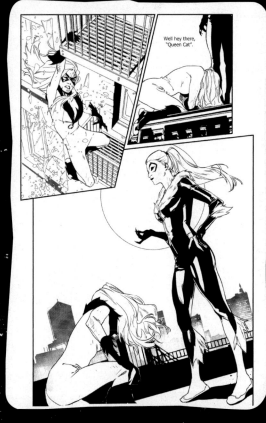

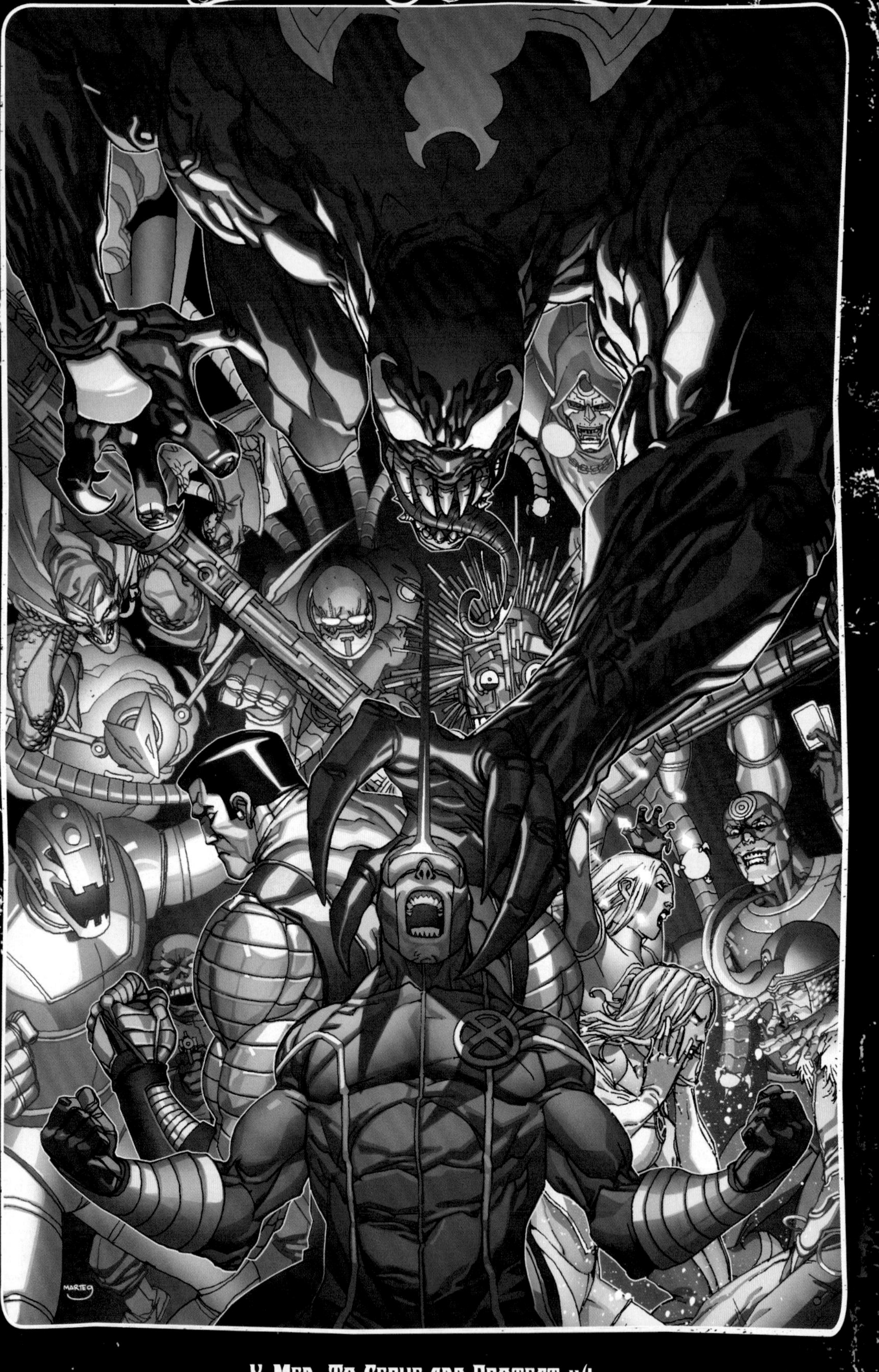

X-MEN: TO SERVE AND PROTECT #4

Dazzler, Misty Knight and Colleen Wing are pulled into the latest Contest of Champions, though it's unlike any held before, in *Black Cat* writer Jed MacKay's first Marvel story!

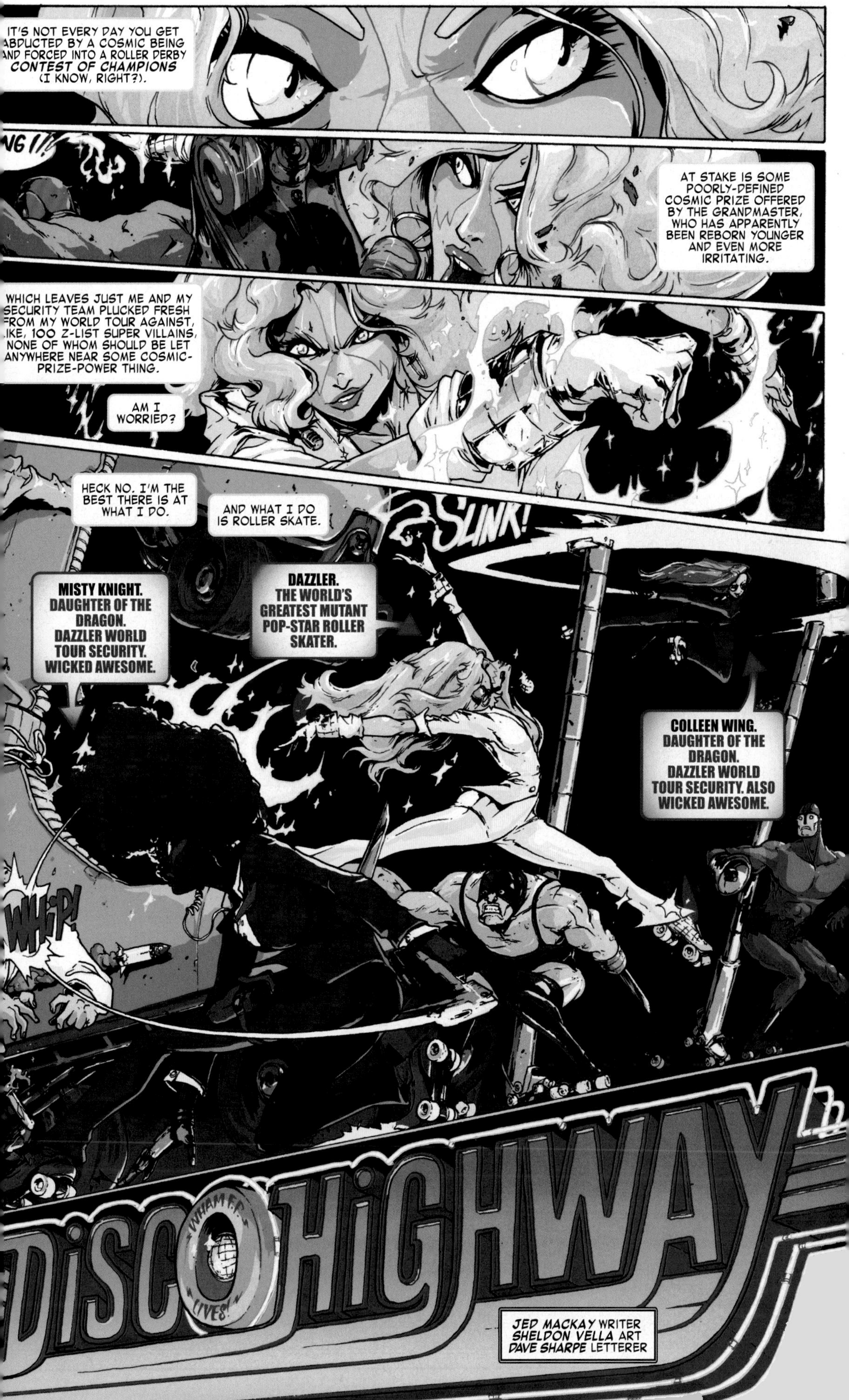

IT'S NOT EVERY DAY YOU GET ABDUCTED BY A COSMIC BEING AND FORCED INTO A ROLLER DERBY CONTEST OF CHAMPIONS (I KNOW, RIGHT?).
AT STAKE IS SOME POORLY-DEFINED COSMIC PRIZE OFFERED BY THE GRANDMASTER, WHO HAS APPARENTLY BEEN REBORN YOUNGER AND EVEN MORE IRRITATING.
WHICH LEAVES JUST ME AND MY SECURITY TEAM PLUCKED FRESH FROM MY WORLD TOUR AGAINST, LIKE, 100 Z-LIST SUPER VILLAINS, NONE OF WHOM SHOULD BE LET ANYWHERE NEAR SOME COSMIC-PRIZE-POWER THING.
AM I WORRIED?
HECK NO. I'M THE BEST THERE IS AT WHAT I DO.
AND WHAT I DO IS ROLLER SKATE.
SLINK!
MISTY KNIGHT. DAUGHTER OF THE DRAGON. DAZZLER WORLD TOUR SECURITY. WICKED AWESOME.
DAZZLER. THE WORLD'S GREATEST MUTANT POP-STAR ROLLER SKATER.
COLLEEN WING. DAUGHTER OF THE DRAGON. DAZZLER WORLD TOUR SECURITY. ALSO WICKED AWESOME.
WHIP!
DISCO HIGHWAY
WHAM F.P. LIVES!
JED MACKAY WRITER
SHELDON VELLA ART
DAVE SHARPE LETTERER

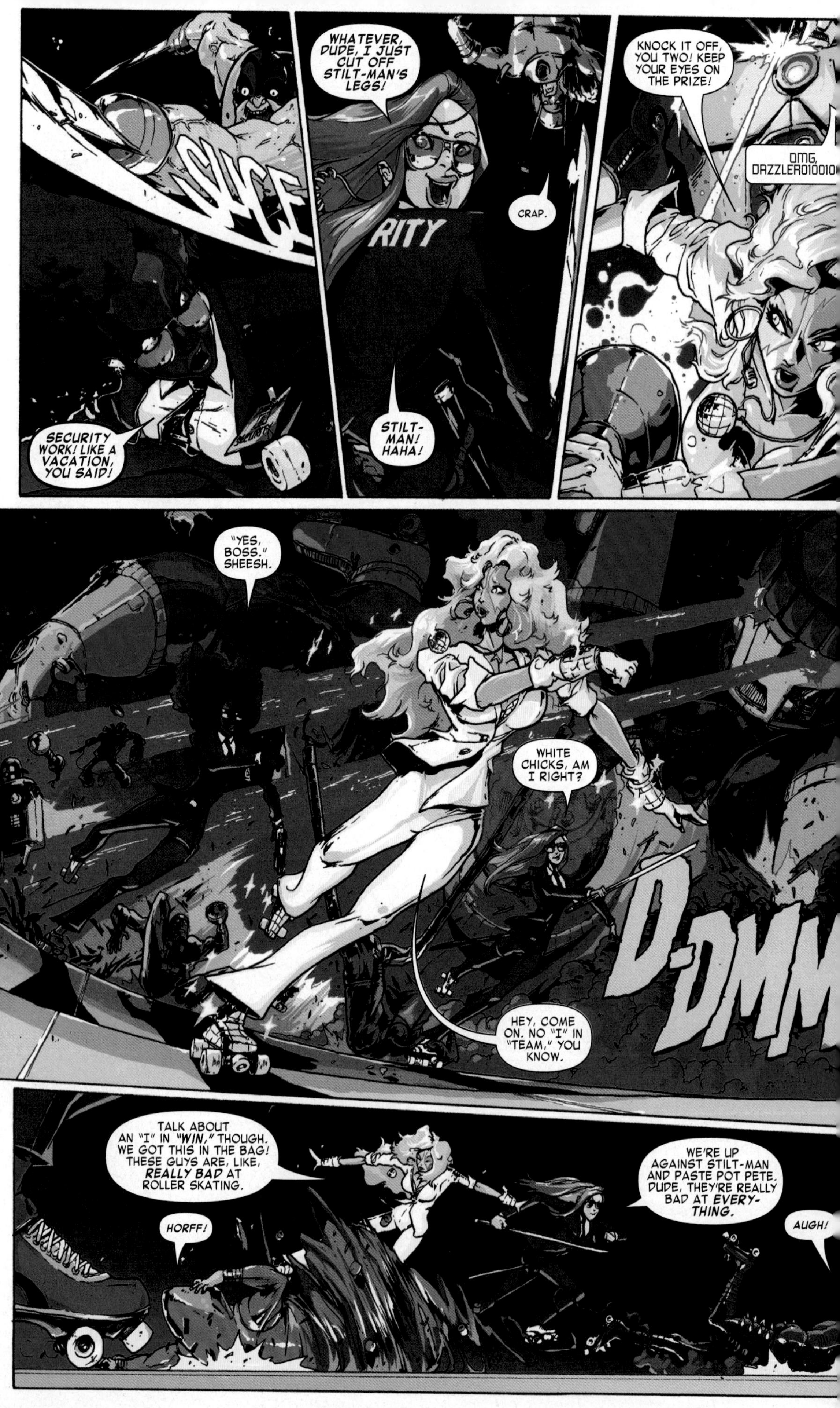
SLICE
SECURITY WORK! LIKE A VACATION, YOU SAID!
WHATEVER, DUDE, I JUST CUT OFF STILT-MAN'S LEGS!
RITY
STILT-MAN! HAHA!
CRAP.
KNOCK IT OFF, YOU TWO! KEEP YOUR EYES ON THE PRIZE!
OMG, DAZZLER010010
"YES, BOSS." SHEESH.
WHITE CHICKS, AM I RIGHT?
HEY, COME ON. NO "I" IN "TEAM," YOU KNOW.
D-DMM
TALK ABOUT AN "I" IN "WIN," THOUGH. WE GOT THIS IN THE BAG! THESE GUYS ARE, LIKE, REALLY BAD AT ROLLER SKATING.
HORFF!
WE'RE UP AGAINST STILT-MAN AND PASTE POT PETE. DUDE, THEY'RE REALLY BAD AT EVERY-THING.
AUGH!

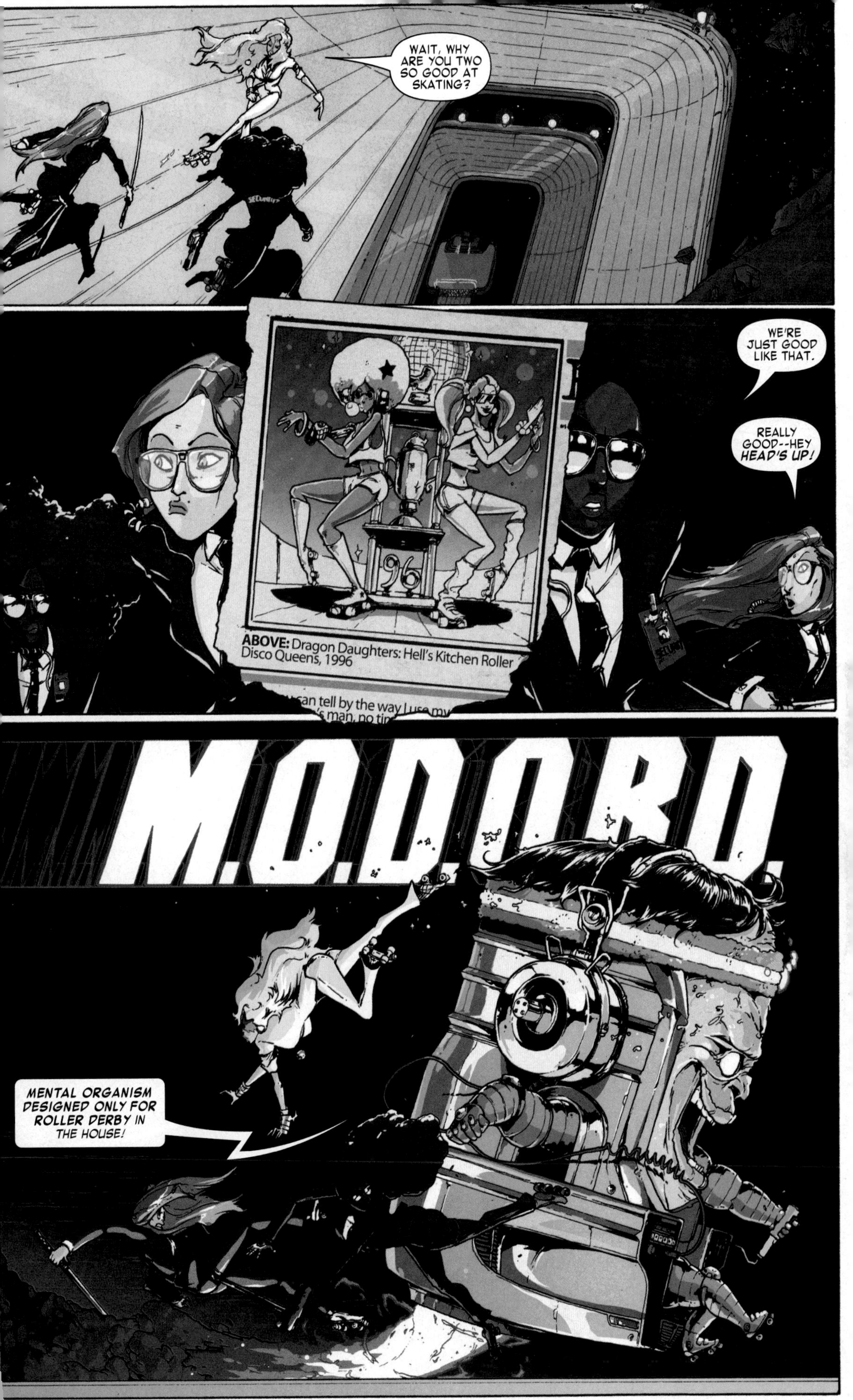
WAIT, WHY ARE YOU TWO SO GOOD AT SKATING?
WE'RE JUST GOOD LIKE THAT.
REALLY GOOD--HEY HEAD'S UP!
ABOVE: Dragon Daughters: Hell's Kitchen Roller Disco Queens, 1996
M.O.D.O.R.D.
MENTAL ORGANISM DESIGNED ONLY FOR ROLLER DERBY IN THE HOUSE!

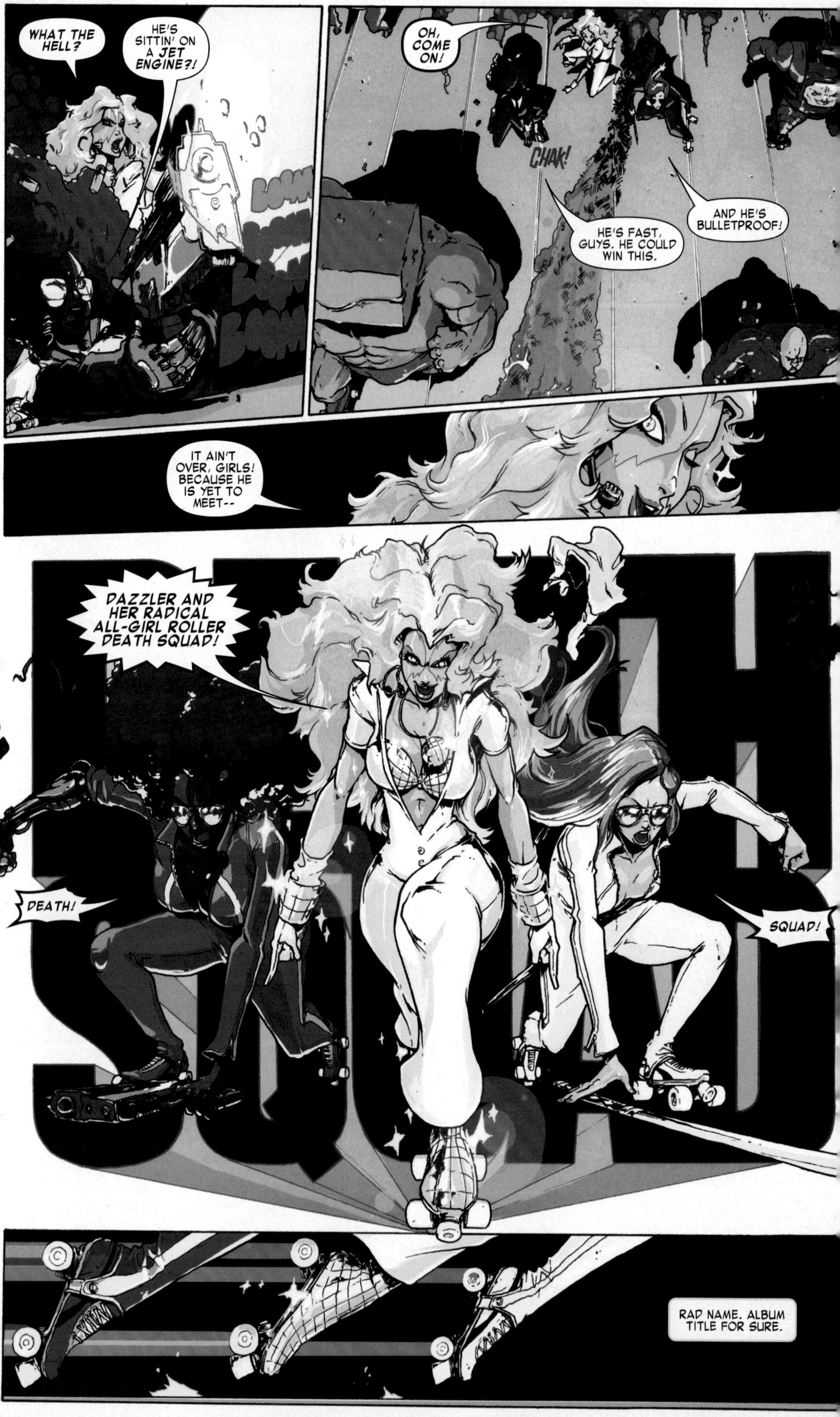
WHAT THE HELL?
HE'S SITTIN' ON A JET ENGINE?!
OH, COME ON!
CHAK!
HE'S FAST, GUYS. HE COULD WIN THIS.
AND HE'S BULLETPROOF!
IT AIN'T OVER, GIRLS! BECAUSE HE IS YET TO MEET--
DAZZLER AND HER RADICAL ALL-GIRL ROLLER DEATH SQUAD!
DEATH!
SQUAD!
RAD NAME. ALBUM TITLE FOR SURE.

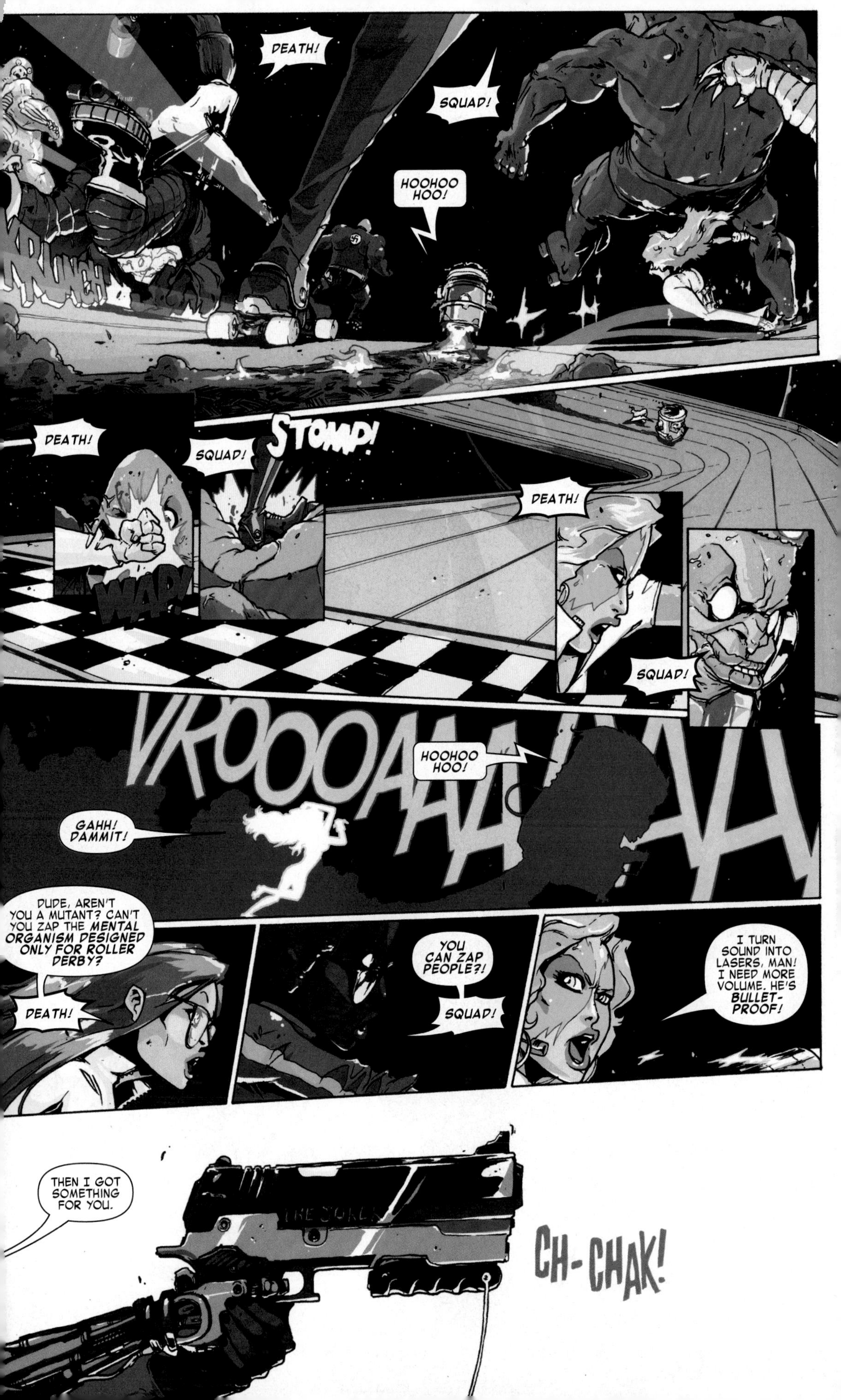
KRUNCH
DEATH!
SQUAD!
HOOHOO HOO!
DEATH!
SQUAD!
STOMP!
WAP!
DEATH!
SQUAD!
VROOOAAAAAAAH
HOOHOO HOO!
GAHH! DAMMIT!
DUDE, AREN'T YOU A MUTANT? CAN'T YOU ZAP THE MENTAL ORGANISM DESIGNED ONLY FOR ROLLER DERBY?
DEATH!
YOU CAN ZAP PEOPLE?!
SQUAD!
I TURN SOUND INTO LASERS, MAN! I NEED MORE VOLUME. HE'S BULLET-PROOF!
THEN I GOT SOMETHING FOR YOU.
CH-CHAK!

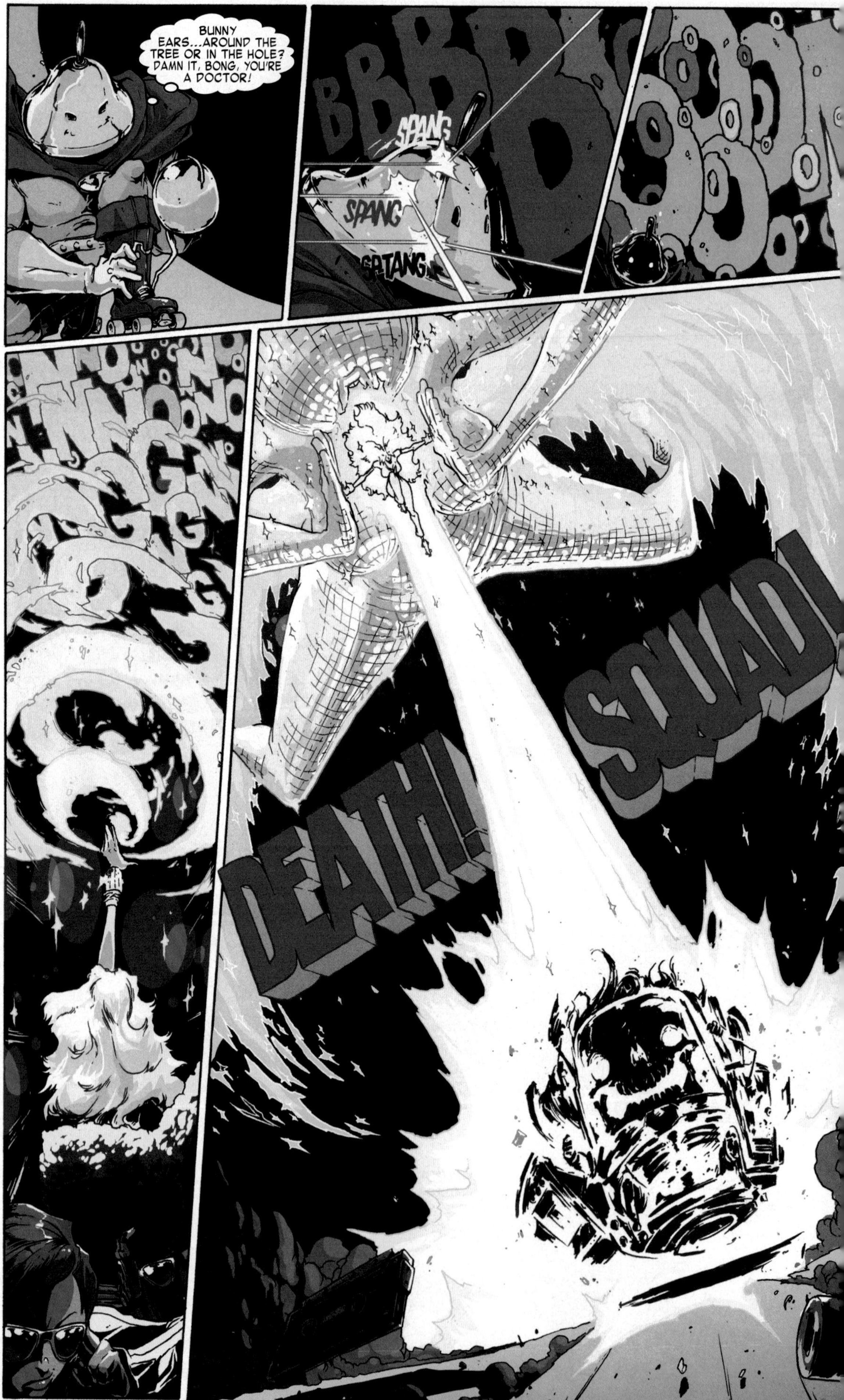

BUNNY EARS...AROUND THE TREE OR IN THE HOLE? DAMN IT, BONG, YOU'RE A DOCTOR!
BBBB
SPANG
SPANG
SPTANG
DEATH!! SQUAD!!

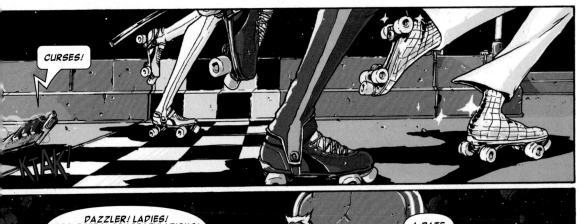

CURSES!

KTAK!

DAZZLER! LADIES! BRO-ETTES! CONGRATULATIONS! YOU HAVE TOTALLY BESTED YOUR COMPETITORS AND WON RIGHTS TO THE MOST ULTIMATE OF PRIZES!

A DATE WITH--

THE SHADMASTER!

WHAT? ARE YOU KIDDING ME?

DAZZLER, BABE, COME ON! I SET THIS WHOLE THING UP FOR YOU! WHY DO YOU THINK NO ONE ELSE COULD SKATE? (EXCEPT FOR THE BIG HEAD GUY. I THOUGHT HIS NAME STOOD FOR MENTAL ORGANISM DESIGNED ONLY FOR ROUTINE DIAGNOSTICS. MY BAD.)

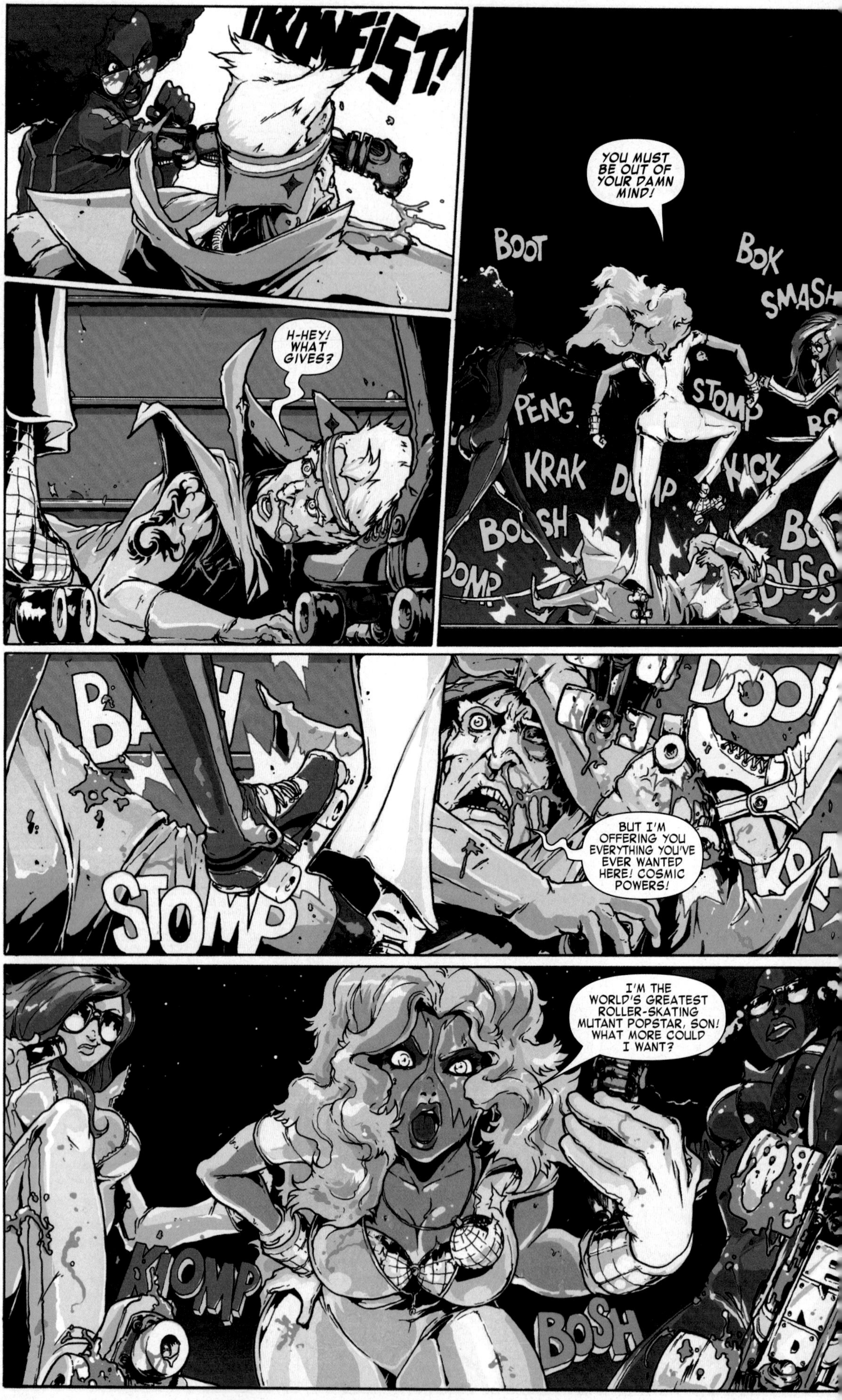
IRONFIST!
H-HEY! WHAT GIVES?
YOU MUST BE OUT OF YOUR DAMN MIND!
BOOT
BOK
SMASH
PENG
STOMP
KRAK
DUMP
BOOSH
DOMP
DUSS
STOMP
BUT I'M OFFERING YOU EVERYTHING YOU'VE EVER WANTED HERE! COSMIC POWERS!
I'M THE WORLD'S GREATEST ROLLER-SKATING MUTANT POPSTAR, SON! WHAT MORE COULD I WANT?
KLOMP
BOSH